AF718226

The Protection of Working Relationships

Volume 39

Series Editors

Prof. Dr Alan C. Neal
Prof. Dr Manfred Weiss
Prof. Dr Birgitta Nyström

Launched in 1997, the Studies in Employment and Social Policy series now boasts over thirty titles, addressing key policy and development issues in the fields of Industrial Relations, Labour Law, Social Security, and International Labour Regulation.

Under the direction of its General Editors, Professor Alan Neal (Founding Editor of the International Journal of Labour Law and Industrial Relations, and Convenor of the European Association of Labour Law Judges), Professor Manfred Weiss (past-President of the International Industrial Relations Association) and Professor Birgitta Nyström (Professor of Private Law at the Law Faculty, University of Lund, Sweden), *Studies in Employment and Social Policy* seeks to provide a forum for highlighting international and comparative research on contemporary areas of significance for evaluation and regulation of the world of work.

With contributors from leading figures in the field, *Studies in Employment and Social Policy* brings together key policy-makers, academics, and regulators, providing a unique context in which to analyse and evaluate the rapid and dramatic work and social policy developments taking place across the globe.

The Protection of Working Relationships

A Comparative Study

Edited by

Frans Pennings

Claire Bosse

Wolters Kluwer
Law & Business

Published by:
Kluwer Law International
PO Box 316
2400 AH Alphen aan den Rijn
The Netherlands
Website: www.kluwerlaw.com

Sold and distributed in North, Central and South America by:
Aspen Publishers, Inc.
7201 McKinney Circle
Frederick, MD 21704
United States of America
Email: customer.service@aspenpublishers.com

Sold and distributed in all other countries by:
Turpin Distribution Services Ltd.
Stratton Business Park
Pegasus Drive, Biggleswade
Bedfordshire SG18 8TQ
United Kingdom
Email: kluwerlaw@turpin-distribution.com

Printed on acid-free paper.

ISBN 978-90-411-3289-5

© 2011 Kluwer Law International BV, The Netherlands

All rights reserved. No part of this publication may be reproduced, stored in a retrieval system, or transmitted in any form or by any means, electronic, mechanical, photocopying, recording, or otherwise, without written permission from the publisher.

Permission to use this content must be obtained from the copyright owner. Please apply to: Permissions Department, Wolters Kluwer Legal, 76 Ninth Avenue, 7th Floor, New York, NY 10011-5201, USA. Email: permissions@kluwerlaw.com

Printed in Great Britain.

List of Authors

Claire Bosse	Legal Advisor of a Belgian employer federation, formerly employed as a researcher at the University of Tilburg (Department of labour law and social policy); observer during the ILO-conference on the Employment recommendation 198 of 2006.
Isabelle Daugareilh	CNRS research direktor, COMPTRASEC UMR 5114, Bordeaux IV Montesquieu University, France.
Wolfgang Däubler	Professor emeritus of labour law, civil law and economic law at the University of Bremen; Visiting professor at the University of Shanghai.
Patrick Humblet	Professor at the Law Faculty of Ghent University; Visiting Professor at the University of Antwerp Management School and at the Royal Military Academy.
Alan C. Neal	Professor of Law and Director of the Employment Law Research Unit at the University of Warwick, United Kingdom. He sits as an Employment Judge in London, and is the Convenor of the European Association of Labour Court Judges. Together with a Visiting Chair in the University of Paris II, since 2006 he has held a Lifetime Visiting Chair in the Zhejiang University, PRC, and is a Visiting Professor in the Beijing Jiao Tong University, PRC. He was the founding editor, and is now Scientific Director, of *The International Journal of Comparative Labour Law and Industrial Relations.*

Frans Pennings	Professor of Labour Law and Social Security Law at Utrecht University; Professor of International Social Security Law at Tilburg University. Member of the Central Appeals Court of the Netherlands. Editor of *European Journal of Social Security*.
Isabel Plets	Researcher at the Law Faculty of Ghent University, lawyer at the Brussels Bar (Lydian).
Andrzej Marian Świątkowski	Jean Monnet Professor of European Labour Law and Social Security Law. Jagiellonian University, Krakow, Poland. First Vice-president of the European Committee of Social Rights, Council of Europe, Strasbourg.

Summary of Contents

Table of Contents

List of Abbreviations

ABU	Algemene Bond Uitzendondernemingen (Federation of Temporary Work Agencies)
AuR	Arbeid und Recht
BAG AP	Bundesarbeitsgericht (Federal Labour Court)
BAG DB	Der Betrieb
BetrVG	Betriebsverfassungsgesetz
BGB	Bürgerliches Gesetzbuch
BGBl	Bundesgesetzblatt (Federal Law Gazette)
BGH	Bundesgerichtshof
BIT	Bureau International du Travail (ILO office)
Bull civ.	Bulletin Civil
BW	Burgerlijk Wetboek (Civil Code)
CEEP	European Centre of Employers and Enterprises Providing Public Services
DG	Directorate General
DTI	Department of Trade and Industry
EAT	Employment Appeal Tribunal
ECR	European Court Reports
EESC	European Economic and Social Committee
EP	European Parliament
ETUC	European Trade Union Confederation
EU	European Union
EWCA	England and Wales Court of Appeal (Civil Division) Decisions
HCSESMSB	High Council for the Self-employed and Small and Medium Sized Businesses
HMSO	Her Majesty's Stationary Office
HR	Hoge Raad (Supreme Court)

ILO	International Labour Organisation
IRLR	Industrial Relations Law Reports
JAR	Jurisprudentie Arbeidsrecht (Journal on Labour Case Law)
JCP Social	La Semaine juridique sociale (JCP S)
Ktr.	Kantonrechter (District Court)
LAG	Landesarbeitsgericht
LJ	Lord Judge
NGO	Non-government Organisation
NJ	Nederlandse Jurisprudentie (Case Law Journal)
NLC	National Labour Council
NSSO	National Social Security Office
NZA	Neue Zeitschrift für Arbeitsrecht
OJ	Official Journal of the EU
OMC	Open Method of Coordination
Or.	Orientations (Journal)
PRC	People's Republic of China
RJS	Revue de jurisprudence sociale (Journal)
S.I.	Statutory Instrument
SMA	Sociaal Maandblad Arbeidsrecht (Journal)
Soc.	Chamber for Social Affairs of Court
Stb.	Staatsblad (Official Journal)
TFEU	Treaty on the Functioning of the European Union
TNO	Nederlandse Organisatie voor Toegepast Natuurwetenschappelijk Onderzoek (Netherlands Organisation for Applied Scientific Research)
TUC	Trade Union Congress (British Trade Union)
TVVS	Corporate Law Magazine
UK	United Kingdom
UNICE	Union of Industrial and Employers' Confederations of Europe
UNIZO	Unie van Zelfstandige Ondernemers (Belgian Employers Federation)
ZZP	zelfstandigen zonder personeel (Self-employed without Staff)

Preface and Acknowledgement

The employment relationship is an essential element of labour law since it defines who has access to labour law protection and who does not have such protection or who is only to a limited extent protected. It is also a difficult concept since it is not always easy to define when a person performing work is doing so under a contract of employment or under another type of civil law contract. This uncertainty is not only due to academic problems of providing an adequate definitions but is to a large extent due to the inherent tensions of the labour market, where businesses, in order to reduce their costs, try to escape labour law rules. This is done, *inter alia*, by creating new types of relationships which do not or, where there is uncertainty, whether they satisfy the conditions for a contract of employment.

Another factor is that new forms of work now exist, which were developed in response to new needs on the labour market and technological developments. These new forms satisfy the traditional criteria for the employment contract hardly better than many of the self-employed relationships do.

An attempt by the International Labour Organisation to introduce more clarity in this area by its Recommendation 198 was the direct reason for undertaking this study. The study is, however, not limited to an investigation of the impact of this recommendation, but analyses all developments in the field of the protection by the contract of employment even if not instigated by the said Recommendation. For this purpose we asked a group of noted European labour law experts to describe and analyse the discussions on the contract of employment in their country and to recommend labour law reforms based on a close examination of existing conditions. These experts are Patrick Humblet, Isabel Plets, Isabelle Daugareilh, Wolfgang Däubler, Andrezj Świątkowski and Alan C. Neal. We are very grateful to them for their willingness to contribute to this volume.

We are also grateful to Mr Bertrand Muller-Schleiden, working at the DG Employment, Social Affairs and Equal Opportunities of the European Commission, and Ms Alette van Leur, Director of the Department of Partnerships and Development Cooperation of the ILO for their indispensable advice and information. Mr Giuseppe Casale, Ms Corinne Vargha, Mr Tayo Fashoyin, Mr Humberto Villasmil and Mr Colin Fenwick provided us also with very useful help. We are indebted to Ms Catelene Passchier, working for the European Trade Union Confederation, who clarified the background of the discussions at the EU level.

Of course, the responsibility for the chapters written by the editors is entirely ours. We hope that the result is a useful contribution to the intriguing issue of the protection by labour law and we are looking forward to comments on the result.

Antwerp/Utrecht, January 2011

Claire Bosse

Frans Pennings

Chapter 1

The Legal Status of Persons Performing Work Personally: The Topic of This Book

Claire Bosse and Frans Pennings

1. INTRODUCTION

The regulation of the employment relationship goes back to the nineteenth century, when factory workers in industrialising countries were working many hours a week in unsafe and unhealthy conditions. Their situation was often one of exploitation and poverty. To redress this abuse, national governments adopted laws and regulations in order to protect the weaker party in the employment relationship.[1]

Over the years, this protection became stronger and stronger and a 'building' of labour law emerged, accompanied by another 'building' of social security law.[2] However, only workers in a formal employment relationship have full access to these two buildings. Self-employed persons and informal workers are not entitled to the advantages of labour law, and are supposed to create their own safety net in case of illness, unemployment, disability or old age.

1. 'The main object of labour law has been, and . . . will always be a countervailing force to counteract the inequality of bargaining power which is inherent and must be inherent in the employment relationship', Sir Otto Kahn-Freund, *Labour and the Law*, Hamlyn Lectures (London: Stevens and Sons, 1972), 7.
2. The idea of labour law as a building is inspired by P.F. van der Heijden, *Naar een nieuwe rechtsorde van de arbeid*, Hugo Sinzheimer Institute (Den Haag: SDU Uitgevers, 1999), 4.

Frans Pennings & Claire Bosse, *The Protection of Working Relationships*, pp. 1–4.
© 2011 Kluwer Law International BV, The Netherlands.

Currently, in most legal systems, workers are divided into two major categories: those with an employment contract or employment relationship (also called 'employees') and those without such a contract/relationship (also called 'autonomous workers', 'independent contractors' or 'self-employed persons'). Persons in the first category are protected by labour law; those in the second are not, although they may be protected by commercial or civil law. This is an important distinction, because employees are much better protected than other workers. An effect of this is that employees are therefore also more expensive.

Since the 1980s, businesses felt a growing need for more flexible working arrangements due to the globalisation of the economy. The number of temporary workers, on-call workers and cross-border subcontracting agreements grew considerably. These arrangements do not always fit in the existing legal framework, in which employed and self-employed persons (or own-account workers) are treated differently. The first are protected by labour law, as we have seen above, the second by civil or commercial law, in which the contracting parties are considered to have equal bargaining power. This means that the rules on minimum wage, maximum working hours, protection against dismissal, etc., only apply when an employment relationship exists. By giving the working arrangement an 'independent look' businesses try to avoid the rigidity of labour law and the price-tag associated with labour law and social security.

New forms of labour often represent a mix of dependent and independent work and/or involve more than two contracting parties. This creates a 'grey area' outside the building of labour law, in which it is not clear whether the worker should be classified as an employee or as an own-account worker.

This uncertainty gradually undermines the existence of labour law and social security law, especially in countries with a large informal economy. Some even argue that 'the erosion of the employment relationship and the failure of labour law to keep pace with evolving labour market issues is the most important industrial relation issue of our time'.[3]

A very important issue is the problem of a grey zone between dependent work and self-employment where it is not clear whether a contract is an employment contract or not. It has already attracted the attention of several authors, whose analyses and proposals will be discussed in Chapter 2. Progress in this area seems, however, to be slow and it is hard to find consensus on particular proposals.

In addition, in 2006 the International Labour Organisation (ILO) adopted a Recommendation on this topic, the Employment Relationship Recommendation (Recommendation 198). The objective of this Recommendation is to guarantee effective protection for workers who perform work in the context of an employment relationship. The Recommendation will be discussed in more detail in Chapter 3. It mentions some criteria for bringing hidden forms of employeeship under the protection of labour law.

3. Ibrahim Patel, workers' spokesperson at the ILO conferences of 2003 and 2006 and currently Minister of Economic Development, Republic of South Africa. See ILO 2003, Provisional Record 26, 26.

This Recommendation triggered this study, as it asked ILO Member States to undertake action to reduce disguised employment relationships. It also mentioned an interesting series of instruments to distinguish employment relationships from other contracts and to ensure that those really working in an employment relationship are actually given the corresponding legal status.

In order to contribute to this discussion, we undertook a study of the developments in a number of EU countries. These studies were made by the national labour law experts, thus ensuring an in depth study of the developments that are put in the relevant context. The studies are certainly not limited to the contents of this Recommendation, but take more generally into account which measures are undertaken and which instruments are used to disclose the bogus self-employed and to cover persons performing personal work by an employment contract.

This study addresses the topic at two different levels. One is that of international organisations, in particular the ILO (Chapter 3) and the European Union (Chapter 4).

The other level is that of country studies (Chapters 5–10), in which national labour law experts describe which developments have taken place in their country and which instruments are used in order to ensure the protection of labour law to dependent workers.

The reason for the double level approach is that it appears to be very difficult to take measures for increasing the protection of dependent workers at the international level. Political support for such measures at these levels is very limited. Therefore the study also discusses the question at which level which measures could be taken.

2. RESEARCH QUESTIONS

In this study we will address the following research questions:

(1) Which proposals have been made by the ILO and EU in order to ensure the protection of labour law to persons performing work personally?
(2) Which methods are used or proposed in order to extend the coverage of employment protection, both by the international organisations and in the selected countries?
(3) Which conclusions and recommendations follow from these findings?

3. THE CONTENTS OF THIS BOOK AND ACKNOWLEDGEMENTS

In order to obtain information from single countries we asked academics from a number of countries to contribute to the discussion. The selection of the countries is, as always, somewhat arbitrary, and restricted to European countries. Although this can be seen as a limitation, this selection is useful since in these countries labour law has been developed to a high level, and in these countries in particular the undermining of labour law seems serious. For this reason we can expect here new roads for realizing labour law protection for dependent workers.

With the results in hand we are convinced that the selected countries are representative for the various ways in which labour law has developed in the EU.

The country chapters include contributions on:

- Belgium by Patrick Humblet and Isabel Plets;
- France by Isabelle Daugareilh;
- Germany by Wolfgang Däubler;
- the Netherlands by Frans Pennings;
- Poland by Andrezj Świątkowski;
- the United Kingdom by Alan Neal.

The chapters on the international organisations were written by the editors of the book. As part of the research we interviewed Mr Bertrand Muller-Schleiden, working at the DG Employment, Social Affairs and Equal Opportunities of the European Commission, and Ms Alette van Leur, Director of the Department of Partnerships and Development Cooperation of the ILO and Chair of the Conference on the Recommendation on the Employment Relationship. We wish to thank her colleagues at the ILO who were very helpful in providing us with information: Mr Giuseppe Casale, Ms Corinne Vargha, Mr Tayo Fashoyin, Mr Humberto Villasmil and Mr Colin Fenwick. We also talked to Ms Catelene Passchier, working for the European Trade Union Confederation.

The persons mentioned here provided us with useful background information. However, the way in which we used the information in the relevant chapters is of course entirely our own responsibility. We wish to thank all our respondents for their helpful comments.

Chapter 2

The Various Categories of Persons Performing Work Personally

Frans Pennings

1. INTRODUCTION

The limitation of the protection by labour law and social security law of employed persons has been under discussion since the creation of labour law.

It was argued that the newly created discipline of labour law was simply unable to cover all working relationships, and therefore had to focus on the employment relationship. Sometimes the need of employers for flexible workers is also mentioned as a reason for the limitation in protection of persons performing work personally.

In many, if not all countries, persons can be found who perform work without a contract of employment, even though they depend to a large extent on one or only a few work providers for work and income. These workers are often not given a contract of employment, since this type of contract is much more expensive and/or causes more responsibilities for the work provider than engaging them under a civil or commercial contract. No matter what the reason is for not giving them a contract of employment, these workers are in most legal systems not protected by labour law. However, these workers are often just as dependent for income and work on their work provider(s) as employees. Also in respect of income risks following from accidents at work and diseases, they are often as dependent as employed persons.

Frans Pennings & Claire Bosse, *The Protection of Working Relationships*, pp. 5–14.
© 2011 Kluwer Law International BV, The Netherlands.

In this book we will use the terms 'those having a contract of employment', 'employees', 'employed persons' and 'persons working in an employment relationship' interchangeably. Persons who perform work personally are called 'workers'; this is an umbrella term for both persons under a contract of employment and persons not having a contract of employment who perform their work personally.

In some countries social security compensates for the lack of protection by labour law. Certain categories of workers are brought within the scope of disability schemes or old age pension schemes. This does not take away the main problem, which is that workers without an employment contract are often in a position worse than that of employees. To say it in other words: only persons with a formal employment contract have access to the 'buildings' of labour law and social security law.

The categories of workers who fall outside the scope of labour law keep changing through time. In response, countries take measures to provide protection for the new category of workers; the following chapters will give several examples. Work providers, however, soon find new ways to escape the rules of labour law. This is even easier since legislative measures are often ambiguous in their elaboration: on the one hand they are meant to avoid erosion of labour law, on the other they are not too strict to allow employers to remain competitive.

2. THE DIFFERENT CATEGORIES OF PERSONS PERFORMING WORK

In this book we will distinguish the following categories of persons performing work:

- employed persons;
- dependent workers without a contract of employment;
- bogus self-employed;
- 'genuine' self-employed.

2.1. Employed Persons

Employed persons are persons having a contract of employment. The contract of employment is defined by national labour law; there is no EU or international definition. However, the main criteria which national legislations and case law use, in any case in Western countries, are quite similar, as appears from the studies undertaken so far (see section 3). Broadly speaking, under a contract of employment a person is obliged to perform work personally in return for wages under the supervision of another person.

Questions arise, however, especially in borderline situations: when can it be said that a person works in supervision for someone else? How to define exactly that work is to be done personally? When is remuneration considered as wages?

As a result of the application and/or interpretation of these criteria, there is also a group of persons performing work personally, who do not have a contract of employment. We will discuss this category below.

Also some categories of persons with a contract of employment may be excluded from part of, or from all, labour law and/or social security law. This may be on the ground that they have a contract for a definite period, a low income or small number of working hours. It is also possible that persons are excluded because they have a high income or a special position (e.g., director of a company). However, the first categories are the problematic ones since persons in the high income group can provide for their own solutions in case of problems, whereas this is much more difficult for those in marginal employment. Because of their vulnerable position these marginal workers are also mentioned as part of the problem of the limited scope of labour law.

2.2. Workers without a Contract of Employment

The category of persons performing personal work without a contract of employment includes several categories. These persons often have a contract of services or of civil law, which is denied the status of contract of employment. Sometimes they do not have a contract in writing. The extent of the group workers without a contract of employment may vary considerably from country to country and the group as such consists of many subcategories.

If these workers wish to claim labour law protection and argue that, despite the title of the contract, they are employed persons, several problems arise. One problem is that of persons whose relationship with their work provider is uncertain. Do they have to do the work personally and under supervision of the work provider? Traditional examples are persons who are asked only to do work when work is available (on-call workers) and home workers. Another type of problem occurs if it is clear that a particular criterion for a contract of employment is, strictly speaking, not satisfied. An example is that of persons who work for a work provider, but who are paid directly by the customers. Another example is that of persons who are supervised by a person other than the person who pays the wage.[1] A more recent example of this category is that of temporary agency workers. In the case of temporary agency workers, it can be said that they are not working in a supervision relation for the user company and that this company is therefore not their employer. It can also be said that these workers are not working for the agency itself. Therefore, it is argued that they do not have a contract of employment. In the case of freelancers it can also be said that they are not working under the supervision of their user company. That company does not decide on the times of the day they

1. In some countries the national legislation has found a solution by defining that such persons should have a contract of employment too or in the case law a broad interpretation of the criterion is accepted. That does not take away that such uncertainties have, in general, lead to the distinction of the various categories of workers.

work and whether they are assisted by others. Moreover, it is possible that they have more than one principal. There can also be a dispute on whether they are obliged to actually perform work in case they are called to do so. For this reason in the situation of freelancers there can be several reasons to argue that they do not have a contract of employment. In some situations, however, it is assumed that they have a contract of employment.

In some countries it is defined by an Act or decided in case law that one or more of these categories of persons still have a contract of employment. It is also possible that they are treated as specific categories and that the Act provides that part of the labour law applies to them. A common example concerns the health and safety rules. Sometimes they are even protected by collective agreements. Still, if they do not have a contract of employment, the major part of labour law does not apply to them.

2.3. The Bogus Self-employed

A third category is that of the bogus self-employed. These persons differ from the other categories in that they are called self-employed and treated in this way by the work provider. In fact, however, they are wholly dependent on the work provider and their position is not different from that of employed persons. Some of the bogus self-employed accepted this position out of free will, as they expect a higher net income and more freedom than workers. Others were forced to accept this position by the employer by whom they were previously employed, since it is cheaper for the latter to engage these workers in a self-employment relationship.

The bogus self-employed are mentioned here as a separate category, even though one may argue that they are subcategories of the two previous ones. However, they are different from the other two since they have formally an independent position, and therefore the legal approach is different than in the case of the other two categories.

2.4. The Genuine Self-employed

The fourth category is that of the genuine self-employed: persons working on their own account for several work providers. Among this category there may be many subcategories, varying from persons with a weak economic position to those who have been able to protect themselves against the risks and uncertainties of their position.

A recent development is the rapid growth of workers who are self-employed but do not have staff. In other words, they do all the work themselves. Often their position is very similar to workers and they are in an economically dependent position. If they have more than one work provider and equipment of their own they are genuine self-employed; however, their economic situation also closely resembles that of workers and the question arises whether they need some protection. There are also self-employed who have chosen their new status out of their own free will, as this gives them a higher net income and more freedom and they do not need further protection. These different groups of self-employed make the analysis more complicated.

The real self-employed are as such not the subject of our research, as this is limited to the protection of persons who work for work providers on whom they are dependent. Still this category is mentioned here because of the problem of delineating the various categories.

3. PROPOSALS FOR DISTINGUISHING THE VARIOUS CATEGORIES

It is often difficult to distinguish employed persons and workers, since the criteria for the contract of employment are subject to large margins of interpretation. A university professor, for instance, often has the freedom to decide what research project he[2] undertakes and with whom. He also decides whether he travels to a conference or not and whether he gives advice or does consultancy work for third parties, etc. He is in many respects a self-employed person with a salary.

In many other professions we can nowadays also find examples of highly skilled or educated persons who have a large freedom to perform their work, including medical doctors, lawyers, managers and persons who nurse others at home.

Below I will discuss some of the analyses which have so far been made in the literature. Inevitably, this description is far from exhaustive. The contract of employment is, of course, the basis of labour law and therefore there are numerous publications on this issue. The proposals selected here are those we considered the most fruitful in discussions on extending the protection by the contract of employment. In our conclusions, made in the last Chapter, we will come back to these proposals.

3.1. The Framework Elaborated by Mark Freedland

An interesting framework for looking at the personal work relationships was developed by Mark Freedland.[3] Although he does not give (nor does he intend to do so) new criteria for distinguishing the various categories, his analysis encourages us to look from new angles at the various relationships under which work is done.

---

2. For the purpose of making the text more readable, the personal pronouns he and him also refer to she and her, where appropriate.
3. M. Freedland, 'From the Contract of Employment to the Personal Work Nexus', *Industrial Law Journal* 1 (2006), 1. See also, from the same author, *The Personal Employment Contract* (Oxford: Oxford University Press, 2003).

Freeland argues that in the realm of personal work contracts, there is an enormous variety of factual patterns of work arrangements. This means that there may be large variations in the rights and duties that are connected with a particular personal work contract. He therefore suggests that employment relationships must be considered from five dimensions:

(i) that of the worker;
(ii) that of the employing enterprise;
(iii) that of the duration and continuity;
(iv) that of personality and substitutability; and
(v) that of purpose and motivation.

The dimensions are relevant in respect of all types of working relationships, but they are useful to identify the classification problems which occur in relation to a specific type of working relationship and to compare them with types of employment relationships.

The fourth dimension, for instance, of personality and substitutability (iv), is particularly relevant in the case of on-call workers, since in their situation it is disputed whether they really have to do the work personally or can be substituted by another worker. By placing this question in the personality dimension, and comparing it to other types of contract, we have to notice that in employment relationships, work is not always done in the modality of subordination or autonomy of the worker either. Instead there can be a variety of purposes and modalities. Training contracts, apprenticeships, and contracts for writing a PhD at a university are examples of contracts where personal autonomy may be large.[4] This is also true for our example of the university professor.

In this way also the dimension of duration and continuity (iii) may be relevant, particularly in the case of on-call workers and casual workers. In case of temporary work agencies, for instance, the disputed facts lie, in particular, in the dimension of the employing enterprise (ii).

Although the framework is made for analysis and not as a decision model, we can use it as a way to broaden the interpretation of the criteria. For instance, the purpose of a particular working relationship, for example, of writing a PhD thesis, may be to increase the expertise of the person concerned and to add to the increase of knowledge. In this case doubts on whether this person works in all respects in subordination to another person should not – given this particular objective of the contract – be the decisive criterion for whether it is a contract of employment or not. The other dimensions should be more relevant.

Another way of using the dimension approach may be to establish more variations between the working relationships. For instance, fixed-term contracts may as well occur in the form of a contract of employment as in the form of an independent personal services contract. If, from this point of view, these contracts

4. M. Freedland, 'From the Contract of Employment to the Personal Work Nexus', *Industrial Law Journal* 35, no. 1 (2006), 12.

have elements in common (e.g., the uncertainty of work at the end of the contract) the law may treat these forms of contract in the same way.

These dimensions are thus not criteria to be fulfilled, but elements which may be useful to address in a factual situation.

Thus, Freedland does not give the ultimate criteria to distinguish the various categories of work relationship, but his analysis is useful to show that when analysing a particular work relationship we have to consider the various dimensions and take these into account in our description. It does, at the moment, not lead to clear cut solutions but it may be a sound basis for further research.

3.2. The Supiot Report

A study more aimed at analysing the existing working relationships was undertaken by Alain Supiot. Supiot was commissioned with a study for the European Commission on this topic, and this led to a book in collaboration with several labour law experts.[5]

Supiot argued that workers in traditional employment relationships nowadays experience greater operational independence. In addition, the appearance of third parties, that is, subcontractors and temporary work agencies, have led to more complex relations between employers and workers. As a result bogus self-employment and a grey area between dependent employment and self-employment may occur. *Supra*, we already mentioned temporary agency workers and home workers; they also fit in this grey area.

These developments mean that the scope of labour law often does not cover all workers who are in a position comparable to that of employees. This was found unjustified and problematic and therefore Supiot made the following proposals:

1. The European Union has to make a Community definition of the notion of employee (p. 219).
2. In addition the power of the courts to reclassify a civil law contract as an employment contract must be upheld. These proposals intend to ensure that the protection available in labour law will indeed be given to persons working *de facto* in an employment relationship (p. 220).
3. The scope of labour law must be expanded to cover all kinds of contracts involving the performance of work for others. Labour law must not be limited to persons working as employees (p. 219).
4. Certain aspects of labour law must be extended to workers who are neither employees nor self-employed. Workers who cannot be regarded as employed persons, but are in a situation of economic dependence

5. Alain Supiot, *Beyond Employment. Changes in Work and the Future of Labour Law in Europe* (Oxford: Oxford University Press, 2005). The original report was published in French in 1999, *Au-delà de l'emploi* (Paris: Flammarion, 1999).

vis-à-vis a principal, should be able to benefit from the social rights to which this dependence entitles them (p. 220).

3.3. The Perulli Report

Another interesting report is by Adalberto Perulli,[6] who was also commissioned by the European Commission to make a study of working relationships. Perulli studied the labour markets of several European countries from the point of view of protection of the economically dependent workers.

He concluded that the following indicators are used in Member States to establish the condition of economic dependency: a person performs mainly personal work; there is continuity in time; the work performance is coordinated with the activity of the client; he performs work mainly for one single client (mono-commitment), which provides a major source of the worker's income.

By and large, Perulli argued, the European countries under study identify self-employment through 'inverse' categorisation, that is, by ascertaining that certain work does not have the characteristics of subordinate work. In other words, what is not considered as subordinate work is self-employment. As a consequence, self-employment does not constitute a general and a unitary category, but a theoretical abstraction which includes multiple and fragmented judicial regimes. It is a complex and diversified phenomenon. He concluded that self-employment is a concept that comprises a growing number of different types of work and legal regimes regulating them. Therefore, it would be a methodological error, he argued, to start from the presupposition that self-employment is a compact and unitary category which can be contrasted with subordinate work.

Perulli added that bogus self-employment is conceptually different from economically dependent work. Bogus self-employed are workers who are treated as self-employed, but who, from the legal perspective, clearly fall within the category of subordinate employment. These two phenomena require different responses from the legal system. The first requires interpretation (or up-dating) of the criteria used for defining subordinate work whereas the second concerns the application of legislation in force.

He also discussed the grey zone between self-employment and subordinate work. New forms of work organisation have been developed such as outsourcing and contracting out. This development led to the emergence of economically dependent work which represents a form of work falling within a grey zone between dependent work and self-employment. This grey zone has, according to Perulli, two different characteristics:

(1) There are forms of work having characteristics of both subordinate work and self-employment and therefore cannot easily be fitted into the binary model (in other words, it is an uncertain status).

6. Adalberto Perulli, *Study on Economically Dependent Work/Parasubordinate (Quasi-subordinate) Work* (Brussels: European Commission, 2002).

(2) In addition there is bogus self-employment. This is a form of subordinate employment disguised as self-employment.

In his report Perulli developed the following scenarios:

(1) One is to maintain the status quo. For instance, the general contractual principles of civil law and in particular the general clause on good faith and correctness can be applied to economically dependent workers. According to Perulli, however, this is a weak way of ensuring protection. Maintaining status quo leaves economically dependent workers at the mercy of market forces.
(2) A second scenario is to create a new type of work (a new legal category) in-between subordinate work and self-employment. Certain forms of protection would be extended through legislation and/or case law to cover this new type of work. According to Perulli this option should be avoided, for it would create new legal problems related to the qualification of a relationship in one of the categories.
(3) A third suggestion is to redefine (enlarge) the notion of subordinate work: to up-date the notion of subordinate work (by adding other criteria for subordination), so that the notion corresponds with the changed socio-economic context. The objective of this option would be to impede the diffusion of 'apparent autonomy' and to support 'real autonomy'. This solution, however, is not widely supported. Furthermore, the enlargement of the definition of subordinate work could result in the excessive expansion of the notion of the subordination.
(4) A fourth scenario is to create a 'hard core' of social rights which are applicable to all work contracts irrespective of their formal qualification in terms of autonomy (self-employment) or subordination.

4. CONCLUSIONS

The previous sections described that, as a result of changing labour market needs, new forms of work were created which are often not covered by labour law. I made a distinction between the categories involved and discussed solutions suggested in recent studies and reports.

From the categorisation of work relationships and the studies mentioned, we can conclude that there are several topics for study:

- the interpretation of the criteria for the contract of employment are often unclear and/or not adjusted to new forms of work; as a result persons in a similar position as employed persons are not given the protection by labour law;
- there are persons who are treated as self-employed and have a contract to that effect, but their position fits with all the criteria of the contract of employment;

- there are persons in an economical dependent position who cannot be brought under the criteria of the contract of employment, even with a broad interpretation of these criteria, most often on the ground that they have more than one principal.

It is important to keep these distinctions in mind, as the legal position of the distinguished categories varies to a large extent. Also the measures which can be taken to improve their position may be very different. Finally, there may also be differences in political support for extending labour law protection depending on the category concerned.

The proposals suggested were:

- To make a Community definition of the notion of employee and to support the power of the courts to reclassify a civil law contract as an employment contract if the person concerned is working de facto in an employment relationship.
- To expand the scope of labour law to cover all kinds of contracts involving the performance of work for others.
- Certain aspects of labour law must be extended to workers who are neither employees nor self-employed. Workers who cannot be regarded as employed persons but are in a situation of economic dependence *vis-à-vis* a principal should be able to benefit from the social rights to which this dependence entitles them.
- To redefine (enlarge) the notion of subordinate work, (by adding other criteria for subordination), so that the notion corresponds with the changed socio-economic context.
- To create a 'hard core' of social rights which are applicable to all work contracts irrespective of their formal qualification in terms of autonomy (self-employment) or subordination.

In the following Chapters we will first discuss the actions taken by the International Labour Organisation and the EU. Then the actual developments in several EU countries are analysed in order to determine whether the proposals which were suggested were implemented in one way or another and also to determine whether in the national context there are additional developments which can contribute to the objective of clarifying the scope of the contract of employment and possibly extending the protection by labour law.

Chapter 3

ILO Recommendation 198, the Employment Relationship Recommendation

Claire Bosse

1. INTRODUCTION

As was discussed in the previous chapters, currently, in most legal systems, workers are divided into two major categories: those with an employment contract or employment relationship (also called 'employees') and those without such a contract/relationship (also called 'autonomous workers', 'independent contractors' or 'self-employed persons'). Persons in the first category are protected by labour law; those in the second are not, although they may be protected by commercial or civil law. By giving working arrangements an 'independent' look, businesses try to escape the costs following from the application of labour law and social security law.

Since this is a threat to labour law and social security law, this development was addressed by the International Labour Organisation. In the ILO Declaration on Social Justice for a Fair Globalisation, adopted by the International Labour Conference on 10 June 2008, representatives of governments, employers' and workers' organisations from all over the world agreed that 'the importance of the employment relationship should be recognised as a means of providing legal protection to workers'.

Frans Pennings & Claire Bosse, *The Protection of Working Relationships*, pp. 15–28.
© 2011 Kluwer Law International BV, The Netherlands.

In this Chapter I will investigate how the ILO dealt with the issue of the employment relationship since it first appeared on the agenda. The background of the current Recommendation will be discussed in Sections 2–5. In Section 4, a table is reproduced representing the different points of view of workers' and employers' representatives. The content of the Recommendation will be discussed in Section 6, where I will highlight some of the legal instruments proposed in the Recommendation. In the final section I will present some elements for a future Convention on disguised employment. For the ILO, this could be an interesting initiative to redress the widespread problem of disguised employment and combat further erosion of the employment relationship.

2. THE CONFERENCE ON CONTRACT LABOUR IN 1998

In the early 1990s, a tripartite technical meeting on the construction industry drew the attention of the Governing Body (the executive body of the International Labour Office) to the problem of contact labour. The term 'contract labour' generally refers to workers engaged by a contractor for user enterprises. Contract workers are workers who operate outside the framework of an employment relationship, but under conditions similar to those of employees. Contract labour is a significant and growing form of employment, especially, but not exclusively, in Asian countries. There are millions of contract workers and they are engaged primarily in agricultural operations, plantation, construction industry, ports and docks, oil fields, factories, railways, shipping, airlines and road transport. This kind of labour is often used to deny or avoid the rights and obligations under labour law and social security regulations. In India, the Contract Labour (Regulation and Abolition) Act 1970 was enacted to protect and safeguard the interests of these workers. It applies to every establishment or contractor in which twenty or more workmen are employed. It also applies to establishments of the Government and local authorities.[1]

In response to this discussion, in 1998, the ILO proposed a convention on contract labour. The Office came up with the following definition:

> Contract labour is work performed for a natural or legal person (referred to as a 'user enterprise') by a person (referred to as a 'contract worker') where the work is performed by the worker personally under actual conditions of dependency on or subordination to the user enterprise and these conditions are

1. See Ministry of Labour Annual Report 2008–2009, Part I (Labour), Chapter 10 (contract labour), <http://labour.nic.in/annrep/annrep0809/Chapter-10.pdf>. A recent study suggests, however, that many of the stipulations made in the Act to safeguard contract labourers are not followed in practice; see Meenakshi Rajeev, *Contract Labour Act in India: A Pragmatic View, IGIDR Proceedings/Project Reports Series PP-062-33* (August 2009), <www.igidr.ac.in/pdf/publication/PP-062-33.pdf>.

similar to those that characterise an employment relationship under national law and practice and where either: (i) the work is performed pursuant to a direct contractual arrangement between the worker and the user enterprise; or (ii) the worker is provided for the user enterprise by a subcontractor or an intermediary.[2]

During the conference it soon became clear that the concept of contract labour was not suitable for standard setting. The main reason was that the term *contract labour* has different meanings in different languages, covers a variety of conditions and circumstances, and is inconsistent with national law and practice. Employers' organisations and many governments argued that the proposed convention would hamper business opportunities, economic growth and the creation of new employment. Some employers' organisations even suggested that the ILO was operating outside its mandate.

At the end of the conference, the reporter of the committee spoke of a 'highly complex area', in which 'the only common view shared by all constituents has related to the need to combat the use of disguised employment as a means of avoiding legal obligations'. The employers' spokesman confirmed that 'disguised employment is the only issue which can be sensibly and practicably addressed'.

The draft convention on contract labour was thus rejected. I will leave this issue here and focus on the issue of disguised employment. At the end of this chapter I will propose some elements for a future convention on this subject (see Section 7).

3. EXPERT REPORT ON DISGUISED EMPLOYMENT RELATIONSHIPS

Following the failure of the conference to adopt an international instrument on contract labour, the Governing Body was asked to put the issue on the agenda of a future session. In the meantime a group of international experts would study the situation of disguised employment. The ILO commissioned thirty-five country studies and appointed a group of experts to identify situations in which workers are in need of protection.[3]

These experts first met in May 2000 and reported on situations of disguised, ambiguous and triangular employment relationships where it is unclear whether an employment relationship exists or not.[4] Workers in these relationships are often not

2. See *Contract labour*, Report V (2A), (Geneva: ILO 1998), <www.ilo.org/public/english/standards/relm/ilc/ilc86/comreps.htm>.
3. The national studies are available at the website of the ILO, <www.ilo.org/public/english/dialogue/ifpdial/areas/legislation/employ.htm>.
4. ILO, *Basic technical document*, Meeting of experts on workers in situations needing protection (the employment relationship: scope) (Geneva: ILO 2000) <www.ilo.org/public/english/dialogue/ifpdial/publ/mewnp/index.htm>.

aware of their rights; do not know who their employer is or who is accountable for their rights. The experts also pointed out that the administrative and legal procedures for the establishment of an employment relationship are often expensive and ineffective, which makes it difficult for workers to realise their rights.

As can be expected, employers' and workers' experts differed in their views on how to address these problems. Worker-experts saw the need for an international instrument to clarify national standards and adjust the limits of labour legislation. Employer-experts agreed on the need to combat fraudulent practices and enforce existing laws and regulations, but saw no need for an international instrument. They argued that the cost of regulating all workers would be too high, regulation would negatively affect competition and employment, and independent contractors did not want to be protected by labour law. The government experts were divided: some of them emphasised the economic perspective, as defended by the employers; others emphasised the social perspective, as defended by the trade unions.

4. THE FIRST CONFERENCE ON THE EMPLOYMENT RELATIONSHIP

In 2003, the discussion was back on the Conference agenda. After two weeks of debate, the Committee on the Employment Relationship managed to lay the foundation for a future Recommendation. The Provisional Record shows once again that employers' and workers' organisations looked at the issue from different angles.[5] The employers emphasised the economic point of view, according to which flexibility and new forms of labour outside the scope of the employment relationship are a prerequisite for economic growth. For them, the ILO should focus on better enforcement of existing laws. The workers emphasised the social point of view, from which flexibility and new forms of labour are only acceptable if combined with security for workers. For them, better enforcement is not enough, as there is also an urgent need to readjust the limits of labour law. The workers put forward a number of proposals, based on successful experiences at the national level, such as the use of tests and criteria to determine the existence of an employment relationship, the introduction of a legal definition of the employment relationship and the presumption of employment in certain cases.[6]

The different points of view are reflected in Table 3.1.

5. Provisional Record 21 (ILO 2003) <www.ilo.org/public/english/standards/relm/ilc/ilc91/pdf/pr-21.pdf>.
6. Provisional Record 21 (ILO 2003), 18–19.

Table 3.1. Points of View of Employers' and Workers' Organisations on Employment Relationship Recommendation

Employers	*Workers*
The employment relationship is a national subject and therefore not suitable for international regulation	The employment relationship is a universal subject; international action is necessary because of the consequences for international competition
Changing employment patterns brings about economic growth, employment and the improvement of living conditions	Changing employment patterns cause greater inequality and a lack of protection
International regulation impedes economic growth and employment creation	International regulation prevents unprotected labour from growing
The focus should be on the application and enforcement of existing legislation	The focus should be on the application and enforcement of existing legislation, but also on international regulation
The diversity and complexity of modern employment relations stand in the way of a uniform approach or single definition	A uniform approach is possible because of common factors and problems
The principle of 'primacy of facts' does not take into account the will of the parties	The principle of 'primacy of facts' precedes the subjective choice of the parties
The lack of protection has not been proved	The lack of protection has been proved and is at the agenda of the ILO since 1950
Working without the protection of labour law is a free choice and offers advantages in the field of taxation, higher income, greater flexibility and personal freedom	Working without the protection of labour law is a forced choice, because the parties to the employment relationship are not equal. Growing unemployment forces many workers to accept suboptimal or even illegal working conditions
Regulation has a negative impact on economic growth, job creation and leads to the emergence of a third category of workers. Besides, protection is not exclusively linked to the existence of an employment relationship but also exists in other legal areas (such as commercial law or contract law)	The lack of employment protection has negative consequences for employers (unfair competition, lower productivity), governments (less income taxes and social security contributions, unsafe working conditions, discrimination, income inequality, lack of social cohesion, poverty and social exclusion) and workers (abuse and exploitation)

Although employers' and workers' organisations had (and still have) opposite views on the need for international regulation of the employment relationship, they agreed that existing laws and regulations should be better enforced. They also agreed that the personal scope of national labour laws and regulations should be clarified, that the capacity of labour administrations, labour inspections and the judiciary should be strengthened, that the knowledge of labour law should be improved and that clear procedures should be introduced to determine workers' status. Together with the main conclusion of the 1998 conference – the need to combat the use of disguised employment as a means of avoiding legal obligations – these common viewpoints lay the foundation for an international instrument.

At the end of the 2003 session, the committee adopted a resolution concerning the employment relationship, including twenty-five conclusions.[7] The following are the main ones:

- the employment relationship is a notion which creates a legal link between the employee and the employer;
- self-employment and independent work based on commercial and civil contractual arrangements are by definition beyond the scope of the employment relationship;
- the concept of the employment relationship is common to all legal systems and traditions;
- the criteria for determining whether or not an employment relationship exists may vary but in many countries common notions such as dependency or subordination are found;
- due to changes in the structure of the labour market, the organisation of work and the inadequate application of the law, a growing number of workers who are in fact employees, find themselves without the protection of an employment relationship;
- it is in the interest of all labour market actors to ensure that the wide variety of working arrangements be put within an appropriate legal framework;
- clear rules are also indispensable for fair governance of the labour market.

The committee concluded that a recommendation would be an appropriate instrument:[8]

> This Recommendation should focus on disguised employment relationships and on the need for mechanisms to ensure that persons with an employment relationship have access to the protection they are due at the national level. Such a Recommendation should provide guidance to Member States without defining universally the substance of the employment relationship. The Recommendation should be flexible enough to take account of different

7. The report, the resolution and the conclusions paras 1–25 were adopted on 18 Jun. 2003, without any objection. See *Provisional Record* 26 (Geneva: ILO, 2003a), 34.
8. ILO 2003, Provisional Record 21, 21/57, para. 25.

economic, social, legal and industrial relations traditions and (. . .) should not interfere with genuine commercial and independent contracting arrangements.

This last conclusion, on which all parties agreed, played an important role in the second discussion on the employment relationship.

5. THE SECOND CONFERENCE ON THE EMPLOYMENT RELATIONSHIP

In 2005, the ILO Office distributed a report on law and practice in more than sixty Member States, including a questionnaire on the employment relationship.[9] In spring 2006, the Office published a draft Recommendation on the employment relationship. When the government delegates and the representatives of employers' and workers' organisations finally gathered in Geneva for the Committee on the employment relationship, they all knew it was going to be a difficult discussion. At first sight, the office proposal went much further than expected and included a number of 'contagious' subjects, such as the idea of legal presumptions or the enumeration of criteria for the existence of employment relationship. It also touched upon the subject of the triangular employment relationship (a labour agreement involving three or more parties), an issue that was not resolved during the first conference. So, when the Committee on the employment relationship started its work, some of the participants were already in a 'state of alarm'. The pressure to reach an agreement was high, not only because of the earlier failure of the conference to adopt a convention on contract labour (see Sections 2 and 3), but also because of the costs of an international conference.

After two weeks of formal and informal meetings in the Palais des Nations and the ILO building, the Committee adopted a Recommendation with 329 votes in favour, ninety-four votes against (including practically all employers' organisations) and forty abstentions. Although the parties agreed to nearly three quarters of the text, there was no consensus on the Recommendation as a whole. What is more, the fact that there was no consensus – a keyword to any successful action within the ILO – has not been forgotten since.

6. CONTENT OF THE RECOMMENDATION

The Recommendation (see Annex) is divided in four parts: (1) the preamble, containing fourteen considerations; (2) the first part, calling for a national policy to guarantee effective protection for workers in an employment relationship; (3) the second part, containing guidelines for the determination of the existence

---

9. ILO, *The employment relationship*, Report V (1), International Labour Conference, 95th Session (Geneva 2006), <www.ilo.org/public/english/standards/relm/ilc/ilc95/pdf/rep-v-1.pdf>. See also the replies in Report V (2A), <www.ilo.org/public/english/standards/relm/ilc/ilc95/pdf/rep-v-2a.pdf>.

of an employment relationship; and (4) the last part, holding provisions on monitoring and implementation. In this section I will concentrate on some of the major (legal) issues of the Recommendation.[10]

6.1. National Policy

The core of the Recommendation is the appeal to ILO Member States to formulate and apply a national policy for reviewing and, if necessary, clarifying and adapting the scope of labour laws and regulations to guarantee effective protection for workers in an employment relationship (Section 1). The nature and extent of this protection should be defined by national law and/or practice (Section 2). The reference to national practice is particularly important for countries such as Denmark and Sweden, where legislation traditionally plays a minor role in the regulation of industrial relations.

According to Section 4, the national policy should at least include measures to:

- provide guidance for employers and workers on the existence of an employment relationship and the distinction between employed and self-employed workers;
- combat disguised employment relationships;
- ensure standards applicable to all forms of contractual arrangements, including those involving multiple parties;[11]
- provide access to employers and workers to speedy and inexpensive procedures for the settlement of disputes on the existence and terms of an employment relationship;
- ensure compliance with and application of laws and regulations concerning the employment relationship.

The national policy should pay special attention to women workers, migrant workers and other vulnerable groups of workers, who are more likely to be involved in disguised or unclear employment relationships (Section 7).

6.2. Primacy of Facts

Section 9 of the Recommendation recalls the principle of 'primacy of facts', according to which the judge has to take into account all the relevant facts and circumstances of the case. This principle is widely accepted among ILO Members. In case of a dispute, the judge will consider the intention of the parties as expressed in the name or text of the contract. In the end, however, the appreciation of the facts

10. In 2008 the ILO published a guide with information on the recommendation: ILO, *The employment relationship. An annotated guide to ILO Recommendation No. 198* (Geneva: ILO 2008), <www.ilo.org/public/english/dialogue/ifpdial/downloads/guide-rec198.pdf>.
11. This formulation replaces the Office references to the triangular employment relationship.

will prevail as intentions can be fraudulent, for example, evasion of income taxes and social security contributions.[12] Therefore, if the contract does not reflect the reality of the facts, it can be put aside by the labour judge. In legal practice, not all the facts are taken into consideration. The judge can only reach a conclusion on the basis of non-disputed or proven facts put forward by the parties in dispute. In most cases, the worker will claim there is (or has been) an employment relationship between the parties, entitling him or her to the benefits of labour law and social security law. The supposed 'employer' will then argue that there is no such relationship as parties had the intention to cooperate on an independent basis. In most of these cases, the dispute turns around the existence of subordination, which is one of the essential features of the employment relationship. In some legal traditions, such as the United Kingdom, the judge will use tests to take account of all relevant facts and circumstances (see also Chapter 10).

6.3. Conditions

As part of their national policy, governments can define the conditions applied to determine the existence of an employment relationship. Paragraph 12 gives two examples: subordination and dependence. During the conference, the employers were not able to accept references to specific conditions, not even as an example. They had already stated this in 2003, and could not be persuaded by the fact that the instrument was only a Recommendation with vague and flexible wording. The introduction of criteria would, in their view, create an imbalance in national legal systems. Employers' spokesman Finlay argued that the Recommendation would be used by national courts and tribunals and result in pressure on governments to adapt or adopt national criteria. It would also make the instrument inflexible and undermine small business agreements.[13] The employers' group proposed to delete the examples from the text, but a majority of governments and workers did not support this amendment. In their view the text would be meaningless without examples.

An employment relationship usually exists when the following conditions are met: work, remuneration, subordination and personal performance. In some countries a certain duration or continuity is required; in other countries it is possible to have an employment relationship for one day. The existence of work, personal performance and remuneration are usually not difficult to establish. In legal practice, most disputes involve the element of subordination.

The notion of subordination has two aspects: (1) the will of the employee to work under the direction and control of the employer and (2) the authority of the employer to instruct the worker, control the work and take disciplinary measures if

12. See, for instance, the judgment of the Assemblée Plenière of the French Cour de Cassation of 4 Mar. 1983, in which the Court ruled that: 'La seule volonté des parties est impuissante à les soustraire du statut qui résulte des conditions d'execution du travail'.
13. ILO, *Provisional Record 21* (Geneva: ILO 2006), no. 399.

the work is not performed according to the instructions. The employer can also give instructions regarding the internal organisation of the enterprise (e.g., determine working hours, collective holidays, protective measures, etc.). However, it is important to note that these are *legal* competences, which means that even if the employee never receives instructions and the employer never controls the work, there can still be an employment relationship if the employer has the legal ability to do so.

6.4. Indicators

Section 13 recommends the use of specific indicators of the existence of an employment relationship, such as the fact that the work:

- is carried out according to the instructions and under the control of another party;
- involves the integration of the worker in the organisation of the enterprise;
- is performed solely or mainly for the benefit of another person;
- must be carried out personally by the worker;
- is carried out within specific working hours;
- is carried out at a workplace specified or agreed by the party requesting the work;
- requires the worker's availability;
- involves the provision of tools, materials and machinery by the party requesting the work.

Other indicators that are often taken into account are:

- periodic payment of remuneration to the worker;
- recognition of weekly rest and annual holidays;
- absence of financial risk for the worker.

This section does not specify how many indicators are needed or whether some of the indicators are more important than others. In practice, the judge will be confronted with a variety of facts, some of them indicating the existence of an employment relationship, others the existence of another contractual arrangement (or at least the non-existence of an employment relationship). As he has to account for his decision, he will carefully weigh the relevant facts. According to Davidov, indicators can sometimes be helpful to identify the existence of subordination or dependency, but judges should not rely too heavily on them.[14] Instead of defining specific indicators in laws or regulations, governments can also develop a code of practice, following the examples of Ireland or South-Africa.[15]

14. European Network of Legal Experts in the field of Labour Law, *Characteristics of the Employment Relationship*, Thematic Report 2009 (Leiden: 2009), 27.
15. See ILO 2003, Report V, 57–60.

6.5. Burden of Proof

Section 11 mentions a number of legal instruments which could relieve the burden of proof for the plaintiff: allowing a broad range of means, providing for a legal presumption and/or deeming workers with certain characteristics to be either employed or self-employed. This can be necessary in order to obtain a fair distribution of the burden of proof among the parties in conflict. In legal proceedings, the burden of proof generally rests with the party that brings the action before the court (the plaintiff). In labour disputes, this is often the worker, even though the employer (the defendant) generally has better access to documentary evidence. Besides, the plaintiff's (former) colleagues are not always willing to testify against their employer for fear of retaliation.

The introduction of a legal presumption is an interesting tool to facilitate the burden of proof for the worker. If the court decides that one or more indicators are present, the existence of an employment relationship is presumed, unless the employer proves otherwise. There is one important detail: a presumption only 'works' if the indicators put forward by the worker are sufficiently substantiated and convincing. In other words, if the court is not convinced that one or more indicators are present, the burden of proof will stay with the plaintiff. This is necessary to protect the defendant from a reversal of the onus of proof in the case of false allegations and will also prevent the courts from a flood of legal proceedings introduced by self-employed workers claiming the existence of an employment relationship.[16] There is also another preventative effect in that employers will carefully define the nature of the relationship to avoid being surprised by a legal presumption. This clarity is in the interest of both parties.

6.6. Disguised Employment Relationships

Section 17 recommends Members to develop effective measures aimed at removing incentives to disguise an employment relationship. A disguised employment relationship occurs when the employer treats an individual as other than an employee in a manner that hides his or her true legal status as an employee (section 4). There are a number of differences between the employment relationship and other forms of contractual arrangements, which could constitute possible incentives to disguise the employment relationship. The fact that this happens deliberately makes it an offence, but the effect of depriving workers from the protection of labour law also arises when the employment relationship is unintentionally disguised.

According to the ILO:

> A disguised employment relationship is one which is lent an appearance that is different from the underlying reality, with the intention of nullifying or

16. See C. Bosse, *Bewijslastverdeling in het Nederlandse en Belgische Arbeidsrecht* (Deventer: Kluwer, 2003), 312.

> attenuating the protection afforded by the law. It is thus an attempt to conceal or distort the employment relationship, either by cloaking it in another legal guise or by giving it another form in which the worker enjoys less protection.[17]

Employment relationships can be disguised by giving it another legal nature (e.g., service, franchise, distribution or training contracts) or by manipulating the form or the contract (e.g., chains of fixed-term contracts). Changes in the legal status of dependent workers are commonly observed in traditional sectors such as construction and clothing, but also in newer areas such as transport, department stores and private security agencies. The case of truck drivers in transport firms is illustrative: in several countries they have been 'transferred' to work for contractors or 'converted' into self-employed drivers required to own or lease their own vehicles. The most visible effect of contract manipulation is that the worker does not obtain the benefits provided to employees by labour legislation or collective bargaining.[18]

For the employer, subcontracting may seem advantagious: no collective bargaining, no strikes, no trade union representation, no fixed working hours, no annual leave, no holiday allowances, no period of notice or severance pay, no personnel department, no training facilities, no social security contributions, no pension allowances. There are even more 'advantages' when subcontractors are working at home, which often happens in manufacturing such as the textile industry: no factory buildings, no maintenance of tools and machinery, no safety regulations, and no visits from the labour inspection. If there is no need for personal instructions and control, the manufacturer may as well choose a subcontracting arrangement. In addition to regulations imposing liability in subcontracting chains, there are also other major disadvantages to this kind of arrangement: the worker is autonomous, which means that the 'employer' has only limited powers to instruct the worker and control the work. The worker will only be available for the agreed task and might be less loyal towards the company. The worker is free to use his knowledge and skills the way he likes, which means that he can terminate the contract as soon as better opportunities arise. Knowledge and skills will gradually decrease by lack of training and workers will become less motivated. In the end, companies might suffer from a bad image and subsequent boycott of their products if they do not control the labour conditions of their subcontractors.

7. A PROPOSAL FOR A FUTURE CONVENTION ON DISGUISED EMPLOYMENT

The ILO Recommendation on the employment relationship was adopted without consensus (Section 6). Difficult legal issues such as presumptions and criteria for the existence of an employment relationship turned out to be major obstacles for the employers' representatives, while the workers' representatives were determined to force the Office Proposal through. As a result, the employment

17. ILO 2003b, 24–25.
18. ILO 2003b, 26 and 40.

relationship is still considered a 'no-go-area', which is obviously not what the Office had in mind when starting the discussion in 2006. It seems that the office underestimated the resistance of the employers' group after the relatively successful outcome of the 2003 conference.

Given the contradictory objectives and the divergent concerns of employers and workers no one is to blame for this debacle. On the other hand, the employment relationship cannot be left in the middle of a no-go-area, as in most countries it is the only entrance ticket to the protection of labour law and social security law. The introduction of a national policy involving one or more elements of the ILO Recommendation can help to improve the protection of workers in an employment relationship. However, to redress the widespread problem of disguised employment relationships, more has to be done. I will therefore turn back to the conclusions of the 2003 conference and formulate some elements for a future convention on disguised employment relationships.

Proposal for a Convention on the Elimination of Disguised Employment Relationships

Considering that:

- the protection of workers is at the heart of the mandate of the ILO and in accordance with the principles set out in the ILO Declaration on Fundamental Principles and Rights at Works and in the Decent Work Agenda;
- the ILO Declaration on Social Justice for a Fair Globalization recognises the importance of the employment relationship as a means of providing legal protection to workers;
- a disguised employment relationship has the appearance of another working arrangement to avoid the application of labour laws and regulations and avoid costs that may include taxes and social security contributions;
- disguised employment, whether deliberately or not, can undermine the protection offered to the worker and cause unfair competition to law-abiding employers.

Each Member which ratifies this Convention shall take effective measures to eliminate disguised employment relationships;:

- by improving the application and enforcement of national laws and regulations in the field of labour law;
- by ensuring that persons in an employment relationship have access to the protection they are entitled to at the national level;
- by improving the capacity of the labour administration, labour inspection and judiciary to recognise and effectively combat disguised employment;
- by informing employers and workers on the negative effects of disguised employment;
- by maintaining a clear distinction between employment relationships and independent contracting.

In a recent report, the ILO points out that 'the potential increases in vulnerable employment and working poverty (...) are likely to affect larger numbers of workers, particularly in view of the decent work deficits that were already evident prior to the economic crisis.'[19] This situation needs serious actions. It has taken many years for governments, employers and workers to adopt an international instrument concerning the employment relationship. It will take even more time to reach the main objective of the Recommendation and provide clarity on the scope of the employment relationship. Combating disguised employment relationships is part of the same strategy. It requires sustained action by national governments, employers' and workers' organisations. Making labour law more effective also means that we have to face the problem of the informal economy.

19. *Global Employment Trends* (Geneva: ILO, 2010), 42.

Chapter 4

The European Union and the Issue of the Employment Relationship

Frans Pennings

1. INTRODUCTION

In the previous chapters we saw that the coverage by the employment relationship and the protection of the economically dependent are complicated issues. In this chapter, I will investigate whether and to which extent the European Union (EU) has undertaken measures to make the concept of the contract of employment clearer and which policy this organisation follows to realise this objective.

First, I will discuss the meaning of the terms worker and self-employed in EU instruments (Section 2), then I will go into the discussion at the EU level to influence the protection by the employment contract in the Member States (Section 3). Since some EU instruments refer to these national definitions, the relevance of the meaning of workers in national law does not only concern the protection of the workers, but it also concerns the proper application of EU instruments. Therefore, we must also pay attention to this aspect (Section 4).

2. THE TERM WORKER OR EMPLOYEE IN EU INSTRUMENTS

Although EU instruments in the area of labour law frequently use the term worker or employee, these terms do not have a uniform meaning. One area of law where

Frans Pennings & Claire Bosse, *The Protection of Working Relationships*, pp. 29–41.
© 2011 Kluwer Law International BV, The Netherlands.

the term worker is used is that of freedom of movement of workers, that is, Article 45 of the Treaty on the Functioning of the European Union (TFEU) and in particular the instrument based on this article, Regulation 1612/68. In these provisions the term *worker* has a uniform meaning, developed by the Court of Justice. In other EU instruments, to be discussed below, the meaning of this term depends on the national laws in which it has to be implemented. This meaning is based on the criteria for an employment relationship which can also be found in many national systems, as we will see elsewhere in this book too: a person performs work for wages under supervision of another person. An example of this interpretation can be found in the *Blum* judgment,[1] in which the Court of Justice ruled that an employment relationship must be defined in accordance with objective criteria which distinguish it by reference to the rights and duties of the persons concerned. The essential feature of an employment relationship, however, is that for a certain period of time a person performs services for and under the direction of another person in return for which he receives remuneration. Any person who pursues activities which are effective and genuine, to the exclusion of activities on such a small scale as to be regarded as purely marginal and ancillary, must be regarded as a worker.

Consequently, part-timers are workers for the purpose of these provisions, provided that they perform genuine activities and which are not purely marginal. Also an on-call worker can be a worker for the free movement of workers provisions, although it depends on the actual circumstances whether this is actually the case. In the *Raulin* case the Court considered that in order to decide whether there are genuine and non-ancillary activities during the eight months that Ms Raulin worked as an on-call worker in the Netherlands, the Dutch court must take account of the fact that during this period she only worked a total of sixty hours. Although this fact could be an indication that it was marginal and ancillary work, the court had also to take into account whether Raulin had to be available for work and was obliged to answer a call of her employer to come to work.[2]

The reason that the term *worker* in the free movement provisions was given a Community meaning was that, without such common meaning, the right of free movement of workers would be infringed. Since free movement within the EU context means that at least two Member States are involved, it was to be ensured that this movement is not hindered in the case of a person who, although doing dependent work for another person, is not considered as an employed person according to a particular national system.

In the Equal treatment directives a definition of the term worker or employee can be found, which is to ensure a broad coverage of these instruments. For instance, Chapter 2 of the Recast Directive[3] applies to members of the working

1. Case 66/85, *Blum* [1986] *ECR* 2121.
2. Case C-357/89, *Raulin* [1992] *ECR* I-1027.
3. Directive 2006/54/EC of 5 Jul. 2006 on the implementation of the principle of equal opportunities and equal treatment of men and women in matters of employment and occupation (recast), (OJ 2006, L 204/23).

population, including self-employed persons, persons whose activity is interrupted by illness, maternity, accident or involuntary unemployment and persons seeking employment and to retired and disabled workers, and to those claiming under them, in accordance with national law and/or practice.

In other EU directives a different approach is followed. The Directive on Collective Redundancies[4] does not define the term *worker*, but only provides which types of contracts are not included: contracts of employment concluded for limited periods of time or for specific tasks and workers employed by public administrative bodies or by establishments governed by public law. This means that in this case for the interpretation of the term *worker* the national legislation is to be applied.

Another example concerns the Directive on the Transfer of Undertaking.[5] Instead of the term *worker*, the word *employee* is used. This term is to be interpreted in the same way as in the national legislation into which the directive is to be implemented,[6] in which respect the directive requires that it applies to any person who, in the Member State concerned, is protected as an employee under national employment law (Article 2(1)(d)). The directive shall be without prejudice to national law as regards the definition of contract of employment or employment relationship, but it does not allow Member States to exclude from the scope of this directive contracts of employment or employment relationships solely because (a) of the number of working hours performed or to be performed; (b) they are employment relationships governed by a fixed-duration contract of employment; or (c) they are temporary employment relationships and the undertaking, business or part of the undertaking or business transferred is, or is part of, the temporary employment business which is the employer. Thus this directive mentions some minimum harmonisation criteria for the term worker: some situations or work relationships cannot be excluded.

Article 2(2) of the Posting Directive[7] provides that for the purposes of this Directive, the term *posted worker* means a worker who, for a limited period, carries out his work in the territory of a Member State other than the State in which he normally works. Consequently, persons who are not workers according to the national criteria of the State of employment (host country) are not covered. It can thus happen that a person is considered an employed person in the sending State and a self-employed person in the host State, or the other way around.

It is remarkable that the Posting Directive does not give a uniform interpretation, since, as in the case of free movement, here also cross-border situations are involved. We will come back to this issue in section 3.2.

---

4. Directive 98/59/EC of 20 Jul. 1998 on the approximation of the laws of the Member States relating to collective redundancies, (*OJ* 1998, *L* 225/16).
5. Directive 2001/23/EC of 12 Mar. 2001 on the approximation of the laws of the Member States relating to the safeguarding of employees' rights in the event of transfers of undertakings, businesses or parts of undertakings or businesses (*OJ* 2001, *L* 82/16).
6. See Case 105/84, *Mikkelsen* [1985] *ECR* 2639.
7. Directive 96/71/EC of the European Parliament and of the Council of 16 Dec. 1996 concerning the posting of workers in the framework of the provision of services (*OJ* 1997, *L* 18/1).

3. EU INITIATIVES AND THE SCOPE OF THE PROTECTION BY LABOUR LAW

3.1. Studies Initiated by the European Commission

An important milestone in the discussion on the employment contract was the report by a group of experts presided by Alain Supiot, *Beyond Employment. Changes in Work and the Future of Labour Law in Europe* (1999).[8] This report was prepared for the European Commission (EC) and we mentioned it in Chapter 2. The report noted increasing personal insecurity as a result of changes in the supervision relation, which can result, for instance, in false self-employment. The second effect is the coming into existence of a grey area between dependent employment and self-employment. The Supiot Report proposed a reassertion of the essential principle whereby the parties to an employment relationship are not vested with the power to establish the legal status of that relationship; and a desire (with an eye to the future) to expand the scope of labour law to cover all kinds of contracts involving the performance of work for others, not only to strict worker subordination. It also suggested the adoption of a Community definition of the notion of employee; upholding the power of the courts to redefine an employment contract; consolidation of a specific status for temporary employment agencies; and the application of certain aspects of labour law to workers who are neither employees nor employers.

In 2002, the EC published a study by Adalberto Perulli, in which the developments in respect of the employment relationship in the Member States were compared.[9] The Perulli Report concluded that new forms of work organisation, such as outsourcing and contracting out, lead to the emergence of a new category of economically dependent work, which represents a form of work falling within a grey zone between dependent work and self-employment. In line with the earlier proposal by Supiot, Perulli was in favour of creating a 'hard core' of social rights, which are applicable to all work contracts irrespective of their formal qualification in terms of autonomy (self-employment) or subordination. Currently, as for contractual terms and conditions applicable to economically dependent work, regulation is lacking. The study suggests that in this field there should be a greater determination to remodel existing protection. This presupposes legislative intervention at national level. This intervention should concern, for instance, the form of the contract (it should be in writing); the object of the contract (the contract should state the professional objective, indicate the characteristics of the autonomy of the performance); rules on remuneration (the contract should indicate the criteria for determining the remuneration). It should also mention the time when

8. Alain Supiot, *Beyond Employment. Changes in Work and the Future of Labour Law in Europe*, (Oxford: Oxford University Press, 2005). The original report was published in French in 1999, *Au-delà de l'emploi.*
9. Adalberto Perulli, *Study on Economically Dependent Work/Parasubordinate (Quasi-subordinate) work* (Brussels: European Commission, 2002), DV/47999.

payments are due (sanctions for late payments); it should regulate the effects of maternity, sickness, accident, serious family reasons (the contract should include a right to suspension of contract in these cases); it has to regulate the termination of the contract (the contract should regulate this and provide for a obligatory notice); deal with training and the right to organise and to participate in trade union activities.

As we saw in Chapter 2, Perulli proposed some solutions. One of them was to create a 'hard core' of social rights which are applicable to all work contracts irrespective of their formal qualification in terms of autonomy (self-employment) or subordination. This prospect is increasingly acquiring credit in the European doctrine.

The *Perulli Report* was discussed in the European Parliament in June 2003. This did not lead to particular choices for the solutions to be followed. After this report several studies were initiated by the Commission on the development of labour law in EU Member States,[10] whose purpose was mainly to make an inventory of the developments. In section 4 the most recent study will be discussed.

3.2. The EU and the ILO Recommendation on the Employment Relationship

In Chapter 2 the Recommendation on the employment relationship was introduced. Some Member States of the EU participated actively in this discussion and were the driving force behind the insertion of Article 7 of this recommendation. This article reads that in the context of the transnational movement of workers, in framing national policy, a Member should, after consulting the most representative organisations of employers and workers, consider adopting appropriate measures within its jurisdiction, and where appropriate in collaboration with other Members, so as to provide effective protection to and prevent abuses of migrant workers in its territory who may be affected by uncertainty as to the existence of an employment relationship. Where workers are recruited in one country for work in another, the Members concerned may consider concluding bilateral agreements to prevent abuses and fraudulent practices which have as their purpose the evasion of the existing arrangements for the protection of workers in the context of an employment relationship.

This provision was made in view of the Posting Directive of the EU (mentioned in Section 2 *supra*), which guarantees some minimum labour rights of the State of employment for workers who are covered by this directive, that is, 'posted' to another EU Member State. Examples of these minimum rights are maximum work periods and minimum rest periods; minimum paid annual holidays; the minimum rates of pay, including overtime rates; health, safety and hygiene at work; protection of pregnant women, children and young people; and equal

10. See, for instance, the conference *Labour Law in Europe: Steps towards 2010* which was organised by the Dutch Presidency of the EU, Leiden, 2004.

treatment between men and women. This protection is given to those who are considered worker by the law of the host State.

Article 7 was written, in particular, with a view to this directive, as one problem with its implementation is that its scope depends on the interpretation of the term *worker*. A limited interpretation of the term *worker* in the host country can thus limit the effect of the directive. Moreover, a difference between the term *worker* in the sending State and the host State can cause problematic situations, as a person who is a worker in the sending State may not have labour law protection in the host State on the basis of the directive. The reversed situation is also possible. Moreover, there may be complicated differences with the scope of the coordination regulation for social security if the meaning of the term *worker* differs from country to country.

The proposal to include this issue in the recommendation was accepted, but the issue as such was seen as a typical EU issue. Although migrant workers occur also in other regions of the world, their legal position is very different, since the EU concern was directly related to the Posting Directive.

For the EU this is an important issue, as it is related to the problem of social dumping, which may arise if the Posting Directive is not applicable to a particular situation. In discussions on the Posting Directive at several occasions reference is made to the Recommendation on the employment relationship, particularly by the European Parliament.

An example is the motion of the European Parliament on the application of Directive 96/7 of 28 September 2006.[11] In the Motion it is concluded from reports based on actual practice that sham self-employment (in Chapter 2 we used the term *bogus self-employment*, which has the same meaning) is a strategy commonly used to circumvent the minimum standards of Article 3(1) of the Posting of Workers Directive. It calls on the Member States, with reference to the Perulli Study on *Economically dependent/quasi-subordinate (parasubordinate employment: Legal, social and economic aspects)*, to adjust their definitions of *employees* so that a clear distinction can be made between the status of entrepreneurs, comprising economically independent businesses working for several mutually independent undertakings on the one hand, and employees, working in an organisationally and economically dependent manner under supervision and for remuneration on the other. It also asked the EC to initiate negotiations with the Member States as a matter of urgency, with the aim of establishing transparent and consistent criteria for determining the status of workers and self-employed persons with regard to employment law. The Parliament pointed out that proving that a sham self-employed person is a de facto employee, is at present a difficult and lengthy process. The posted worker may have completed the job and returned home by the time the necessary evidence has been established. For this reason it asked for exchanges between the employment inspection services to enable a joint campaign against sham self-employment.

11. P6_TA(2006)0463.

So far this has not led to an initiative for a more convergent approach of the terms of the Posting Directive.[12] Still, it is an interesting example of the interaction of the Recommendation on the employment relationship with EU instruments.

3.3. The Green Paper

In the Green Paper *Modernising Labour Law to meet the Challenges of the 21st Century*[13] of 2006, the EC discussed, among several other issues, the protection by the employment relationship and the distinction between employed and self-employed persons.

First, however, we have to clarify the context of the Green Paper as this context is not the same as that of the studies[14] mentioned in Section 3.1 *supra*. The objective of the Green Paper was to encourage the development of labour law, in the sense that it supports economic growth and the increase of employment. The Paper mentions that the traditional model of the employment relationship might not prove well-suited to all workers in view of the challenge of adapting to change and seizing the opportunities that globalisation offers. Alternative models of contractual relations could enhance the capacity of enterprises to foster the creativity of their whole workforce for increased competitive advantage. Thus the Paper focused on an increase of flexibility of the work force and approached the difference between those who are protected by labour law and those who are not protected from that angle.

The Paper argues that the emergence of diverse forms of non-standard work has made the boundaries between labour law and commercial law less clear. As a result, the traditional binary distinction between employees and self-employed is no longer an adequate depiction of the economic and social reality of work.

The Commission also mentioned the problem of disguised employment and noted that action at national level to combat the phenomenon of disguised employment has ranged from the introduction of mandatory legal presumption rules[15] to improving enforcement mechanisms including targeted campaigns and special information and awareness initiatives. Unclear legal definitions of the status of self-employment in national legal and administrative frameworks may result in situations in which persons, believing they are self-employed, subsequently find themselves to be classified by social security agencies or tax institutions as a dependent employee. This can result in an obligation for the self-employed/employee and his main client/employer to pay additional social security contributions. The Commission stressed that the problem of persons posing falsely as

12. Resolution 2006/2038(INI), Text P6_TA(2006)0463, adopted 26 Oct. 2006.
13. COM (2006) 708 final.
14. See studies mentioned in fns 8 and 9.
15. The Commission mentions in a footnote the example of the Dutch Flexibility and Security Act (1999), that introduced a mandatory legal presumption whereby an employment contract exists when work has been carried out for another person in return for pay on a weekly basis, or for at least twenty hours per month during three consecutive months (see also Ch. 6).

self-employed workers to circumvent national law should be dealt with primarily by Member States. Accordingly, the Commission noted in a footnote to welcome the adoption in June 2006 of the ILO Recommendation on the Employment Relationship. This promotes the formulation and adoption by Member States, in consultation with the social partners, of national policies for regularly reviewing the scope of their laws, and where necessary clarifying and adapting them, in order to guarantee effective protection for workers who perform work in the context of an employment relationship.[16] This non-binding instrument takes a strategic approach, it adds, leaving the nature and extent of protection given to workers in an employment relationship to be defined by national law and practice.

The Commission added that the concept of economically dependent work covers situations which fall between the two established concepts of subordinate employment and independent self-employment. These workers do not have a contract of employment and may not be covered by labour law since they occupy a 'grey area' between labour law and commercial law. Although formally 'self-employed', they remain economically dependent on a single principal or client/ employer for their source of income. The Commission distinguished this phenomenon from the deliberate misclassification of self-employment. The Commission mentioned some examples of legislative measures to safeguard the legal status of economically dependent and vulnerable self-employed workers: the concept of employee-like workers corresponding to the civil law notion of *parasubordination* in Italy and Germany. The Commission admits that these approaches have been somewhat tentative and partial, but they reflect efforts on the part of legislators, the courts and the social partners to tackle problems in this complex area.

The Commission concluded this section of the Green Paper by mentioning several questions to be discussed. The first is whether greater clarity is needed in the legal definitions of employment and self-employment in national legislation in order to facilitate bona fide transitions from employment to self-employment and *vice versa*.

The second is whether there is a need for a floor of rights dealing with the working conditions of all workers regardless of the form of their work contract.

Further, in the Green Paper the Commission addressed the issue of the Three Way Relationships, notably that of temporary agency workers.

3.4. Reactions to the Green Paper

The reactions to the Green Paper were laid down in the *Outcome of the Public Consultation on the Commission's Green Paper 'Modernising labour law to meet the challenges of the 21st century'*.[17] The EC received over 450 responses, which showed a large divergence of views and opinions among Member States and other actors involved. The EU Ministers for Employment and Social Affairs had a

16. See also Ch. 2.
17. COM (2007) 627 final.

preliminary discussion of the Green Paper; in their conclusions they stressed the value of the standard full-time, open-ended contract as the cornerstone of employment relationships in the EU, while allowing for other more flexible forms to cater for specific needs and individual situations.[18]

3.4.1. Flexicurity

In the meantime the Commission had published the *Communication Towards Common Principles of Flexicurity: More and better jobs through flexibility and security*, which was adopted on 27 June 2007.[19] This 'flexicurity' approach, which was already hinted at in the Green Paper, had a large impact on the discussion of the Green Paper, for which reason it is mentioned here as an intermezzo. In the communication the Commission mentions some principles of 'flexicurity': which concept basically is meant to introduce more flexibility, and at the same time to introduce more security, in particular by a better training so that persons who have to leave their job are prepared for a new job.

3.4.2. The Political Context

In the *Outcome* Paper the Commission concluded that trade union stakeholders, a number of Member States and academic experts warned against viewing the standard indefinite employment contract as somehow obsolete, or as an obstacle to the creation of jobs. In their view, the Green Paper could be interpreted as expressing a preference for more diverse contractual forms and for the introduction of weaker employment laws. Many respondents, including the EP, EESC and Member States stressed the stability and security offered by the standard work contract. Conversely, employer stakeholders, together with some Member States, considered that flexible work contracts had not been treated in a sufficiently positive light.

The Commission concluded that there was no agreement on the application of the concept of 'insiders' and 'outsiders' to segmented labour markets. In the view of employers, the only real 'outsiders' are the unemployed and the 'insiders' are all those legally employed. Trade unions maintained that the gap between 'insiders' and 'outsiders' can only be eliminated by improving the protection of precarious workers.

Many business submissions, recalling the limitation of EU competences, called for labour law reform to be pursued exclusively within a *national* context.

Most Member States, the EP and the EESC, national parliaments and the EU social partners recalled, the *Outcome* Paper continues, the division of

18. Presidency Conclusions, Informal Meeting of Ministers for Employment and Social Affairs, Berlin, 19 Jan. 2007.
19. Brussels, 27 Jun. 2007, COM (2007) 359 final; Communication from the Commission, towards Common Principles of Flexicurity: More and better jobs through flexibility and security (Brussels: European Commission 2007).

responsibilities between EU and Member States. The development of labour law within the EU is generally viewed as falling within the competence of the Member States and the social partners, with the role of the Community *acquis* being to complement the actions of the Member States.

EU level activity on key issues of employment rights should not be confined to the Open Method of Coordination (OMC), in the view of trade union stakeholders, academics, and several other Member States. Trade unions emphasised that emerging European labour markets can no longer be managed by relying on national rules in the social sphere as internal market and competition rules are being accorded primacy over national social policy provisions.

3.4.3. Uncertainty with regard to the Definition of the Employment Relationship

Many stakeholders, in their reaction to the *Green Paper*, acknowledged that it was complex to define 'workers' and 'self-employed persons' under Community law. This complexity was acknowledged to have increased as a consequence of the cross-border provision of services. Most Member States wanted to rely upon national law and well-tested legal procedures to resolve such problems. Together with many social partner organisations they favour the position whereby the definition of worker under most labour law directives remains at the discretion of the Member States. While employer interests at EU and national levels generally dismissed the need for more convergent national definitions, social partner interests in the service, entertainment, media and retail sectors considered that the definitions used in different Member States to define the status of those referred to as *freelancers, casual or independent workers* might be listed and explained to facilitate a better understanding of the employment status of the persons concerned.

The EP called for an initiative towards convergence in the national definitions of worker status to ensure a more coherent and efficient implementation of the Community *acquis*. It urged the Member States to promote the implementation of the 2006 ILO Recommendation on the employment relationship.

Some Member States also suggested that the Recommendation be used as a basis for discussion among the Member States and social partners about how to cope better at a European level with the phenomenon of concealed employment relationships.

Most Member States and social partners were opposed to the introduction of any third intermediary category, such as the so-called 'economically dependent worker', alongside those of dependent workers and independent self-employed workers. Even in Member States where such a concept already exists in national law, such as Italy, there were reservations about whether an unequivocal definition could be devised at European level. However, BusinessEurope accepted that some added value could be gained by sharing experience on the impact of such measures, so that Member States might learn from each other. Trade unions favour re-focusing the scope of labour law through national reforms to extend the protection associated with the standard employment contract to all workers.

The ETUC called upon the EU Institutions, together with the Social Partners at EU level, to develop an EU-wide supportive legal framework, consisting of a combination of EU 'rules of the game' and certain EU minimum standards to establish a 'core of rights' while ensuring respect for national social policies and industrial relations. Social NGOs also supported the idea of a common set of rights, linked to a commonly agreed definition of 'worker' established under Community law, in order to underpin the principle of freedom of movement.

On the basis of these findings the Commission announced that it will continue working with the Member States with a view to reach conclusions on common principles of 'flexicurity'. One of the announced measures was the clarification of the nature of the employment relationship to promote greater understanding and facilitate cooperation across the EU.

3.5. Conclusions on Green Paper Discussions

From the document that summarised the reactions on the Green Paper, discussed in Section 3.4, we can conclude that the political views on the employment contract vary largely. There is no consensus that the formulation of a Community definition of the contract of employment is desirable. A definition of employee is left as a matter of the Member States, even though the Commission wishes to clarify the nature of the employment relationship. The employees' and employers' organisations (the so-called social partners) at the EU level are largely divided. Employers are averse to extend the scope of labour law, as this may decrease flexibility and competitiveness. Trade unions fear that changes in labour law, for instance to give protection to the persons in the grey area, may introduce 'flexicurity' elements, and these are seen as weakening the position of the workers. Although they would support proposals to extend the traditional protection of labour law, they are reluctant to discuss any compromise strategies. This leaves very little political room for activities at the EU level, even where the European Parliament asks for initiatives. Legal activities are therefore to be expected from Member States only; the EC will only encourage discussions and comparative studies.

In 2009 EP member Mr Jan Cremers referred to the need for a proper application of the Posting Directive to have a European definition of self-employment; he also referred to ILO Recommendation 198 and the report by Adalberto Perulli, which suggested a new form of work category: 'a form of work falling within the grey zone between subordinate work and self-employment'. He asked whether the Commission takes the view that introducing such a category at European level would be a useful instrument for tackling the problem of disguised employment.[20]

The EC answered that it was aware of the uncertainty in the definition of an employment relationship and the consequences on certain categories, such as the 'economically dependent workers' and 'bogus' self-employed workers.

20. Question of 14 Jan. 2009, E-0019/9.

Furthermore, acknowledging the complexity of attempting to define workers and self-employed persons under Community law, it stressed the need to clarify the situation of dependent employment and the grey areas between self-employment and employees with a dependent employment relationship in order to combat the phenomenon of disguised employment. The Commission therefore envisaged to focus the follow-up actions planned in 2009 on obtaining a more comprehensive overview of the legal concept, the main characteristics, the trends and problems encountered in the regulation of the employment relationship in the different Member States, and drawing up an inventory of the main measures taken, including indicators to determine the existence of an employment relationship. The Commission added that the outcome of the public consultation on the Green Paper indicated that most Member States and many social partners were of the view that national law and well-tested legal procedures at national level should be relied upon to resolve problems and uncertainty in the definition of an employment relationship and were opposed to the introduction of an intermediate category. On the basis of the above, the Commission did not envisage, at this stage, introducing a European definition of self-employment or specific indicators at European level.

4. THE PRESENT STATE OF AFFAIRS

As we saw in the previous section, given the little support that exists in the EU Member States and among the social partners for making a Community definition of employee or extending the scope of employment law, the EC limits itself to investigations of the concept of the employment contract in the Member States. For this purpose the academic European Labour Law Network was given the task to write a report on the developments in the Member States. This report was published under the title *Characteristics of the Employment Relationship*.[21]

On 12 and 13 November 2009 a seminar took place based on this report. A main result of the seminar was that most participants were reluctant to make a uniform European definition of employee. The report includes some interesting presentations, including the one by Guy Davidov. Davidov discussed the possibility to create one or two intermediate categories, that is, instead of a binary divide between ‘employees’ who are entitled to *all* labour rights and independent contractors who have no labour-related rights, to add another group (or two groups) of people who are entitled to *some* rights. This may be the concept of a dependent contractor or an employee-like one. This refers to persons who have some characteristics of independent workers, but at the same time some of the vulnerabilities of employees, in particular that they depend entirely or mostly on a single supervisor. Technically, this can be achieved by stating in specific laws that they apply not only to employees but also to dependent contractors, or that for the purpose of the specific law, the term employee also includes dependent contractors.

21. European Network of Legal Experts in the field of Labour Law, *Characteristics of the Employment Relationship* (s.l. [Leiden] 2009); <www.labourlawnetwork.eu> (under Publications).

He remarks that a similar result can be achieved by the introduction of a term broader than the regular employee. For example, in the UK some labour laws apply to all workers. As a result, there is the group of employees who enjoy all labour laws, and those who are workers but not employees who enjoy only some labour laws. The technique is slightly different, but the result is the same. He concludes that the question still remains whether in practice there is some discernible difference between different groups of workers that can justify the application of some labour laws but not others.

A second working group of the conference, engaged in the theme 'Specific labour rights for special groups, but a floor of rights for all dependent persons?', concluded that it is very complicated to define a so-called 'in-between-group' of workers who should need only part of the protection of employees. The criterion 'economically dependent workers' is hard to define; there is also a lack of consensus relative to which rights should be part of the floor.

The working group on 'tackling bogus self-employment' discussed that many countries have means to tackle bogus self-employment. Also tax and social security legislation can be used for this. The problems with bogus self-employment are quite different per Member State and the solutions should in first instance be found on the national level.

Thus, the value of this report is that it gives a good insight in the various labour law systems of the Member States and the problems in finding consensus in making proposals for improving protection by labour law. The lack of recommendations also shows that there is a strong need for further in-depth research, which is undertaken by the present study.

5. CONCLUSIONS

Although several studies showed the need for a modernised concept of the contract of employment, there is no consensus among social partners and in Member States on how to proceed. Social partners take strongly differing positions, i.e., refusal of any measures to broaden protection to workers (employers' organisations) and refusal to seek any compromise other than by means of the contract of employment, since otherwise the latter may be weakened (workers' organisations).

As a result the EC limits itself to investigations of the concept of the employment contract in the Member States, but this is unlikely to lead to EU legislative initiatives. It is up to the Member States to undertake actions.

In order to contribute to this discussion this in depth study of systems of some EU Member States was undertaken. In Chapter 11 we will make suggestions, on the basis of the outcomes of these studies, what the tasks of the ILO and the EU must be in order to realise the protection by the contract of employment and the protection of the economically dependent.

Chapter 5

Protection of Working Relationships in Belgium

Patrick Humblet and Isabel Plets

1. INTRODUCTION TO THE BELGIAN LABOUR LAW SYSTEM

In Belgium a person can work as a voluntary worker; under a specific civil law contract; as a civil servant; under an employment contract; or as an independent contractor, that is, as a self-employed worker.

Since 1 August 2006, the status of voluntary workers has been regulated[1] and those who perform unremunerated work enjoy protection. From then on certain provisions made for the protection of employees also apply to voluntary workers. A pregnant voluntary worker, for example, may not perform work from seven days prior to the anticipated date of delivery to nine weeks after the birth of the child. Despite the fact that the principal does not pay any salary to the voluntary worker, he may give him a compensation of around EUR 1,000 per year, for example, for travel expenses.[2]

1. Act of 3 Jul. 2005, *Belgisch Staatsblad* (hereafter *Belgian Official Journal*) 29 Aug. 2005. See D. Frère, 'La loi du 3 juillet 2005 relative aux droits des volontaires', in J. Clesse and F. Kefer (eds), *Questions de droit social* (Liège: Anthémis, 2007), 7–48; K. Goossens, *Het vrijwilligersstatuut* (Mechelen: Kluwer, 2006), 96; K. Goossens, 'Spelregels voor organisaties en hun vrijwilligers', *Or.* 5 (2007): 103–114; M. Davagle, *Vrijwillige arbeid*, Reeks Sociale Praktijkstudies (Mechelen: Wolters Kluwer, 2008), 214.
2. Article 10 Voluntary Workers Act.

Frans Pennings & Claire Bosse, *The Protection of Working Relationships*, pp. 43–59.
© 2011 Kluwer Law International BV, The Netherlands.

Civil law contracts (e.g., mandates) are regulated by the provisions of the Civil Code and are not necessarily remunerated.

Since the impact of ILO Recommendation 198 is the starting point of this study, we focus on individuals who are paid for their work and more specifically on employees and (bogus) self-employed.

It makes little sense to discuss the regulations applying to civil servants. Due to the complex State structure in Belgium, there is no uniform civil servant status. Describing its essentials within a brief space would therefore be impossible. Moreover, there is hardly any discussion on who is a civil servant, and friend and foe alike agree that the status of civil servant offers sufficient protection. The only problem worth noting is that in recent years the different governments have recruited virtually no officials with civil servant status, but are concluding more and more straightforward employment contracts, although a contractual status is supposed to remain the exception for persons in the public service.[3] In general, these employees enjoy inferior working conditions as compared to those of their colleagues who are civil servants[4] and often also worse than those of employees in the private sector who are employed under similar conditions. For example, they do not fall within the scope of application of the Collective Labour Agreements Act. This implies an absolute freedom of negotiation, often resulting in low(er) salaries being paid.

For a limited number of professions special regulations exist, for instance for seafarers and barge masters. However, the majority of employees fall under the Act of 1978 on Employment Contracts. Even within this group of employees, however, there are a number of different regulations. First, a distinction is to be made, based on the nature of the activity: blue-collar workers, white-collar workers, sales representatives, domestic workers, students and homeworkers. The Act of 1978 on Employment Contracts also applies to teleworkers and temporary workers,[5] but there are additional provisions applicable to them.

The different rules relate to the specific situation in which the work is performed and they offer additional protection. There is one major exception to this principle. The status of blue-collar workers differs sharply from that of white-collar workers. For example, in the event of dismissal without notice a blue-collar worker with 31 years of seniority receives compensation equal to (at most) 112 days of wages. For a white-collar worker, this compensation would be a minimum of twenty-one months' wages, and if it involves an employee who, on an annual basis, earns more than EUR 30,327[6] (a so-called executive white collar) this

3. For a critical analysis, see R. Janvier, 'Over vrijheden, contractanten en ambtenaren: geen vrijblijvende "ménage à trois" ', in M. De Vos and I. Plets (eds), *Contractuele tewerkstelling in de overheid* (Bruges: die Keure, 2005), 1–35.
4. See D. Delvax, 'Le recours au contrat de travail ou au statut de la fonction publique. Prolégomènes', in J. Jacqmain (ed.), *Une terre de droit du travail: les services publics* (Brussels: Bruylant, 2005), 1–30.
5. For an overview, see P. Humblet, 'Employment through Temporary Staff Agencies in Belgium', *Europäisches Arbeits- und Sozialrecht* 10 (2002): 183–196.
6. Since 1 Jan. 2010.

amount will be even (much) higher. Blue-collar workers thus receive far less protection against dismissal than white-collar workers.[7]

This is just one of many differences. In the past this discrimination was already brought, with varying degrees of success, to the Constitutional Court.[8] In 2005 the government appointed a commission with the task to make proposals for harmonisation of the status, but this has so far not produced any results, because the employers' and employees' organisations are not at all on the same wavelength. Nevertheless, the opposition against the distinction between white-collar and blue-collar workers is quite strong, so there is a genuine chance that a breakthrough will be achieved in the short term.

2. LIMITATIONS TO THE USE OF FLEXIBLE CONTRACTS

In Belgium the standard contract is a full-time employment contract for an indefinite period. Such a type of contract is subject to few formal requirements. For example, it is not necessary for the contract to be in writing, except for categories of employees who are specifically protected, such as students, or when certain clauses are included in the contract, such as on a probation period. Part-time employment contracts and fixed-term contracts are the exception to the standard.

The legislature has imposed extra obligations on the validity of these contracts. For both types of contract the agreement must be in writing, for each employee individually, and has to be made at the latest by the time when the employee enters into force. If these requirements are not fulfilled, an employment contract for an indefinite period is automatically deemed to have been concluded.[9]

Two fixed-term employment contracts concluded one after another are considered as an employment contract for an indefinite period, unless the different agreements are justified because of the nature of the work or for a legally valid reason.[10] However, courts are very selective in accepting exceptions. Because the statutory rules reduce flexibility, an escape possibility was provided: contracts for a fixed term may be cumulated on condition that this involves a maximum of four contracts of at least three months, without exceeding a period of two years.[11]

7. For a comparison between Belgian law on termination of employment contracts and other Member States of the European Union, see European Commission. Directorate General Employment, Social Affairs and Equal Opportunities, *Termination of employment relationships. Legal situation in de Member States of the European Union* (Brussels: 2006) 136.
8. Among others R. Leysen, 'Het Arbitragehof: 15 jaar rechtspraak in sociale zaken', *Tijdschrift voor Sociaal Recht/Revue de Droit Social* (2000) 546 et seq.; M. De Vos, 'Het Arbitragehof en het arbeidsrecht', in M. Rigaux and P. Humblet (eds), *Actuele problemen van het arbeidsrecht VI* (Antwerp: Intersentia, 2001), 89 et seq.
9. Articles 9 and 11*bis* of the Act of 1978 on Employment Contracts.
10. Article 10 of the Act of 1978 on Employment Contracts.
11. Article 10*bis*(2) of the Act of 1978 on Employment Contracts. See also Art. 10(3) of this Act concerning the combination of jobs up to three years, with employment contracts of less than six months and with the social inspector's consent.

However, if these conditions are not satisfied the contract is deemed to be a contract for an indefinite period.

Making on-call contracts is also made more difficult, because the weekly working hours of a part-time employee may not be less than one-thirds of the weekly working hours of a full-time employee.[12] In addition, the duration of a working period may not be shorter than three hours, unless exemptions to this rule are made at the sectoral level, which means that the employees' organisations are involved.[13] Discrimination of part-time work is expressly prohibited.[14]

There is no legislation with regard to the relationship between the self-employed person and his principal, which relationship is exclusively governed by civil law. Whatever the parties have agreed to thus applies as law between them. An exception to this rule is the agency agreement. A self-employed commercial agent enjoys a protection closely resembling that of a sales representative.[15]

On the basis of the number of work positions, the jobs in 2008 were distributed as follows:[16]

Table 5.1. Distribution of Jobs over Blue Collar and White Collar Workers

Private sector:	2,697,024
– blue collar workers	1,243,786
– white collar workers	1,453,238
Public sector:	744,665
– officials under contract (blue-collar)	51,317
– officials under contract (white-collar)	236,283
– officials with civil servant status	457,065
Self-employed individuals[17]	923,946

About 25% of the wage-earners work part-time.[18] The share of women[19] (40.8%) working part-time is much higher than that of men (7.5%). There has been a clear increase over the years. The reasons why part-time work is chosen are diverse. However, it is not always an intentional choice. Thus, only 11% of the women who

12. Article 11*bis* of the Act of 1978 on Employment Contracts.
13. *Ibid.*
14. Act of 5 Mar. 2002, *Belgian Official Journal* of 13 Mar. 2002.
15. Act 13 Apr. 1995, *Belgian Official Journal* of 2 Jun. 1995. See, among other authors, P. De Keyser and N. Beaufils, 'Agence commerciale et représentation commerciale. La loi du 13 avril 1995', *Journal des Tribunaux du Travail* (1996): 1–13; C. Willems, 'Le contrat d'agence commerciale: la formation et l'exécution du contrat', *Orientations* 2 (1996): 25–40.
16. X., *Vade Mecum van de financiële en statistische gegevens over de sociale bescherming van België* (Brussels: Federale Overheidsdienst Sociale Zekerheid, 2009), <www.socialsecurity.fgov.be/docs/nl/publicaties/vademecum/2010/II_C_1StatNl_VMed2010.pdf>.
17. <www.socialsecurity.fgov.be/docs/nl/publicaties/vademecum/2010/III_C_1StatNl_VMed2010.pdf>.
18. <statbel.fgov.be/nl/statistieken/cijfers/arbeid_leven/werk/deeltijds/perrcentage/index.jsp> (2009).
19. <www.werk.be/c-en-o/cijfers/kerncijfers/flexibele_arbeid/deeltijdarbeid.htm> (2008).

work part-time indicate that they do not wish to work full-time, while amongst men this figure is 9%.[20]

3. DETERMINATION OF THE EXISTENCE OF AN EMPLOYMENT RELATIONSHIP

3.1. Introduction

The existence of an employment contract[21] is an important element for the application of labour law and its protective provisions.[22] For example, employees enjoy a limited liability for harm they cause within the company and to third parties.[23] In addition, the wage they receive within the framework of an employment contract is the basis for calculating the social security contributions and the reference wage for social security benefits, such as unemployment benefits. Finally, the employment contract is very important in situations of restructuring of the enterprise. In the event of bankruptcy, for instance, employees receive better treatment than ordinary creditors and enjoy a wage guarantee for outstanding wages through the Company Closing Fund.

3.2. The Presumptions

To minimise discussions about whether or not an employment contract exists, a number of presumptions were written into the Act of 1978 on Employment Contracts. First, these are refutable presumptions with regard to pharmacists,[24] sales representatives[25] and students.[26] For example, a pharmacist working in a pharmacy, which is open to the public, is deemed to be bound by an employment contract with the owner or the lessee of the pharmacy, unless the opposite is proven.

In addition, a number of statutes provide for irrefutable presumptions. Article 5a of the Act of 1978 on Employment Contracts provides, for instance, that additional services cannot be performed on a self-employed basis (and thus refuting evidence is excluded), when the person who performs the services and the person for whom the services are performed are bound by an employment contract

20. <igvm-iefh.belgium.be/nl/statistieken> (2004).
21. In the scope of this contribution we consider employees who are bound by an employment contract by virtue of the 1978 Act on Employment Contracts. Special contracts as for seamen will not be taken into account.
22. R. Blanpain, 'Ondergeschikt verband: de sleutel op de deur van het arbeidsrecht', *Tijdschrift voor Sociaal Recht/Revue de Droit Social (special issue)* (1998): 1–14.
23. Article 18 1978 Act on Employment Contracts.
24. Article 3*quater* of the Act of 1978 on Employment Contracts.
25. Article 4 of the Act of 1978 on Employment Contracts.
26. Article 121 of the Act of 1978 on Employment Contracts.

for similar services. This prevents an employee from working more than the legally allowed number of working hours by accumulating employment contracts. There is also an irrefutable presumption in Article 8 of the Temporary Jobs Act of 1987. No proof is allowed against the presumption that the agreement with the agency for temporary work is an employment contract. A similar provision applies to professional athletes.[27] In other words, they are employees.

3.3. Subordination

The employment contract is defined in Article 3 of the Act of 1978 on Employment Contracts: 'The employment contract for white-collar workers is the agreement whereby an employee, the white-collar worker, undertakes, in exchange for wages, to perform primarily intellectual labour under the authority of an employer.' Three constitutive elements make an agreement an employment contract: wages, performing work and authority.

The element 'wages' (compensation in whatever form) and 'work' can also be found in other types of contracts. Consequently, these criteria are insufficient to distinguish an employment contract from a contract for services. 'Authority' is therefore the distinguishing criterion.

This criterion came first up in Article 1 of the first Act on Employment Contracts of 10 March 1900:[28] a worker is a person who undertakes to work under authority, direction and supervision. However, nowhere in the Parliamentary Proceedings is it explained what the term *authority* entails. Nor was the relationship of authority with the factors 'direction and supervision' made clear. In 1985 these terms were eliminated.[29]

The case law and legal doctrine generally do not use the term *authority*, but they use *subordination*. An employee is the person who works in a relationship of subordination.

In order to be able to assume the existence of authority and an employment contract, however, it suffices that the employer has the (legal) possibility of giving orders. This often leads to confusion.

The relationship of authority has undergone a major evolution in recent decades.[30] First, the group of persons who qualify to work in a relationship of

27. Article 3 of the Act of 24 Feb. 1978.
28. For the evolution, see P. Humblet, *De gezagsuitoefening door de werkgever. Een juridische analyse* (Antwerp: Kluwer rechtswetenschappen, 1994), 55 et seq. The distinction used to be the pay condition: piecework for the rent of work and time-rates for the rent of services. See K. Nevens, 'De transformatie van het rechtsbegrip "ouvrier": van het Burgerlijk Wetboek naar de eerste arbeidswetgeving (1804–1900)', *Brood en Rozen* 1 (2009): 46.
29. Article 1 Act of 17 Jul. 1985, *Belgian Official Journal* 31 Aug. 1985.
30. See mainly C. Engels, *Het ondergeschikt verband naar Belgisch arbeidsrecht* (Bruges: die Keure, 1989), 644; M. Jamoulle, 'La notion de subordination et son évolution', *Seize Leçons sur le droit du travail* (Liège: Coll. Scientifique de la Faculté de droit, 1994), 109–136;

subordination has greatly expanded. Fifty years ago, it would have been inconceivable that doctors, for example, could be employees.[31] They exercise a 'liberal' profession. At present it is assumed that a contract of employment is possible, in so far as the employer does not intervene in diagnostic work.

Yet, with regard to other liberal professions there is still a taboo on the working relationship. This is illustrated by the profession of lawyers. Although nothing prevents a lawyer from working under the authority of another lawyer, this is still regarded with suspicion.[32]

In 2000, the Industrial Tribunal in Brussels decided that a lawyer was an employee.[33] On 8 June 2005 the Council of the Flemish Bar issued a so-called deontological rule,[34] which said that a lawyer cannot exercise his profession in subordination. The Court of Cassation, however, quashed this regulation.[35]

It was mainly the poor financial situation of trainee lawyers in the past that gave rise to discussions about their subordination.[36] Since the introduction of an obligatory compensation for trainees and the compensation for *pro bono* lawyers, the whole debate appears to have quieted down. The National Social Security

---

P. Humblet, 'Gezag en ondergeschiktheid in de 21e eeuw. Van werknemer naar medewerker?', in M. Stroobant and O. Vanachter (eds), *Honderd jaar Arbeidsovereenkomstenwet* (Antwerp: Intersentia, 2001), 85–96; X., *Le lien de subordination. Actes du colloque organisé le 19 mars 2004 par l'Ordre des Avocats du Barreau de Tournai et le Jeune Barreau de Tournai*, Etudes pratiques de Droit Social n° 18 (Brussels: Kluwer, 2004), 258; V. Vannes (ed.), *Le lien de subordination dans le contrat de travail* (Brussels: Bruylant, 2005), 216.

31. C. Engels, *Het ondergeschikt verband naar Belgisch arbeidsrecht* (Brugge: die Keure, 1989), 281–328.
32. See G. Lauwers, *Schijnzelfstandigheid bij advocaten* (Antwerp: Maklu, 2008), 145.
33. Arbeidsrechtbank (Industrial tribunal) of Brussels 8 Dec. 2000, annotation C. Wantiez, *Journal des Tribunaux du Travail* (2000–2001), 1209, For comments, see P. De Keyser, 'Un avocat peut-il être un employé? Révolution ou fin d'une hypocrisie', *Journal des procès* 408 (2001): 26–27 and 30–31. The court rejected the subordination in appeal. Industrial Court of Appeal (Arbeidshof) Brussels 16 Mar. 2004 (2004) *Nieuw Juridisch Weekblad* 561 and (2005–2006) *Rechtskundig Weekblad* 26. For comments, see M. De Vos, 'De advocaat: zelfstandige of werknemer? Het dogma van de zelfstandige advocaat en het enigma van de ondergeschikte advocaat-stagiair', *Nieuw Juridisch Weekblad* (2004): 542–545; C. De Ganck, 'Intellectuele onafhankelijkheid van de advocaat verhindert de uitoefening van een "vrij beroep" in dienstverband', *Rechtspraak Antwerpen, Brussel, Gent* (2004): 524–525; J. Stevens, 'De uitoefening van het beroep van advocaat in dienstverband', *Rechtskundig Weekblad* (2005–2006): 1–21; W. Van Eeckhoutte, 'Advocaat-medewerker is geen medewerker: een schot naast de roos', *De Juristenkrant* 87 (2004): 1.
34. *Belgian Official Journal*, 30 Jun. 2005.
35. Court of Cassation (Hof van Cassatie) 6 Oct. 2006 (2006) *Journal des Tribunaux du Travail* 391 and *Jurisprudence de Liège, Mons et Bruxelles* (2006), 29. For comments, see E. Breways, 'Cassatie velt principearrest over arbeidsstatuut advocaten', *De Juristenkrant* 138 (2006): 1 and 7; C.E. Clesse, 'L'Ordre des avocats peut-il imposer une relation de travail indépendant malgré les dispositions impératives et d'ordre public?', *Jurisprudence de Liège, Mons et Bruxelles* (2006): 32–43.
36. C.E. Vercammen, 'Beoordelingsvrijheid in dienstverband: na de geneesheer, ook de advocaat onder arbeidsovereenkomst', *Rechtskundig Weekblad* (1992–93): 1353–1366.

Office (NSSO) also appears to have largely accepted that in principle lawyers are not employees.[37]

In qualitative terms, the notion of authority has gone through a certain evolution.[38] For non-intellectual professions, authority is often shown directly. The employer is present in the workplace and monitors the employees personally. In other cases, it is the work organisation itself which exercises the control. For instance, blue-collar workers who work for a car manufacturer cannot possibly leave the assembly line without disrupting the production process.

However, we are evolving towards a service society where routine tasks are being replaced by creative jobs, which are often performed worldwide. The employer hires employees who carry out tasks that he does not know how to do (which makes control difficult or impossible) and often employs them in places where he cannot keep an eye on them. Work is taking on a nomadic aspect. From a culture of obedience we have evolved towards a culture of responsibility. The employee has become a collaborator.[39] Authority has evaporated. The dividing line between an employee and a self-employed person is often difficult to draw.[40]

4. THE BOGUS SELF-EMPLOYED

4.1. General

The discussion on authority would be purely academic were it not for the problem of the bogus self-employed.[41]

---

37. G. Lauwers, *Schijnzelfstandigheid bij advocaten* (Antwerp: Maklu, 2008), 78–80.
38. P. Humblet, 'Gezag en ondergeschiktheid in de 21^e^ eeuw. Van werknemer naar medewerker?', in M. Stroobant and O. Vanachter (eds), *Honderd jaar Arbeidsovereenkomstenwet* (Antwerp: Intersentia, 2001), 85–96.
39. J.L. Dehaene, 'Financiële participatie van werknemers', *Economisch en Sociaal Tijdschrift* (1998): 331. See also M. Jamoulle, 'Le contrat de travail à l'épreuve du temps', *Chroniques de Droit Social* (1998): 473.
40. For a survey, see A. Van Regenmortel, 'Onderscheid tussen werknemer en zelfstandige', in J. Van Steenberge and A. Van Regenmortel (eds), *Actuele problemen van het sociale zekerheidsrecht* (Bruges: die Keure, 1995), 31–100.
41. See the report of the Treasury (Rekenhof) *Prévention et répression du phénomène des faux indépendants* (Brussels: 2004), 62 (<www.ccrek.be/FR/PublicationsEtatFederal.htm>); J. Heynen, 'Schijnzelfstandigheid aan banden. De ervaringen van de inspectiediensten', *Arbeidsblad* (1995): 17–23; J. Schatteman and P. Vanden Broeck, 'Schijnzelfstandigheid aan banden. Het onderscheid tussen werknemer en zelfstandige in de rechtspraak', *Arbeidsblad* (1995): 24–47; A. Van Regenmortel, 'Onderscheid tussen werknemer en zelfstandige', in J. Van Steenberge and A. Van Regenmortel (eds), *Actuele problemen van het sociale zekerheidsrecht* (Brugge: die Keure, 1995), 31–100; H. L'Homme, 'Casuïstiek omtrent enkele aspecten van sociale fraude in het rechtsgebied van het Arbeidshof te Antwerpen', *Rechtskundig Weekblad* (1997–98): 657–665; K. Van den Langenbergh, *Les Faux Indépendants. La différence entre le travail indépendant et le travail dans les liens de subordination* (Brussels: Ministère fédéral de l'Emploi et du Travail, 1999), 252; F. Lagasse, 'Les faux indépendants et le droit du travail: les

In Belgium, the burden of social security contributions weighs quite heavily. The employer's contribution fluctuates around 35% and the employee's contribution is 13.07%. This implies that, for an employee earning EUR 2,000, the total labour cost for the employer is EUR 2,700. Additionally, in some sectors, like construction, employers are obliged – on the basis of sectoral collective labour agreements – to pay extra sums. These are required, for instance, for supplementary social security benefits. It is thus primarily in such sectors that employers often seek to evade the employment contract. One method used is to camouflage an employment contract as a contract for services. This can be a win-win situation for both parties.

If the employee does not earn EUR 2,000 per month, but rather EUR 20,000 the social security contribution rises proportionally. This means that each month more than EUR 9,500 has to be paid to the NSSO. However, if the employee were to generate the same monthly income as a self-employed person, he alone would have to pay social security contributions (and not the principal). In 2010 the contribution is set at around EUR 14,700, because no social security contributions have to be paid for an income above (around) EUR 75,246. In this perspective it is easy to understand that employment relationships are construed as contracts for services. An agreement is concluded with the principal/employer to split the difference between the contributions as an employee and as a self-employed person (in our example, almost EUR 100,000). The NSSO disagrees with these practices and vigorously pursues them before the labour tribunals.

4.2. The Case Law

Prior to the Court of Cassation decision of 23 December 2002[42] in determining whether or not there was subordination, judges primarily made use of the so-called indicia method. They looked for elements pointing in the direction of subordination or independence, and on this basis performed an assessment which, depending on the case, inclined in the direction of either an employment contract or a work contract. The characterisation of the agreement by the parties was merely one of the elements which the judge could take into account.

---

frontières du lien de subordination', *Orientations* 5 (2003): 3–15; F. Lagasse, 'Les faux indépendants et le droit du travail (II), quelques cas d'espèces', *Orientations* 5 (2003): 16–24; V. Dooms and T. Messiaen, *Schijnzelfstandigheid*, Bibliotheek Sociaal Recht Larcier (Ghent: Larcier, 2009) 235; C. Clesse, 'Chronique de jurisprudence. Aux frontières de la fausse indépendance', *Orientations* 2 (2009): 1–11 and 3 (2009): 1–9.

42. *Journal des Tribunaux du Travail* (2003): 271. For a complete survey, see K. Nevens, 'Schijnzelfstandigen in het offensief: de analyse van de toepasselijke regelen inzake, bewijs, interpretatie en kwalificatie van de arbeidsovereenkomst', (2004–2005) *Rechtskundig Weekblad* 1201–1213; W. Van Eeckhoutte, "Gezag" in de cassatierechtspraak. Een kwestie van bewijs, interpretatie en kwalificatie', *Nieuw Juridisch Weekblad* 95 (2005): 2–17; O. Langlet, 'L'existence du lien de subordination: recherche d'équilibre entre la Cour de Cassation, le juge du fond et l'exécutif', *Chroniques de Droit Social* (2006): 245–263; W. Rauws, 'De kwalificatie van de (arbeids)overeenkomst', *Journal des Tribunaux de Travail* (2006): 93–101.

However, the judgment of 23 December 2002 introduced a fundamental change. If the parties have characterised their agreement as a contract for services, the judge may not change that characterisation into an employment contract if the other elements do not exclude it. Thus, where earlier the judge had to examine whether or not there was authority or subordination (and thus an employment contract), it now suffices that he follows the characterisation. The party who asserts that there is an employment contract must furnish the proof that there are elements which are incompatible with the existence of an independent collaboration. Freedom of will and liberty of contract have thus been given a larger role. This case law has subsequently been confirmed many times.[43] Obviously, it is now much more difficult than it used to be for a person who has signed an agreement, which says that he is self-employed, to prove that in fact he is a bogus self-employed worker.[44] Some authors have already wondered whether the viewpoint of the Court of Cassation conflicts with ILO Recommendation No. 198.[45]

4.3. Interlude: Techniques for Determining Subordination

In 2001 the UNIZO[46] formula was developed by a number of university professors and others.[47] The model (it is a model rather than a formula) consists of a questionnaire of twelve questions. One gets points (out of a total of 100) for the questions to which one responds 'yes'. Thus the question whether or not someone can freely set his own working hours yields nine points in the event of a positive answer. The question whether there is a substantial participation in the profit or loss is good for thirteen points, etc.

A person who scores more than sixty points is regarded as self-employed; a person who scores less than forty is an employee. For the cases of doubt, between 40 and 60 points, it was proposed to submit the advice to a ruling committee.

---

43. K. Nevens, 'De betekenis van de kwalificatiearresten verduidelijkt', *Rechtskundig Weekblad* (2007–2008): 782–783; V. Dooms (2009), *supra* n. 41, 207 et seq.
44. J. Clesse, 'La qualification juridique de la relation du travail', in J. Clesse and F. Kefer (eds), *Questions de droit social* (Liège: Anthémis, 2007), 232.
45. *Ibid.*, 233.
46. UNIZO is a representative employers' organisation that promotes the interests of small- and medium-sized businesses.
47. I. Baeke et al., 'Werknemer of zelfstandige: met vragenlijsten en puntensysteem naar een voorafgaandelijk bindend advies?', *Tijdschrift voor Sociaal Recht/Revue de Droit Social* (2001): 107–299; W. Van Eeckhoutte, 'La formule dite d'UNIZO', in X., *Le lien de subordination. Actes du colloque organisé le 19 mars 2004 par l'Ordre des Avocats du Barreau de Tournai et le Jeune Barreau de Tournai*, Etudes pratiques de Droit Social n° 18 (Brussels: Kluwer, 2004), 165–179. For a critical view, see K. Van den Langenbergh and A. Van Regenmortel, 'De UNIZO-formule kritisch bekeken. Brengt deze formule de gewenste rechtszekerheid en wordt, gelet op het beschermend karakter van het sociaal recht, voor deze (schijn van?) rechtszekerheid geen al te hoge prijs betaald?', *Tijdschrift voor Sociaal Recht/Revue de Droit Social* (2002): 3–27.

The purpose of the formula was to be converted into a statute. This never happened, but the formula has occasionally been used to base a judgment on.[48]

4.4. Parliamentary Initiatives

During the Verhofstadt-I Government, the successive Ministers of Labour, Onkelinx[49] and Vandenbroucke, engaged in an attempt to curb bogus self-employment.[50] The government finally took an initiative in 2006.

In Title XIII of the Programme Act (I) of 27 December 2006[51] the Employment Relationship Act[52] was incorporated. In principle this Act subjects only employees and self-employed persons to social security.

5. QUALIFYING A WORK RELATIONSHIP

5.1. The Criteria

The parties freely choose the nature of their working relationship (employment contract or contract for services).[53] However, if, from the facts, it appears that there are specific elements which exclude the characterisation of the agreement chosen by the parties, then priority must be given to the characterisation as it appears from

48. Industrial Court Leuven 26 oktober 2001, annotation M. De Vos, *Nieuw Juridisch Weekblad* (2002): 358.
49. F. Lagasse, 'Les faux indépendants et le droit du travail (IV). Les projets de réforme de la ministre Onkelinx', *Orientations* (2003): 16–18.
50. V. Dooms (2009), *supra* n. 41, 33 et seq.
51. *Belgian Official Journal* of 28 Dec. 2006, Arts 328–343.
52. For comments see J. Clesse, 'La qualification juridique de la relation du travail', in J. Clesse and F. Kefer (eds), *Questions de droit social* (Liège: Anthémis, 2007), 229–260; C. Lhoste, 'La loi relative à la nature des relations de travai: vers une plus grande sécurité juridique dans l'exercice d'une activité professionnelle', *Orientations* (2007): 9–15; J. Kerremans, 'De wet betreffende de aard van de arbeidsrelaties: kroniek van een aangekondigde dood?', *Journal des Tribunaux de Travail* (2007): 149–155; G. Lenaerts, '(Schijn)werknemer of (schijn)zelfstandige? . . . Soms een moeilijke evenwichtsoefening!', *Pacioli* 225 (2007): 1–6; C.J. Lorré, 'Aard van de arbeidsrelaties als *deus ex machina*', *Rechtskundig Weekblad* (2006–2007), 1662–1676; W. Van Eeckhoutte and G. De Maeseneire, 'Arbeidsrelatieswet. Het bepalen van de rechtsaard van arbeidsrelaties', *Nieuw Juridisch Weekblad* (2007): 98–119; H. Van Hoogenbemt, 'Zelfstandigheid en schijnzelfstandigheid na de Programmawet (I) van 27 December 2006', *Oriëntatie* 3 (2007): 49–65; P. Verdonck (ed.), *la nouvelle loi sur les relations de travail. Premier état et perspectives* (Louvain-la-Neuve: Anthémis, 2007), 171; M. Rigaux and A. Van Regenmortel (eds), *Rechts(on)zekerheid omtrent (schijn)zelfstandigheid* (Antwerp: Intersentia, 2008), 228; K. Mortier, 'Arbeidsrelatieswet. Twee jaar na de inwerkingtreding', *Nieuw Juridisch Weekblad* (2009): 382–386; K. Van den Langenbergh and A. Van Regenmortel, 'Schijnzelfstandigheid na de arbeidsrelatiewet: een eerste evaluatie', in X., *CBR Jaarboek 2008–2009* (Antwerp: Intersentia, 2009), 503.
53. Article 331 Employment Relationship Act.

the facts.[54] The judge can re-qualify the agreement, with all the attendant consequences for the applicable social security regime.[55] In a sense, therefore, this provision is simply a confirmation of the case law of the Court of Cassation.[56]

The Act gives the judge a foothold for his assessment. The elements which make it possible to evaluate the existence or absence of authority, that is, the so-called general criteria, are:[57]

- the will of the parties;
- the freedom of organisation of the working hours;
- the freedom of organisation of the work;
- the possibility of exercising a hierarchical control.

Other elements, however, are as such not sufficient to qualify a working relationship adequately:[58]

- the title of the contract;
- the registration with a social security institution;
- the registration with the Crossroads Bank for Companies;
- the registration with the VAT Administration;
- the manner in which the earnings are reported to the tax administration.

Although they are, taken as isolated criteria, not decisive to qualify a relationship, they can, together with other elements, be an indication of the intention of the parties.

In addition, the King can prepare a list with specific criteria which relate to a sector, one or several professions, or one or several categories of professions.[59]

This list with specific criteria can *inter alia* include the following elements:[60]

- responsibility and decision-making power over the financial resources in order to keep the company profitable;
- the fixed and/or guaranteed remuneration;
- personal and substantial investment in the company with own resources and personal and substantial participation in the profits and losses of the company;
- the possibility to hire personnel or to have oneself replaced;
- to act as a company vis-à-vis the co-contractor or third parties;
- to work in spaces and/or with equipment the worker owns.

---

54. Article 331 Employment Relationship Act.
55. Article 332 Employment Relationship Act.
56. A. Van Regenmortel, 'De Arbeidsrelatieswet: continuering van de cassatierechtspraak', in M. Rigaux and A. Van Regenmortel (eds), *Rechts(on)zekerheid omtrent (schijn)zelfstandigheid* (Antwerp: Intersentia, 2008), 91–143.
57. Article 333 § 1 Employment Relationship Act.
58. Article 333 § 3 Employment Relationship Act.
59. Article 334 § 1 Employment Relationship Act.
60. Article 334 § 3 Employment Relationship Act. For more details, see J. Buelens, 'De normatieve afdeling van de Commissie tot regeling van de arbeidsrelatie: een niet-evidente zoektocht naar specifieke criteria', in M. Rigaux and A. Van Regenmortel (eds), *Rechts(on)zekerheid omtrent (schijn)zelfstandigheid* (Antwerp: Intersentia, 2008), 159–176.

The law includes a special procedure with a view to determine sectoral criteria (see below).

5.2. The Commission

The linchpin of the law is the 'Commission for the regulation of the employment relationship'. This is composed of two divisions:

- a normative division, with a single chamber;[61]
- an administrative division, with several chambers.

The chamber of the normative division is composed of one magistrate, twelve federal civil servants and four experts.[62]

The chambers of the administrative division are presided over by a magistrate and are each composed of an equal number of members, designated on proposal of the Minister of Small and Medium Sized Businesses and the Ministers responsible for Social Affairs and Labour.[63] These civil servants may not perform inspection assignments.[64]

The members of both the normative chambers and the chambers of the administrative division are appointed by the King.

5.2.1. Tasks of the Normative Division[65]

5.2.1.1. Gathering Advice

This chamber gathers advice with a view to making agreements about labour relations in a sector (e.g., the health sector) or for one or several professions.[66] For example, one could agree that physical therapists who fulfil assignments in a hospital are never employees, and that someone who processes meat in a slaughterhouse can never be a self-employed person.

The advice is collected from representative organisations, such as professional orders, professional institutes, joint committees and from public authorities.[67] Individual complaints cannot be submitted.[68]

61. For more details, see P. Humblet and T. Martens, 'De normatieve afdeling van de Commissie ter regeling van de arbeidsrelatie: het organisatorische kader', in M. Rigaux and A. Van Regenmortel (eds), *Rechts(on)zekerheid omtrent (schijn)zelfstandigheid* (Antwerp: Intersentia, 2008), 145–158.
62. Article 329 § 2 Employment Relationship Act.
63. Article 329 § 3 Employment Relationship Act.
64. Article 329 § 4 Employment Relationship Act.
65. Article 330 Employment Relationship Act.
66. Article 330, 1° Employment Relationship Act.
67. *Parliamentary documents*, House of Parliament (*Parl.St.* Kamer), 2006–2007, No. 2773/1, 210.
68. *Ibid.*

5.2.1.2. Issuing a Report

The chamber must, at the request of the competent ministers, or can, upon its own initiative, issue a report on whether there are uncertainties or problems on the nature of employment relations in a particular sector or in one or several professions.[69] In other words, the chamber has to give a signal should a dispute arise.

5.2.1.3. Advisory Role

The chamber must give advice to the High Council for the Self-employed and Small and Medium Sized Businesses (HCSESMSB) and the National Labour Council (NLC) on the determination of the lists with specific criteria (see Section 5.2.1.1).[70]

5.2.1.4. Proposals

The chamber must – if asked to do so by the competent minister – within a certain period prepare a draft list with specific criteria (see Section 5.2.1.1).[71] A highly complicated procedure is followed in which the social partners are involved.[72]

The proposal is submitted for advice to the HCSESMSB and the NLC.[73] The HCSESMSB issues its view only after having consulted the sectors and professions involved and (if there is one) the professional or disciplinary council that is designated for the involved profession by the law.[74] The NLC issues its opinion only after having consulted the competent joint committees.[75]

If the opinions are unanimous, the chamber turns over the draft list with specific criteria, unchanged, to the competent ministers within one month.[76]

In that event, the King may not accept any other criteria.[77] He is obliged to draw up a Royal Decree as a result of this agreement between the social partners.[78] If the advice is not unanimous, the chamber prepares a synthesis. In this situation the King will have much more room for policy-making.

5.2.2. The Tasks of the Chambers of the Administrative Division

The chambers of the administrative division have the task of taking preventive decisions concerning the characterisation of an employment relationship (the

69. Article 330, 2° Employment Relationship Act.
70. Article 330, 3° Employment Relationship Act.
71. Article 330, 4° Employment Relationship Act.
72. See Art. 335 Employment Relationship Act.
73. Article 336 § 1, first subsection Employment Relationship Act.
74. Article 336 § 1, second subsection Employment Relationship Act.
75. Article 336 § 1, third subsection Employment Relationship Act.
76. Article 336 § 3, second subsection Employment Relationship Act.
77. *Parliamentary documents of the Chamber of Representatives* 2006–2007, No. 2773/1, 223.
78. *Ibid.*

so-called 'social ruling').[79] The parties to an agreement – the principal and the performer – can individually or jointly turn to these chambers and ask that a position be taken on whether, in a specific working situation, labour is performed as an employee or as a self-employed individual. These decisions remain in force for a period of three years.

However, absolutely no decision can be given:

- if, at the time of submitting the request, the competent services of the social security institutions had initiated a (criminal) investigation regarding the nature of the employment relationship;
- if the nature of the employment relationship involved was an issue pending before a Labour Tribunal, or the latter has already pronounced on it.

The decisions are binding for the institutions which are represented in the administrative chamber (e.g., NSSO and the National Institute for the Social Security of the Self-employed), as well as for the social insurance funds, except in a number of cases enumerated in the law.

The parties, within the month following the notification of the decisions, can via registered letter file an appeal against these decisions with the labour tribunals.

5.3. Assessment

The parameters which were incorporated into the law are already being used by the labour tribunals;[80] in practice, however, nothing has changed. Formally, of course, the court makes reference to the Employment Relationship Act, but for the substance of the case it still assesses the nature of the employment relationship the way it has always done.

In practice the criteria which were incorporated into the law are not only used in discussions about social security (which was the intention of the legislature), but also in disputes relating to labour law aspects (which was not the intention).

The Commission has still not been formed, despite the fact that this was supposed to have happened by 1 January 2008 at the latest.[81] This means that until today no social ruling can take place and no lists with specific criteria exist.

6. CONFORMITY WITH ILO RECOMMENDATION NO. 198?

The ILO recommendation has two key objectives: improving protection of employees and certainty concerning the nature of the contract.

---

79. Article 338 Employment Relationship Act.
80. Industrial Court Brussels 19 Apr. 2007, *Journal des Tribunaux du Travail* (2007),. 243; Industrial Court Ghent 5 Nov. 2007, (2008) *Journal des Tribunaux du Travail* 28.
81. Article 343 Employment Relationship Act.

Belgium probably offers sufficient protection. Through the Employment Relationship Act an attempt is made to clearly delineate the distinction between employees and self-employed workers. But is this enough?

The Council of State was quite critical in its comments on the draft of the Employment Relationship Act.[82] The Council noted that the law proceeds from an agreement between the parties on the characterisation of their legal relationship, which runs contrary to Article 9 of ILO Recommendation No. 198 that gives priority to the factual situation.[83] In addition, strong emphasis is placed on the legal relationship of authority alone (just as in the case law).[84] However, the Recommendation also allows other criteria, including economic dependency and the indicia criterion.[85]

The Employment Relationship Act makes absolutely no use of these criteria. Only with regard to the specific criteria is reference made to elements of economic dependency (e.g., substantial investment in the company with own resources), but as mentioned above, these specific criteria still do not exist to this day.

From the view of the National Labour Council No. 1657 it appears that the social partners are also not altogether enthusiastic about the present Act,[86] which should not surprise us.

Normally the government submits a bill on labour relations to the National Labour Council. The Council gives its view on the bill, which enables the government to adapt the bill. In the case of the present Act that has not happened, which is in part the result of the fact that the Employment Relationship Act was an initiative of the Minister of Small and Medium-sized Businesses (which has virtually no ties with the NLC), as well as due to the fact that the law came at a time when new elections were imminent. This law was a rush job, with all the consequences as a result.

It really stretches the imagination to simply sell the Act as an implementation of the provisions of the ILO Recommendation, as the government did.[87] The objective of the Employment Relationship Act is not to protect the economically weaker contracting party (which is the starting point of the Recommendation), but solely to create legal certainty for employers.

---

82. Advice of the State Council (Raad van State) No. 41.521/1 published in *Parliamentary documents of the Chamber of Representatives* 2006–2007, No. 2773/2, 453 et seq.
83. *Ibid.*, 455.
84. In the original text the will of the parties was much more (than is the case now) accentuated. As a result of the remark(s) of the State Council some arguments were moderated. See K. Van Den Langenbergh, 'Basisprincipes van de Arbeidsrelatieswet: herkomst en kritische analyse', in M. Rigaux and A. Van Regenmortel (eds), *Rechts(on)zekerheid omtrent (schijn)zelfstandigheid* (Antwerp: Intersentia, 2008), 36–37.
85. *Ibid.*, 454. For critical comments in a similar sense, see M. Rigaux, 'De gespannen verhouding tussen artikel 1134 BW en de sociaalrechtelijke finaliteit. Inleidende beschouwingen', in M. Rigaux and A. Van Regenmortel (eds), *Rechts(on)zekerheid omtrent (schijn)zelfstandigheid* (Antwerp: Intersentia, 2008), 20.
86. <www.cnt-nar.be/ADVIES/advies-1657.pdf>, 5.
87. *Parliamentary documents of the Chamber of Representatives* 2006–2007, No. 2773/1, 215.

The correct implementation of the ILO Recommendation into Belgian law presumes a complete reconsideration of the subordination criterion between employees and independent workers. The Employment Relationship Act certainly does not facilitate this, on the contrary.

For the sake of completeness, we should note that the self-employed enjoy protection in social security, and this protection is progressively being expanded.

Professor of Sociology Bea Cantillon (University of Antwerp) has published some studies which have kick-started the debate about the status of the self-employed.[88] In recent years their situation has greatly improved, and the social security arrangements of the various professional categories will (probably) gradually become more and more alike.

As for the labour law protection, we also note that in the area of safety and health the contractor always remains responsible. If, for instance, a (bogus) self-employed person becomes the victim of harassment at the place where s/he exercises his/her activity, s/he enjoys a protection similar to that of an employee.

Finally, let us point out that a number of structures have been created which are analogous to those of employees. For example, a self-employed worker cannot receive unemployment benefits, but since 1 July 1997 a bankrupt self-employed person is covered by bankruptcy insurance.[89] He thus maintains his rights to specific benefits and enjoys, during a maximum of six months, a benefit which is equal to the minimum pension of the self-employed. The self-employed are still less protected than employees, but they have a higher net income.

---

88. B. Cantillon et al., 'Propositions de réformes dans le régime de pension des travailleurs indépendant: deuxième rapport du Groupe de travail Cantillon', *Revue belge de sécurité sociale* 2 (2002): 229–263; B. Cantillon, 'The Failures of Bismarck and Beveridge: The Case of Old-Age Pensions for the Self-Employed in Belgium', in E. Overbye (ed.), *Pensions: Challenges and Reforms* (Ashgate: Aldershot, 2004), 131–147.
89. M. Goldfays, 'Assurance sociale et travailleurs indépendants faillis', *Journal des Tribunaux de Travail* (1997): 317–322; D. Roulive, 'Les sanctions à charge de l'employeur dans le cadre de la réglementation du chômage', *Orientations* 10 (2008): 10–18.

Chapter 6

Protection of Working Relationships in France

Isabelle Daugareilh

1. INTRODUCTION

Since the 1970s, many new forms of employment relationships have been developed in France. Temporary, fixed-term, and part-time employment contracts have been clearly defined in the Labour Code and are thus protected by law. At the same time, permanent, full-time contracts have received a special position in the Labour Code. In the Code a provision was included stating that: 'permanent employment contracts are the normal, general form of employment relationship'.[1] Although permanent contracts are thus enshrined as the standard, they are constantly becoming less representative of the reality of employment in France. In 1975, 72% of the workers were employed on permanent, full-time contracts, in 1998 this was only 56%.[2] Workers on fixed-term and temporary contracts represented 12.6% of all

1. Article L 1221-2 of the Labour Code.
2. Figures published in J.P. Chauchard, 'Entre travail salarié et travail indépendant: l'émergence du travail autonome', in *Du travail salarié au travail indépendant: permanences et mutations* (Bari: Cacucci Editore, 2003), 1–20.

Frans Pennings & Claire Bosse, *The Protection of Working Relationships*, pp. 61–82.
© 2011 Kluwer Law International BV, The Netherlands.

employees in 2007.[3] Indeed, since 2004 casual employment has become the dominant pattern in some business sectors, such as culture.[4]

In the post-war period, the French working population was almost evenly distributed between employed and self-employed persons. Employment relationships then began to increase considerably and became clearly dominant in the sixties and seventies. They accounted for 82% of the working population in 1982 and 88.6% in 1997.[5] Self-employment became more widespread again in the 1990s, due to a series of factors, including a durable economic downturn and the resulting loss of jobs, the development of subcontracting and the outsourcing of some production. Taking all business sectors together, there were 2,059,000 self-employed workers[6] in 2005 and 1,564,540 enterprises with no employees.[7] In 2007, 25.6 million people had a business activity, including 2.8 million self-employed workers, or 10.8% of the total.[8] Obviously, the category of self-employed workers is heterogeneous (farmers, shopkeepers, tradespeople, professional people, entrepreneurs, etc.) and covers many different working arrangements. Self-employment is not governed by labour law, but by civil or commercial law. However, the French Act of 11 February 1994, which aimed to rein in the case law which reclassified agreements as employment contracts, marked a policy change in favour of self-employment, giving it a legal framework equivalent to that of salaried work. This legislation, that specified the evidence required to prove that a contract was presumed not to be an employment contract,[9] was repealed by the Act of 19 January 2000, but reintroduced by the Act on

3. Figures from Insee-Enquête emploi en continu. Données 2007, quoted by J.-P. Chauchard, 'Les avatars du travail indépendant', *Droit social* 11 (2009), 1065.
4. In the cultural sector, 59% of employees in live and audiovisual entertainment had permanent contracts in 1998, compared to only 48% in 2004, by which time the majority of salaried workers were on fixed-term contracts, irrespective of their qualifications. Figures from the Department of studies, forward planning, and statistics by the Ministry of culture, *Tendances de l'emploi dans le spectacle*, 2007-1 (Paris, 2007).
5. Figures published by J. Barreau & M. Del Sol, 'Les formes hybrides de travail; de nouveaux rapports entre précarité et situations professionnelles', in *Nouvelles dimensions de la précarité* (Paris: PUR, 2001).
6. Figures taken from ACOSS STAT (Agence comptable des organismes de sécurité sociale), n° 61, December 2007 quoted by P.H. Antonmattei & J.C. Sciberras, *Le travailleur économiquement dépendant: quelle protection?* (Paris: La Documentation française 2008), <lesrapports.ladocumentationfrancaise.fr/BRP/084000694/0000.pdf>, *Droit social* (2009), 221–233 at 232.
7. Figures are taken from Insee, *REE* (Répertoire des entreprises et des établissements – Sirene), quoted by P.H. Antonmattei & J.C. Sciberras *Le travailleur économiquement dépendant: quelle protection?* (Paris: La Documentation française, 2008), *Droit social* (2009), 221–233 at 232.
8. Figures cited by J.-P. Chauchard, 'Les avatars du travail indépendant', *Droit social* 11 (2009), 1066.
9. M. Laroque, 'Présentation introductive de la loi du 11 Février 1994 relative à l'initiative et à l'entreprise individuelle', *Droit social* (1995), 631; J.E. Ray, 'De Germinal à Internet. Une nécessaire évolution du critère du contrat de travail', *Droit social* (1995), 634; J.P. Chauchard, 'Le rescrit social, procédure d'interrogation de l'URSSAF', *Droit social* (1995), 642; G. Lyon-Caen, 'Où mènent les mauvais chemins', *Droit social* (1995), 647.

economic initiatives of 1 August 2003.[10] It is now Article L 8221-6-I of the Labour Code. Finally, the Act on modernisation of the economy of 4 August 2008, which came into effect on 1 January 2009, gave the first legal definition of self-employed workers (Article L 8226-1 of the Labour Code).[11]

The absence of a legal definition of the employment contract or of any obligation to establish a written employment contract for permanent, full-time workers raises the important issue how to classify working relationships. Are these persons employed or self-employed? This question reflects the *polarisation* in French law,[12] whereby workers do not have an employment contract if they are self-employed. This approach has already for a long time been adopted by both the courts and the legislature.

The French case law and the Acts are consistent with the provisions of ILO Recommendation 198 on employment relationships, adopted in 2006. This text contains guidelines[13] to assist Member States in clarifying whether a particular working relationship is an employment relationship or not (by defining employment contracts or determining the basic criteria for legal subordination), distinguishing between employed persons and self-employed, and reclassifying these relationships. However, the really problematic issue in France is the polarisation in law between employed and self-employed persons.[14]

In some areas the legal position of employed and self-employed workers has become more similar. For instance, self-employed farmers now receive basic social benefits in case of work-related accidents. Restrictions on HGV drivers' working hours are also applicable to self-employed drivers.[15] Self-employed doctors have gone on strike to demand an increase in their fees and rest periods. To summarise, the boundary between employed and self-employed workers is becoming increasingly fuzzy, both in fact and in law. Some employed persons have acquired a certain autonomy or even freedom in the way they do their work. In contrast, increasing numbers of self-employed workers are giving up their autonomy as they become integrated in production and distribution networks or are bound, in practice, to a single client or main contractor. Under these conditions,

---

10. M. Vericel, 'Le rétablissement de la présomption de non salariat, Art. 23, loi du 1er August 2003 pour l'initiative économique', *Droit social* (2004), 297.
11. J.-P. Chauchard, 'Les avatars du travail indépendant', *Droit social* (2009), 1065. By the same author, 'Eléments pour une définition d'un contrat de travail indépendant', (June 2007) n° 24, *JCP*, 1761.
12. F. Héas, 'Etre ou ne pas être subordonné', *Droit social* (1995), 405.
13. A brochure gives a clarification of the text and many examples from national systems, ILO, *The Employment relationship; an annotated guide to ILO Recommendation No. 198* (Geneva: ILO, 2008), 25–42.
14. In addition, the legislature is reluctant to transpose the European directive of 14 Oct. 1991, concerning the employer's obligation to inform workers about the conditions applicable to the contract or employment relationship more explicitly (OJ 1991, L 288).
15. Directive (EC) 2002/15 of the European Parliament and of the Council of 11 Mar. 2002 on the organisation of the working time of persons performing mobile road transport activities, OJ 2002, L 80/35; Court of Justice 9 Sep. 2004, *Spain and Finland*, case 1/05.

subordination is apparently no longer effective as the distinctive legal criterion for employment contracts and the application of labour law.

Thus, in view of this 'tendency towards hybrid employment situations'[16] the legal distinction between employed and self-employed work is more confused. In 1990, Gérard Lyon-Caen's *Le droit du travail non salarié*[17] (Law on non-salaried work), provided a brilliant premonitory demonstration of all the limitations of this bipolarity. He proposed the adoption of the concept of 'work law' (employed and self-employed work), based on the concept of working people. Twenty years later, the French legislature, unlike its European,[18] German,[19] Italian,[20] English,[21] or Spanish[22] counterparts, has still not proposed an overall legal solution and continues to implement piecemeal measures.

The most eminent French theorists have, however, produced publications and proposals on both national and European level. The Commission of the European Community's Green Paper, *Modernising labour law to meet the challenges of the 21st Century*,[23] issued on 22 November 2006, proposed creating a new category of economically dependent workers, who are neither employed nor self-employed, defined as follows:

> The concept of "economically dependent work" covers situations which fall between the two established concepts of subordinate employment and independent self-employment. These workers do not have a contract of employment. They may not be covered by labour legislation, since they occupy a "grey area" between labour law and commercial law. Although formally "self-employed", they remain economically dependent on a single principal, client or employer for their source of income.[24]

---

16. According to the expression used by J. Barreau and M. Del Sol, 'Les formes hybrides de travail: de nouveaux rapports entre précarité et situations professionnelles', in *Nouvelles dimensions de la précarité* (Paris: PUR, 2001).
17. G. Lyon-Caen, *Le droit du travail non salarié* (Paris: Sirey, 1990).
18. 'Le sort des travailleurs économiquement dépendants en Europe', (January 2009) n° 215–216, *Liaisons sociales*.
19. For *arbeitnemerähnliche Personen* (persons assimilated with employed persons) in the *Tarifvertragsgesetz*, § 12 a (Act on collective agreements).
20. M. Hascoët, 'Le contrat de projet: le nouveau visage de la para subordination en Italie', *Droit Social* (2007), 879; J. Barthélémy, 'Essai sur la para-subordination', *Semaine Sociale Lamy* (2003), 6.
21. On the concept of *workers* in Great Britain, see Ch. Vigneau, 'Les travailleurs précaires face à l'exigence de continuité de l'emploi', *Semaine Sociale Lamy* (2003), 5.
22. Act 20/2007 of 11 Jul. 2007 (OJ 166, 2007), 29964; F. Valdés dal Ré and O. Leclerc, 'Les nouvelles frontières du travail indépendant. A propos du statut du travail autonome espagnol', *Revue de droit du travail* (2008), 296–303; J.M. Goerloch and A. Guamán, 'Le règlement de 2009, une nouvelle étape dans la règlementation espagnole de l'hybride', *Revue de droit du travail* (2009), 337.
23. COM (2006) 708 final. A. Perulli, *Study on Economically Dependent Work Parasubordinate (Quasi-subordinate) Work* (Brussels: European Commission, 2002); see J.P. Chauchard and A.C. Hardy Dubernet (eds), *La subordination dans le travail* (Paris: Cahier Travail et Emploi, 2003).
24. COM (2006) 708 final.

A report was published in France in late November 2008, entitled *Economically-dependent work: what protection?*[25] This report, commissioned by the Minister of Labour, could have been the forerunner of new legislation. However, so far no draft bills on this subject have been brought before the Parliament.

Consequently, for the moment, there is no specific legal framework in France governing the borderline area between subordinate employment and self-employment. There have been a few legislative initiatives, but they were sporadic, partial, and 'tied' to sectoral or even corporatist approaches; none of them have ever challenged the binary analysis of the French legal system. Currently, the courts are mainly responsible for dealing with requests to reclassify employment relationships and to determine the appropriate category for hybrid work situations (discussed in Section 2). Hope for future legislative changes has not been completely abandoned. In addition to the many theoretical studies produced in recent years, reports very recently commissioned by the French authorities indicate that new legislation is imminent (Section 3).

2. A BINARY LEGAL DEFINITION OF EMPLOYMENT RELATIONSHIPS

2.1. Introduction

The Labour Code does not define the contents of employment contracts, which 'are subject to the rules of general law. They may be established in any form that the contracting parties decide to adopt'.[26] Furthermore, France has still not satisfactorily transposed the Directive of 14 October 1991:[27] only atypical (short-term, temporary, and part-time) employment contracts are legally required to be in writing. The only obligation imposed upon employers, which was considered by the French legislature as an adequate transposition of the European norm, is to inform the social protection agency in advance when a new employee is engaged.[28]

In case of a legal dispute, it is, therefore, up to the plaintiff to provide evidence of the existence and effective application of an employment contract. If there is apparently a contract, it is up to the party alleging that it is a fictitious contract to submit evidence to that effect. The courts thus have the main responsibility for classifying employment relationships (section 2.2). However, legislation has also been enacted granting persons in certain professions the same protection as employed persons. In this way, the legislature has contributed to extending the scope of application of labour law (section 2.3).

25. P.H. Antonmattei and J.C. Sciberras, *Le travailleur économiquement dépendant: quelle protection?* (Paris: La Documentation française, 2008). *Droit social* (2009), 221–233 at 232.
26. Article L 1221-1 of the Labour Code.
27. Directive (EEC) 91/533 of the Council of 14 Oct. 1991 on an employer's obligation to inform employees of the conditions applicable to the contract or employment relationship, (*OJ* 1991, *L* 288/32).
28. Article L 1221-10 of the Labour Code.

2.2. Classification of Working Relationships by Courts

2.2.1. Introduction

French law does not allow the parties to freely choose the legal framework for their working relationship, independent of the conditions involved. The courts are responsible for 'determining the precise classification of the disputed facts and actions, irrespective of the terminology used by the parties'.[29] The absence of the free choice for the parties follows from the fact that it is public order legislation. Irrespective of the will of the parties and the principle of freedom of contract, the decisive factors are the actual conditions under which the work is performed. 'The will of the parties is powerless to take away from workers a social status which necessarily results from the conditions under which they carry out their tasks.'[30]

This principle has been unanimously adopted by the various chambers of the Court of Cassation.[31] The courts apply exactly the same principle in judging social security issues.[32] Thus, according to a formula used by the Court of Cassation in many rulings,[33] the existence of an employment contract depends neither on the will expressed by the parties nor on the title of the contract, but on the actual conditions under which the workers carry out their tasks. There is a great deal of case law concerning the reclassification of fictitious or apparent employment contracts, or contracts initially and incorrectly classified by the parties in the following categories: agricultural integration contracts,[34] taxi rental contracts,[35] contract for appearing on a television programmes,[36] business referral contracts,[37] voluntary work contracts,[38] registered HGV rental company contracts,[39] computerised data capture contracts,[40] independent consulting contracts[41] and franchise contracts.[42]

29. Article 12(2) of the New Civil Procedure Code.
30. Court of Cassation, Ecole des Roches judgment, 4 Mar. 1983, *Dalloz*, 1983, 381, Conclusion by J. Cabannes.
31. This was the case in the social chamber (Soc. 27 Oct. 1993), *Droit social* (1993), 960, criminal chamber (Crim. 29 Oct. 1885, *Bull Crim*, no. 335), and civil chamber.
32. J.J. Dupeyroux, M. Borgetto & R. Lafore, *Droit de la sécurité sociale* (Paris: Dalloz, 2008), n° 578.
33. For instance Soc. 15 Mar. 2006, B.V, n° 110p; J. Savatier, *Droit social* (2006), 695; Soc. 25 Oct. 2005, B., V., n° 300, obs. J. Savatier, *Droit social* (2006), 94.
34. Soc. 13 Nov. 2008, JCP 2009, S, 1149, note D. Asquinazi-Bailleux. See also H. Gilbert, 'Contrat et production: l'agriculteur intégré ou un exemple de la dépendance dans l'indépendance', in J.P. Chauchard and A.C. Dubernet (eds), *La subordination dans le travail* (Paris: Cahier Travail et Emploi, 2003), 227.
35. Different:Soc. 17 Sep. 2008, *JCP*, Social, 2008, 1580, note C. Puigelier.
36. Soc. 3 Jun. 2009, *Bull. Civ*, no. 141.
37. Different: Civ. 2nd, 4 Dec. 2008, *RJS*, 2/2009, n° 214.
38. Civ. 2nd, 7 Feb. 2008, *RJS*, 6/2008, n° 715.
39. Soc. 19 Dec. 2000, *Bull. Civ. V*, n° 437. Civ. 2nd, 20 Mar. 2008, RJS 6/2008, No. 715.
40. Different: Civ. 2nd, 20 Mar. 2008, *RJS*, 6/2008, n° 715.
41. Soc. 14 May 2009, *Droit ouvrier*, 2009, 411.
42. Soc. 25 Mar. 2009, *Droit ouvrier*, 2009, 416.

Theorists have developed the following definition of the employment contract: it is a contract by which an individual agrees to carry out tasks for another individual or organisation, within a relationship of subordination, in return for payment.[43] The existence of an employment contract, therefore, requires a combination of three elements: work has to be provided, payment is to be provided in return, and there must be legal subordination. French case law has mainly focused on the third element (section 2.2.2), whereas the reality of the work involved has received very little attention, except in the occasional disputes focusing on this issue (section 2.2.3).

2.2.2. The Existence of a Legally Defined Subordinate Relationship

In a legally defined subordinate relationship, the employer is authorised to give orders and instructions, as well as to organise and control the conditions under which work is carried out; employees are obliged to comply with these arrangements. In the case law the concept of economic dependence has been rejected; it focuses solely on legal subordination:

> The legal relationship of workers with the person for whom they work cannot be determined by their weakness or economic dependence, but only by a contract between the parties; employee status requires a legal subordination relationship between worker and employer.[44]

The case law of the Court of Cassation has evolved from a strict interpretation of legal subordination to a more flexible (pragmatic) approach, aimed at facilitating access for certain workers to the general social security system, as well as reflecting current changes in employment relationships.

Subordination was initially considered to involve actual management and control by the employer of the way work was carried out. Under the terms of an employment contract an employer has the right to interfere or intervene to determine the way the work is carried out and the employee must accept the employer's surveillance and decisions. The Court of Cassation initially accepted that subordination was based on subsidiary obligations. It thus extended general social security coverage to managers of service stations,[45] whereas they were otherwise considered as shopkeepers. At a later stage, the Court of Cassation observed that the employer's interference in the way work was carried out could be considered incompatible with self-employment, technical skills or the freedom necessary to complete certain tasks properly. This is particularly the case in the health, teaching and training professions. The Court of Cassation classified a relationship in which

43. J. Pélissier, A. Supiot and A. Jeammaud, *Droit du travail* (Paris: Dalloz 2008, 24th edn, n° 284.
44. Cass. Civ. 6 Jul. 1931, *Dalloz*, 1931, I, 121, note P. Pic.
45. Soc. 18 Dec. 1975, *Dalloz*, 1976, 399, note A. Jeammaud, Soc. 24 Feb. 1977, *Bull. Civ.* V, n°150.

the work was carried out in the context of a service organised and directed by the contracting party as an employment contract.[46]

This movement of the case law in which coverage was expanded was restricted by the famous Court of Cassation ruling in the *Société Générale* case of 16 November 1996. In this judgment the court gave a definition of a subordinate relationship that was also cited verbatim in later rulings:

> a subordinate relationship exists when work is carried out under the authority of an employer who has the power to give orders and instructions, control the way work is done, and apply penalties if the subordinated person fails to comply.[47]

However, the Court of Cassation adopted certain 'flexibility' with regard to its own definition by deciding that workers should benefit from the 'employee' status if they were in a situation of economic rather than purely legal subordination.[48] Thus taxi drivers' vehicle rental contracts were reclassified as employment contracts, although the rental company did not define their workplace, length of the workday or working hours. However, the important point is that, since this ruling in 1996, the Court of Cassation has made the subordinate relationship the key criterion, not only for employment contracts, but also for coverage under the general social security system. Consequently, 'employee' status is defined in an identical manner in both labour and social security law. Furthermore, the courts now consider that providing work in an organised service is merely an indication of subordination, when the employer unilaterally determines the conditions under which work is carried out.[49]

The courts use a set of criteria to determine the existence of a subordinate relationship or organised service. There is no hierarchy among the many criteria applied: the behaviour of the parties (who signs the employment contract, issues the pay slip, registers the workers with the social security system?), who determines the workplace[50] and working hours, who does the work, who provides the equipment and raw materials, who establishes the payment arrangements, who is responsible for managing and monitoring the work,[51] and who bears the risks (financial and employment) in the enterprise, and who applies penalties for employee misdemeanours?[52] Determining the existence of subordination is a matter of fact, based on practical, material considerations.

The importance and even the existence of these criteria have been modified by new forms of work and employment (multitasking, telework and working for multiple employers), which alter the boundaries of the employment relationship. These new forms of work organisation, particularly the widespread, intensive use

---

46. Cassation full court, 18 Jun. 1976, *Dalloz*, 1977, p. 173, note A. Jeammaud, Cassation full court 4 Mar. 1983, Soc. 20 Nov. 1986, *Droit social* (1987), 379; Soc. 29 Mar. 1994, *RJS*, 5/94, n° 517.
47. *Ibid.*
48. Soc. 19 Dec. 2000, B., V., n° 437.
49. Soc. 13 Nov. 1996, B., V., n°386, *Droit social* (1996), 1067, note J.J. Dupeyroux.
50. Court full chamber 4 Mar. 1983, *Bull. Civ.*, V, n° 3.
51. Soc. 29 Jan. 2002, *Bull. Civ*, V, n° 38.
52. Soc. 13 Nov. 1996, *Bull. Civ.*, V, n° 386.

of new technologies, have modified subordinate relationships and the characteristics of employment relationships. For example, working time, the workplace and management of work, which used to form a whole, are now scattered, looser, and more flexible.[53] Employers increasingly control mainly the results of their workers' activities rather than the process. Workers may be free to set their own working hours or even to decide on their workplace (at home or elsewhere). Corporate networks have developed new configurations, where many tasks are outsourced and only the 'core business', 'brand' or 'label' remain in-house. However, is it possible to reduce the definition of provision of work to a set of criteria indicative of subordination?

2.2.3. The Existence of Provision of Work

The basis of the contract of employment is the provision of work. Neither the French Labour Code nor case law defines what is meant by the provision of work. From a legal theory standpoint, an activity is considered to be professional when the aim is to earn an income or a compensation of normal living expenses.[54] The ruling issued by the Court of Cassation on 3 June 2009,[55] in a case involving the well-known TV reality show 'Ile de la tentation', provided an opportunity to analyse the existence of a provision of work and the concept of work itself. From a logical standpoint it is necessary to determine the existence of a provision of work as a prerequisite for analysing the conditions under which the work is carried out, to determine whether there is a legal subordination relationship.[56] It is one thing to classify a work activity, but quite a different matter to classify the conditions under which an activity is carried out.

Can participation in a reality TV show, where the objective is for the participants to express their own feelings and become involved in interpersonal relationships generated by life in a closed community, under the constant gaze of the cameras, be considered work or is it recreation? Can recreation constitute work? It is not easy to answer that question without making a moral judgment. The Court of Cassation attracted strong criticism from most French authors by refusing to make any pronouncements on this issue and restricting its examination to the existence of legal subordination to deduce the existence of a provision of work subject to an employment contract.[57] The Court of Cassation did not take the risk of defining

53. A. Supiot, 'Les nouveaux visages de la subordination', *Droit social* (2000).
54. J. Pélissier, A. Supiot and A. Jeammaud, *Droit du travail* (Paris: Dalloz, 2008), n° 142.
55. Soc. 3 Jun. 2009, *Bull. Civ*, V. n°, FP-P+B+R+I.
56. J. Barthélémy, 'Qualification de l'activité du participant à une émission de télé-réalité', *Semaine sociale Lamy*, 1382 (2009), 8.
57. In the first place, J.Y. Verkindt, 'Debout! Les damnés de la terre', *JCP* 25 (2009); J.E. Ray, 'Sea, sex . . . and contrat de travail', *Semaine sociale Lamy* (2009), 1403; A. Jeammaud (interview), 'La Cour de cassation escamote le problème', *Semaine sociale Lamy* (2009), 1403; Contra A. Fossaert, 'Télé-réalité et contrat de travail', *Semaine sociale Lamy* (2009), 1403; Ch. Radé, 'La possibilité d'une île', *Droit social* (2009), 930; Opinion given by Advocate General D. Allix, 'Un nouveau passeport pour les loisirs, le vraifaux contrat de travail ?', *Droit social* Avis,

provision of work, generally accepted to be applicable to occasional, manual, intellectual, artistic or even sporting activities. It agreed that even inactivity could be work, when a person is required to remain on call, for example, monitoring an oil depot from home, while carrying out personal occupations and without being obliged to carry out any specific tasks.[58]

In recent years, the court refused to consider activities without any economic purpose as work, which was not the case in respect of the TV reality show. The court followed this approach in the case of work by prisoners,[59] Emmaüs companies,[60] people working in sheltered workplaces,[61] and ministers working in their churches,[62] contrary to lay people 'employed' by religious charities.[63]

The courts consider that legal subordination is an essential criterion that actually determines the existence of an employment relationship. Previously it was only a distinctive criterion, but the ruling of 3 June 2009 made it the 'decisive' factor for accepting an employment contract. As it argued:

> Provided it is carried out, not for private purposes but in a subordinate relationship, on behalf and in the interests of a third party, with a view to producing goods with an economic value, an activity, irrespective of its nature, even if it is recreational or requires no effort, is a provision of work subject to labour law.

Thus, according to this formula, quoted by the Court of Cassation in many rulings, the existence of an employment relationship depends neither on the will expressed by the parties, nor on the title they give to the contract, but on the actual conditions under which the workers carry out their tasks.

A. Jeammaud very rightly remarked that, in this ruling, the Court of Cassation continued a trend that started with the *Leblanne* ruling on 19 December 2000, which analysed the issue from the angle of the employment relationship rather than the employment contract.

The question arises whether this should be interpreted as a change in legal theory, bringing it in line with ILO Recommendation 198 and the related guidelines. Its key terms were quoted in the report by Counsellor Fossaert, but neither of the parties had raised that issue. This may have to do with the fact that the international text is a mere recommendation.[64]

(2009), 780; For a different view J.J. Dupeyroux, 'Observations', *Droit social* (2009), 791; in contradiction, but concerning another television production, D. Cohen & L. Gamet, 'Loft story: le jeu travail', *Droit social* (2001), 791.

58. Soc. 18 Jul. 2000, *Bull. Civ*, V, n° 289.
59. Soc. 17 Dec. 1996, *Droit social* (1997), 544, note by G. Giudicelli-Delage and M. Massé.
60. Soc. 9 May 2001, *Droit social* (2001), 801, note by J. Savatier.
61. Soc. 18 Mar. 1997, *Droit social* (1997), 525; note by P.Y. Verkindt; Soc. 24 Jun. 1998, *RJS* (1998), 1021.
62. Soc. 12 Jul. 2005, *Droit social* (2005), 1035, note by J. Savatier.
63. Soc.. 8 Jan. 1993, *Bull. Civ*, n° 2; Soc. 12 Jul. 2005, *Bull. Civ*, V, n° 243; Soc. 29 Oct. 2008, *Bull. Civ*, V, n° 206.
64. A. Fossaert, 'Télé-réalité et contrat de travail', *Semaine sociale Lamy* 1403 (2009), 3–4.

Counsellor Fossaert drove the point home by quoting a principle stating that 'the employment contract is mainly defined by the conditions under which the obligations are carried out and the type of relationship between the two parties'.[65]

On the contrary, the legislature acted to impose classification as an employment relationship on working situations where subordination was not a characteristic.

2.3. LEGISLATION CLASSIFYING EMPLOYMENT RELATIONSHIPS

In France, the legislature has used a set of presumptions of law to move the boundaries of salaried work. Until recently, the prevailing legal presumption was that of an employment contract or salaried work (Section 2.3.1). The legal presumption that a person is not an employed person has only very recently been included in the Labour Code (Section 2.3.2).

2.3.1. The Legal Presumption of a Contract of Employment

Part 7 of the new Labour Code is a veritable patchwork of provisions specific to certain professions and businesses. It constitutes the highly visible side of legislative action to expand the scope of application of the Labour Code. This part of the Labour Code demonstrates the prevalence of the employed persons' model and its tentacular expansion, sometimes at the expense of forcibly integrating professional situations that are actually much closer to self-employment. These provisions concern professional journalists, show business, fashion, and advertising professions; caretakers and employees in blocks of flats, domestic employees and services; travelling sales representatives, branch managers and home workers. These professions were integrated by the legislature in Article L 311-2 of the Social Security Code and affiliated to the general social security system.

The legislation uses two methods. Either it establishes a simple legal presumption of an employment contract for the professions concerned, for example, journalists, show business artists and models or it imposes a conclusive legal presumption that an employment contract exists, as is the case with travelling sales representatives. Persons in these professions are thus legally fully assimilated to employed persons and benefit from all the provisions in the Labour Code. This simple legal presumption is very favourable to workers, as it places the burden of proof that no employment contract exists on the other party to the relationship (i.e., the employer or client). Some provisions mention reasons which cannot be used, which makes it is almost impossible to refute the presumption, for instance for professional journalists, models and show business artists.[66] In the latter case, the legislation specifies that 'the presumption of an employment contract is maintained irrespective of the method and amount of payment, or the title given to the contract

65. F. Gaudu & R. Vatinet, *Le contrat de travail* (Paris: LGDJ, 2001), n° 31.
66. I. Daugareilh and Ph. Martin, 'Les intermittents du spectacle: une figure du salariat entre droit commun et droit spécial', *Revue française des affaires sociales* 3–4 (2000), 77–92.

by the parties. This presumption is upheld, even if it is proved that the artist is free to express his/her art, owns all or part of the equipment used or employs one or more people to assist him/her, provided he is personally involved in the performance'.[67] In case of conclusive presumption, it is simply impossible to modify the provisions imposed by law.

The legislation also uses another technique, in which certain provisions of the Labour Code are applied to professions which are not entitled to an employment contract, but whose business activity is subject to legal conditions. The professions concerned are self-employed managers, distributors, and service providers, as specified in Article L 7321-1 and following of the Labour Code. These professions are partly covered by labour law and partly by civil or commercial law.[68] This legal provision is sufficiently broad to be applicable to a wide range of self-employed workers, shopkeepers and tradespeople. Thus independent managers of service stations, other exclusive distributors and franchisees may benefit from this law, as they depend exclusively on a single principal who has an indirect, but strong influence on their working conditions and controls the prices of the goods or services they supply to their customers.[69]

There were indications that the employed person's model was losing ground and that the empire of labour law no longer continued to extend its scope via legal presumptions. However, the legislation recently included a profession in the Labour Code by partial legal assimilation to salaried employment.

Umbrella Companies

In this respect the so-called umbrella companies are an interesting phenomenon. Umbrella companies first appeared in France about twenty years ago.[70] Umbrella companies set up a three-way contractual relationship with a worker who finds assignments for one or more corporate clients. The portage firm signs a membership agreement and an employment contract with the worker and a business or service contract with the client firm. As the situation is very comparable to that of temporary work, the legislation included this contract in the legal provisions on temporary work. For people involved in this type of business, the objective was

---

67. Article L 7121-4 of the Labour Code concerning the possible reversal of the presumption on classification; Soc. 1 Feb. 1995, *Bull. Civ.*, V, n° 47; Soc. 8 Mar. 1995, *RJS*, n° 4, 1995, n° 452 (journalist); Soc. 12 Jan. 1995, *RJS*, N° 2/1995, n° 162 (show business artists); Soc. 16 Jan. 1996, *RJS*, n° 3, 1997, n° 326 (models).
68. S. Brissy, 'L'application du droit du travail aux travailleurs indépendants, un régime juridique cohérent ?', *JCP Social* 5 (2006), 1093; A. Jeammaud, 'L'assimilation de franchisés aux salariés', *Droit social* (2002), 158.
69. Soc. 23 Oct. 1968, *Bull. Civ.*, V, n° 455; Soc. 13 Jan. 1972, *Dalloz*, 425, note E. Schaeffer; Soc. 18 Dec. 1975, *Dalloz*, 1976, 399, note A. Jeammaud; Soc. 18 Nov. 1981, *Dalloz*, 1983, 242, note Y. Saint-Jours; Soc. 7 Jul. 1977, *Bull. Civ.*, V., n° 482; Soc. 3 May 1995, *Dalloz*, 1997, 10, note L. Amiel-Cosme; Soc. 25 Feb. 1998, *JCP* 1998, ed. E, 536, note P. Morvan; Soc. 4 Dec. 2001, *Droit social* (2002), 158, note A. Jeammaud.
70. P.M. Menger et al., 'Travailler par mission: qui et comment? Le cas du portage', *Droit social* (2007), 46–57.

mainly to protect people from unemployment, as this type of work is characterised by discontinuity and, as a result, considerable fluctuations in income.[71] Umbrella companies pushed for the legalisation of this form of employment by means of three main arguments. The umbrella company provides assistance to a working person (employee, self-employed, or a starting new enterprise) during a change in status. It facilitates the reintegration of unemployed people into the job market, allows for new forms of independent work and provides support for seniors.[72]

But what are the reality and content of the subordinate relationship? Are workers registered with umbrella companies really employees? The legislation seems to have adopted this formula in the absence of any other legal alternative to being employed or self-employed in France today, considering that the latter status does not offer workers the same protection.

Umbrella companies were legalised by the Act of 23 June 2008, which was intended to modernise the labour market.[73] The contract with the umbrella company is defined by the following terms:

> It covers a set of contractual relations involving an umbrella company, a person providing a service, and a client enterprise, where the person is subject to the employed persons' regime and his/her services to the clients are paid by the umbrella company, in the form of salary. The contract guarantees the person's rights to his/her own clientele.[74]

The legislation also formally excluded umbrella companies, like temporary work or modelling agencies, from labour-only contracting offences.[75] It entrusted the industry considered to be the closest with organising this sector, following consultation with organisations representing umbrella companies, via an extended industry-wide agreement.

2.3.2. The Legal Presumption of Self-Employment

The Act of 11 February 1994 on initiative and sole proprietorships introduced a new provision in the Labour Code, Article L 120-3, which stipulates:

> Individuals registered in the corporate and commercial register, the trade register, the sales agents register or at the URSSAF for the payment of family

71. It is estimated that, in 2005, 15,000 workers worked with an umbrella company for a few hours, weeks or months. Earnings varied considerably and the average income of women working in this way was over one-third lower than that of men. *Ibid.*, 56.
72. Umbrella companies were developed by executives and professional persons of over 50 years of age, who were made redundant and started working as consultants on short-term advisory, audit, engineering or training assignments as a transitional solution prior to finding another job, or registering as self-employed or starting their own firm. However, umbrella companies have also started working with young workers early in their careers, who are generally less qualified and work in sectors other than consulting. *Ibid.*, 57.
73. On the 2008 Act, see J.Y. Kerbourch, 'Le portage salarial: prestation de services ou prêt de main-d'œuvre illicite?', *Droit social* (2007), 72–80.
74. Article L 1251-64 of the Labour Code.
75. Article L 8241-1 of the Labour Code.

> social contributions are presumed not to be parties to an employment contract for the business activity for which they are so registered.

This legal presumption,[76] revoked at one time, was reintroduced in the same terms by the Act on economic initiative of 1 August 2003.[77] The new provision caused some surprise. There were fears that it would lead to an increase in fake self-employment or outsourcing.

However, this did not actually happen, since the legal provision was accompanied by two safety nets. First, the 1994 Act made it possible for a person unsure of his precise legal situation to ask the social security organisation for clarification, according to Article L 311 of the Social Security code. Second, the Act of 11 March 1997 on concealed work applied retroactive social security contributions for the period covered by the contract to clients who worked with a self-employed person 'under conditions that made it possible to establish the existence of an employment contract'.

Today, all French legal provisions on self-employment are included in Chapter II on concealed work, in Book II on combating illegal labour and Book VIII on controlling the application of labour legislation.

The Code initially instituted the presumption that there was no employment contract. Thus, according to Article L 8221-6-I of the Labour Code, the following:

> are presumed not to be bound to the client by an employment contract for the business activity covered by the registration:
>
> 1. Individuals registered in the corporate and commercial register, the trade register (etc.);
> 2. Individuals registered in the transport company registry for good haulage, passenger transport, or operating school buses (etc.);
> 3. Managers of corporations registered in the corporate and commercial register and their employees.

Contrarily, Article L 8221-6-II stipulates that 'the existence of an employment contract may, however, be established when the persons specified provide services to a client, directly or via an intermediary, under conditions that put them in a situation of constant legal subordination. In this case, the employment contract is considered to have been concealed if the client is proved to have intentionally avoided carrying out one of the formalities stipulated in Article L 1221-10 on the New Employee Statement and L 3243-2 on issuing pay slips.'

The existence of a subordinate relationship is established when the clientele, invoicing and pay are provided for self-employed people who work in the same way as company employees, including receiving orders and having their work controlled.[78] There are grounds for reclassifying a contract and convicting an employer for concealed work by concealing employees, if it can be demonstrated

76. By the Act of 19 Jan. 2000.
77. See M. Véricel, 'Le rétablissement de la présomption de non salariat', *Droit social* (2004), 297.
78. Soc. 17 Oct. 1996, n° 3953.

that a subcontractor only provided work under constant legal subordination where he is economically dependent on the client.[79]

To conclude, the law on modernising the labour market of 4 August 2008[80] gives a definition of self-employed workers, inserting the following text in Article L 8221-6-1 of the French Labour Code: 'a person is self-employed if his/her working conditions are defined exclusively by him/herself or by the contract between him/herself and the client company.'

The main purpose of reclassification of contracts into employment contracts in the case law to date has been to provide decent coverage under the general social security system for social and unemployment risks. Today the main issues at stake are individual and collective rights (collective bargaining,[81] strike,[82] etc.) to protect workers from risks encountered during the employment relationship itself (dismissal, pay, rest periods, etc.). This raises the possibility of new solutions besides the historical, outdated alternatives of employed work/self-employment.

3. ALTERNATIVES FOR LEGAL PROTECTION FOR THE EMPLOYMENT RELATIONSHIP

The theoretical approach to employment relationships in France changed considerably between the 1990s and early 2000s. The French legal theory was initially used to analyse the new and diverse forms of employment relationships which could exist throughout working life. The idea was to understand a person's working life as a whole, in all its diversity, while the legal basis of this relationship was relatively unimportant.

Recently, a new, more realistic or pragmatic theory has developed from research into variations in the protection of employment relationships, depending on their legal status (Section 3.1). At the same time, the authorities took up this issue by commissioning a report that came out in favour of a legal recognition of a new category of economically dependent, self-employed workers (Section 3.2).

3.1. Theoretical Analyses of Protection of Employment Relationships

In the 1990s, many reports and theoretical reflections were produced concerning new types of employment and work.[83] Two of these considered employment

79. Crim. 12 Dec. 2006, n° 05-87 125, *RJS* 4/07, n° 463.
80. 2008-776 of 4 Aug. 2008 (Official Journal of 5 Aug. 2008).
81. J. Barthelémy, 'Réflexions à propos des accords du 16 avril 1996 fixant le statut des agents généraux d'assurance', *Droit social* (1997).
82. A. Supiot, 'Revisiter les droits d'action collective', *Droit social* (2001).
83. R. Castel, *Métamorphose de la question sociale*, 2nd edn (Paris: Fayard, 1995); G. Schmidt, 'Le plein emploi est-il encore possible? Les marchés du travail "transitoire" en tant que nouvelle stratégie des politiques d'emploi', *Travail et Emploi* 65 (1995), 5–17; B. Gazier, 'Transitional Labour Markets: From Positive Analysis to Policy Proposals', in G. Schmid and B. Gazier (eds),

relationships as described in ILO Recommendation 198 and proposed quite similar solutions, featuring a 'working individual' status and rights associated with a professional status (Section 3.1.1). Over the past decade, French legal theory has reviewed the Italian concept of para-subordination, making proposals that were less ambitious, but perhaps more practicable, than the previous ones (Section 3.1.2).

3.1.1. Proposals for Legal Recognition of Common Workers' Rights

The project of a 'working individual' status was developed on the basis of research directed by Jean Boissonnat.[84] The idea is to build a career path that takes the non-linear, diverse professional situations of the working population into account, covering alternating periods of training, work in a corporate context, self-employment, or work in associations, leave from jobs working for a series of employers, and intermediate situations between unemployment and employment contracts. While, according to the authors of the report, standard employment contracts are likely to disappear, they may facilitate the emergence and development of a 'working individual' status and constitute a focal point for building careers made up of various types of professional activities. The aim of these contracts would be to 'broaden the objectives of traditional employment contract'. This type of employment relationship would combine the legal characteristics of employed work and self-employment.[85] These 'working individual' contracts would facilitate the social management of 'diversity, hazards, and movement or instability'.[86] In particular, this type of contract would 're-establish a minimum of public social order for the benefit of self-employed people and their employees'.[87]

Alain Supiot[88] considered that the aim was to recognise the 'professional status' of employees accompanied by social rights (time-off rights, training leave, time-savings accounts, etc.), that is, rights transferable from one company to another, usable within or outside employment contracts and jointly funded by the State, social security, enterprises, and the joint social institutions. Supiot felt that:

> labour law is certainly likely to become the general law governing all work relationships, both employment and others', due to changes in substantive law,

The Dynamics of Full Employment. Social Integration through Transitional Labour Markets (Cheltenham and Brookfield: E. Elgar, 2002); B. Gazier, 'Flexisécurité et marchés transitionnels du travail: esquisse d'une réflexion normative', *Travail et emploi* 113 (2008), 117.

84. J. Boissonnat, 'Le travail dans vingt ans', in O. Jacob (ed.), *Rapport pour le Commissariat général du Plan* (Paris: La Documentation française, 1995); F Gaudu, 'Du statut de l'emploi au statut de l'actif', *Droit social* (1995), 535; Th. Priestley, 'A propos du "contrat d'activité" proposé par le rapport Boissonnat', *Droit social* (1995), 955.
85. J. Boissonnat, *ibid.*, 286.
86. J. Boissonnat, *ibid.*, 960.
87. J. Boissonnat, *ibid.*, 299.
88. A.Supiot, *Au-delà de l'emploi, Transformations et devenir du droit du travail en Europe, Rapport pour la Commission européenne* (Paris: Flammarion, 1999); A. Supiot, 'Les nouveaux visages de la subordination', *Droit social* 131, in particular 133.

which have extended the right to social security, professional training, and collective bargaining to certain categories of self-employed workers. This general law will consist of a set of fundamental rights and principles, combined with some specific rights.

In contrast to Jean Boissonnat, Supiot defended the idea that these fundamental rights should not be dependent on a contract (making them subject to the risk of termination, juxtaposition, gaps or imbalances, depending on the person's status – employed or self-employed – or the type of work) but should take the form of a personal right. Thus, these rights and principles 'must target the individual and ensure the continuity of a real professional status, irrespective of the diversity of a person's situation in the work market'.[89]

3.1.2. Para-subordination in French Legal Theory

The concept of para-subordination presupposes a third category of work, called para-subordination, which may take several forms. According to E. Peskine, the term 'describes all the cases in which non-salaried workers may benefit from certain protective provisions, based on or even taken from labour law, due to the dependent status resulting from their work situation'.[90]

This author bases his theory on legislative practice, which stipulates that workers must legally be treated like employees, without reclassifying the work relationship as an employment contract, and disconnecting the work relationship from any legal subordination. This is the case for branch managers[91] and self-employed managers of retail food outlets.[92]

A. Jeammaud noted very clearly that: 'while the four conditions stipulated in the 1941 Act constitute both factors and indicators of great dependence, that does not mean that the people to whom they apply have employee status'.[93] Some labour law provisions (working hours, rest periods, holidays, minimum wage, and dismissal) are applicable to these professions.[94] Industrial tribunals have jurisdiction over disputes on aspects concerning labour law, while all other matters are referred to commercial courts. We are 'dealing with mixed situations, calling for the distribution or cumulative application of the key points of general labour law, as well

89. A. Supiot, *ibid.*, in particular 144 and report, in particular 83–85.
90. E. Peskine, 'Entre subordination et indépendance: en quête d'une troisième voie', *Revue de Droit du Travail* (2008), 371–377.
91. Article L 7321-2 of the Labour Code. This text was originally designed for managers of station kiosks supplied by newspaper distributors and lottery ticket sellers. Today it is also applicable to self-employed managers of service stations who have management lease contracts with oil companies, owners of business premises, exclusive agents or distributors, and certain franchisees.
92. Article L 7322-1 of the French Labour Code.
93. A. Jeammaud, note in Soc. 14 Oct. 1976, *Dalloz*, 1977, J. 356.
94. Real and serious grounds must be given for terminating a contract, leading to the payment of severance pay and requiring compliance with a specific procedure. Including self-employed managers, Soc. 15 May 2007, *Bull.*

as aspects of civil and commercial law governing management leases, common interest mandates, or franchise contracts'.[95] They are not employees, but they benefit from some aspects of labour law via their integration in the Labour Code.

While case law and legislation do not recognise the application of workers' rights to self-employed workers, they apply the principles. One of these principles is the requirement to give grounds for termination of the contract. The Court of Cassation did not hesitate to insist that grounds, and even legitimate reasons, must be given.[96] Furthermore, via the Act of 2 August 2005, the French Commercial Code set up a legal regime for managing agents. This was done in order to put an end to reclassifications as employment contracts. The new provision did not import dismissal law into the French Commercial Code; instead, Article L 146-4 stipulates that the contract 'may be terminated at any time under the conditions determined by the parties'. However, in case of termination by the principal, the managing agent must be paid compensation, except in cases of serious misconduct.

According to Elsa Peskine, a law on dependence, applicable to contracts with the same name, is thus being developed. The way is being prepared for a new law on dependence, based on civil law mechanisms, but frequently reflecting labour law provisions, either by means of legislation or case law. This necessary adaptation is leading to labour law being taken more widely into account, contributing its specific features to the mechanisms of civil law. Altogether, the combined application of commercial and labour law provisions, or even the transposition of certain labour law mechanisms, is starting to outline the status of parasubordinate workers.[97]

How can these workers be identified? Economic dependence is only one indicator among others in this new theory. Indeed, the particular feature of para-subordination is the link between the exercise of power and the distribution of business risks. In contrast to salaried status, sharing in corporate and employment risks appear to be evidence that the contract in question should be reclassified.[98] 'This specific combination of subordination to authority and non-liability for risks is reviewed in parasubordinate work situations. (...) The key feature of dependent, self-employed workers lies in the separation of risk and power. (...) Like in the case of employees, someone has power over them but, as self-employed workers, they are liable for their own business risks.'[99] This power is less visible and tangible in their case than that of even highly autonomous employees.

95. A. Jeammaud, 'L'assimilation de franchisés aux salariés', *Droit social* (2002), 158.
96. Com. 20 Jan. 1998, *Bull. Civ.* IV, N° 40, *Dalloz*, 1988, J., 413, note by C. Jamin; see also M. Fabre-Magnan, 'Pour une obligation de motiver la rupture des contrats de dépendance économique', *Revue Droit commercial* 2 (2004), 573.
97. E. Peskine, 'Entre subordination et indépendance: en quête d'une troisième voie', *Revue de Droit du Travail* (2008), 374.
98. M.L. Morin, 'Partage des risques et responsabilité de l'emploi. Contribution au débat sur la réforme du droit du travail', *Droit social* (2000), 733.
99. M.L. Morin, 'Partage des risques et responsabilité de l'emploi. Contribution au débat sur la réforme du droit du travail', *Droit social* (2000), 736.

Beyond the criterion of power, which may be common to all para-subordinate workers, the evidence quickly becomes heterogeneous. This power could be considered protean, depending on the sector and its structure, the product concerned, and the position of the self-employed worker in the chain of subcontractors. However, in general, this power concerns the freedom to establish contracts with other enterprises or not, set the price of goods, organise production, specify the conditions for doing the work or providing the service, etc.

The French legislature had never previously shown any real interest in these theoretical proposals. However, they may at present be ready to adopt a third way, as outlined by the experts who wrote a recent report on self-employed but economically dependent workers, based on the most recent theoretical research (see below).

3.2. A New Category: Self-employed but Economically Dependent Workers

A report commissioned by the Ministry of Labour recently proposed a third solution, which may receive legislative support.[100] On the one hand, it does not overturn existing provisions and, on the other hand, it avoids a multiplicity of scattered legislative measures to meet the needs of specific professional situations. The authors recommend a global legal solution for economically dependent work, not by recognising a general law, but by setting up an intermediate category between employed workers and self-employment, economically dependent workers. They also propose criteria for (1) identifying and (2) protecting these people.

3.2.1. Criteria for Self-employed but Economically Dependent Workers

Self-employed economically dependent workers are self-employed workers, and not concealed employees. The authors propose that self-employed workers could be identified by taking the elements of the legal presumption of self-employment cited above. They state that self-employed workers are persons who have personally defined their own working conditions or established them in a contract with their clients. In addition to this criterion taken from the law, the authors propose another criterion, derived from case law, namely that the person is carrying out work on his/her personal behalf.[101] However, is it necessary for self-employed workers to provide the service or do the work themselves, which would prohibit or exclude those who use labour? Excluding all forms of company would create the risk that they hide behind company law to escape the protection of social law.

100. P.H. Antonmattei & J.C. Sciberras, *Le travailleur économiquement dépendant: quelle protection?* (Paris: La Documentation française, 2008); *Droit social* (2009), 221–233.
101. Com. 11 Mar. 2008, n° 06-20089, *JCP, E*, 2008, 2050, note Ch. Lebel.

Should this system simply be restricted to forms of sole proprietorship, preventing the use of labour?

This was the argument retained by the Court of Cassation in a dispute concerning the classification of a tradesperson,[102] whereas the legislation envisaged this possibility. Thus, Article L 7322-2 of the Labour Code considers that freedom to hire labour is part of the legal definition of self-employed managers of retail food outlets, who benefit from the protection on the basis of economic dependence. Similarly, show business artists benefit from the legal presumption of an employment contract, even if it can be proved 'that they employ one or more persons to support them, provided they are personally involved in the show'.[103] The authors prefer, therefore, to include micro-enterprises in which the self-employed work themselves, although the threshold headcount remains to be defined, with all the perverse effects that can be imagined.

Self-employed workers are economically dependent. How can economic dependence be determined? The criterion of power used to define legal subordination does not seem operational. Economic dependence may exist when a single client accounts for most of a self-employed worker's turnover. The authors clearly decide in this case in favour of 'calculating the business ratio' at 50% of the total income. They also consider the length of the working relationship and make a real distinction in this case between economic dependence and legal subordination. Indeed, legal subordination bears no relation to the length of the working relationship: it is applicable from the outset. In contrast, economic dependence develops completely and absolutely over time: the longer the working relationship, the greater the economic dependence. Italian law applies this principle. The authors of the report recommended a minimum period of two months. Another criterion is the specialisation of the production tools used by self-employed workers to meet the client's expectations, as demonstrated by examples of industrial outsourcing.

3.2.2. Factors in Legal Protection of the New Category

What protection is not available to economically dependent workers? Until the 1990s, the key attraction of employed workers was the resulting social protection. Article L 311-3 of the Social Security code was the vector for continuous extension of the scope of application of the general social security system.[104] Today, two risks are not yet covered when a worker is considered to be self-employed: loss of income and work-related accidents or diseases.[105] The authors recommend leaving self-employed workers in their existing social security system, adding specific

102. Com. 11 Mar. 2008, n° 06-20089, JCP, E, 2008, 2050, note Ch. Lebel.
103. Article L 7121-4 al.1 of the Labour Code.
104. See J.J.H. Dupeyroux, M. Borgetto & R. Lafore, *Droit de la sécurité sociale*, 16th edn (Paris: Dalloz, 2008), n° 568 et seq.
105. The exception is when a business project support contract (CAPE) is signed by an enterprise or association and a project initiator intending to set up or take over a company, under the law dated 1 Aug. 2003 on economic initiatives.

coverage for loss of income and work-related accidents, for which the social contribution charges will 'naturally' be paid by the client.

The authors also consider whether the protection of the business relationship should be based on the Labour Code, although it is probably not the ideal system. They agree that some rights may be common to all workers, irrespective of their status, for example, fundamental workers' rights. The authors also note that '(. . .) the practice of strike has become common among self-employed workers'[106] and propose that these workers should have a recognised right to collective action, which would, in particular, make it possible to maintain the contract in case of a strike and prevent the client from replacing a self-employed worker who was on strike. Similarly, the right to collective bargaining is not reserved for employed persons and has already been used to negotiate the status of general insurance agents.[107] Indeed, industry-wide collective bargaining is the way in which they envisaged that rights common to all self-employed workers could be adopted and legalised. In the same way, the right to professional training is not linked to employed persons.[108]

While pay is a key element in economic dependence, the demand for a common minimum pay for all self-employed workers may be highly desirable, but is extremely difficult to implement in practice. Therefore the authors recommend collective bargaining on company level.

The authors propose several measures concerning contracts, including the right to information on the client, a reconsideration period, and a contract in writing, specifying the key elements of the working relationship. The authors envisage applying the legal provisions already adopted for sales agents[109] and agency managers[110] concerning notice for termination and severance pay, possibly calculated as a percentage of the order of 10% of the turnover achieved during the contract. There was even some question about whether grounds should be required for unilateral termination by the parent company, which would make the system similar to the law on dismissal. They very clearly rejected this approach to avoid a too close similarity to the situation of salaried workers. They suggested it would be preferable to adopt the standard solution of penalties for wrongful breach of contract.

On the issue of working conditions, especially those concerning health and safety at work, there is no indication that these are reserved solely for employed persons. Furthermore, when self-employed workers work on company premises, they are subject to the provisions of the Labour Code. However, if this is not the case, there is no reason for the client enterprise to accept any obligations in this area. This also marks the difference between the two types of work relationships.

106. A. Supiot, 'Revisiter les droits d'action collective', *Droit social* (2001), 687, in particular 696.
107. J. Barthélémy, 'Une convention collective de travailleurs indépendants? Réflexions à propos des accords du 16 avril 1996 fixant le statut des agents généraux d'assurance', *Droit social* (1997), 40.
108. Article L 6312-2 of the Labour Code.
109. Article L 134-12 of the Commercial Code.
110. Article L 146-4 of the Commercial Code.

However, on the basis of European law,[111] the authors consider that the only applicable provisions on working hours were those concerning minimum rest periods, which could be imposed on the grounds of health and safety. Finally, they recommend that industrial tribunals should not have jurisdiction in this area.

All these recommendations may be included in an inter-industry collective bargaining agreement, followed by the adoption of new legislation. These proposals are quite similar to a new theoretical concept, which is becoming influential in France: para-subordination.

The report was strongly influenced by examples from Italy and Spain. It has the advantage of being relatively pragmatic and practical, proposing a reform that does not cause a major upheaval in the framework of French labour law. This is likely to ensure its acceptance by French legislators and the social partners.

111. Directive (EC) 2003/88 of the European Parliament and of the Council of 4 Nov. 2003 concerning certain aspects of the organisation of working time (*OJ* 2002, *L* 299/9).

Chapter 7

The Protection of Working Relationships in the Netherlands

Frans Pennings

1. INTRODUCTION

In Dutch law, there are three types of contract under which a person can perform work. The first to be mentioned, the most important one, is the contract of employment. Only persons working under this type of contract are employees and receive labour law protection under, *inter alia*, the *Burgerlijk Wetboek* (BW – Civil Code). The protection by the Dutch Civil Code and other labour Acts and regulations includes provisions regulating dismissals, a restriction of successive fixed term contracts, health and safety and codetermination, and minimum wage protection.[1] Social security protection is also to a large extent linked to the status of employee.[2]

A contract of employment requires, in particular, that a person works in a subordinated position for another person and has the obligation to do the work personally, that is, he cannot ask somebody else to do the work instead.

The other types of contract under which work can be done are the contract for services and the contract to realise a certain work (e.g., a house); under these types

1. See, for an English language overview of Dutch labour law, A. Jacobs, *Labour Law in the Netherlands* (The Hague: Kluwer Law International, 2004).
2. See, on the Dutch law, also Robert Knegt (ed.), *The Employment Contract as an Exclusionary Device* (Antwerp: Intersentia, 2008).

Frans Pennings & Claire Bosse, *The Protection of Working Relationships*, pp. 83–107.
© 2011 Kluwer Law International BV, The Netherlands.

of contract the work is not done in subordination to another person and the work does not have to be done personally. Work that is done by self-employed persons for a principal is done under one of these two types of contract.

If for a working relationship a contract of services or assignment is made, but the actual circumstances in which the work is done has all characteristics of a contract of employment, such as that work is done in subordination, the contract concerned is considered a contract of employment. Sometimes this is called: 'lifting the veil'; the veil (the name of the contract) is lifted and on the basis of the facts of the case it is concluded that there is an employee relationship.[3]

Through time (the effects of) some escape routes have been closed, limited or mitigated by statutory instruments and/or court decisions. However, this does not mean that now all dependent work is always done under a contract of employment and that the protection is always satisfactory.

In particular in case of flexible workers, it can be uncertain whether they have a contract of employment or not. Examples of flexible contracts under which these workers are engaged are on-call contracts, freelance contracts and homeworker contracts. These contracts may be contracts of employment, but this is not necessarily the case, depending on whether the worker works in subordination to another person or not and whether he is obliged to do the work personally.

A special category of flexible worker is the worker engaged by an agency for temporary work (henceforth: agency worker). Until 1998 it was regularly disputed in Dutch law whether the agency worker was an employee or not; the Flexibility and Security Act (to be discussed in Section 3 *infra*) introduced provisions to regulate his legal status. Agency workers will be discussed in Section 6 *infra.*

Some workers prefer not to work under a contract of employment, as it may give them more freedom and a higher net income to work as 'self-employed'. However, when a particular risk materialises (invalidity, unemployment), or the contract with the principal ends, the person is confronted with the fact that he does not have social security or labour law protection. If this happens, some of these quasi self-employed persons try to be recognised as employee.

A special category consists of self-employed people without staff. A self-employed person without staff is often dependent on his/her principal in a way that to a very large extent resembles the position of employees, since he may be very dependent for his/her income on the work given by this principal. It may also happen that he/she does the same work for this principal as his/her employees.

In view of these different types of legal relationships in which work can be done and given the limitation of labour law in the protection of employees, the research question of this contribution is: how is the labour law protection of dependent work organised and are there gaps in this protection? How is this situation to be assessed vis-à-vis Recommendation 198?

---

3. An example from the case law is a judgment of the *Hoge Raad* (Supreme Court) of 17 Nov. 1978, *NJ* 1979/140 (*IVA-ponstypiste*), concerning a homeworker working for a particular enterprise. On the basis of the circumstances the court decided that the worker was to be considered an employee.

In order to be able to answer these questions I will first discuss the criteria which are applied in order to determine that there is a contract of employment or not (Section 2). Then I will discuss the measures in favour of the flexible workers (Section 3), including the introduction of legal presumptions that there is a contract of employment (Section 4). Subsequently, I will discuss the position of persons who are designated as employees on the basis of an Act, that is, the postmen (Section 5) and temporary agency workers (Section 6). In Section 7, I will analyse the position of the self-employed, with special attention to how the protection of workers is or can be extended to them and which are the pros and cons of such protection. Finally, I will analyse the position of the dependent workers in view of the ILO Recommendation.

First I will give some figures on the flexible workers and the self-employed without staff.

1.1. Figures

Since the 1960s there has been an important change from permanent and full-time jobs to more flexible jobs. In 1969, 82% of the jobs were permanent; 14% was part-time and 5% was flexible. The absolute number of permanent and full-time jobs has not changed since 1969, but its share in the total number was reduced to 47% in 2005; in this year the share of flexible work was around 9%.[4] For this purpose, flexible workers are agency workers, on call workers and workers with a fixed-term contract. On call workers predominantly work in middle-sized firms (ten – ninety-nine employees), such as restaurants and cafes.

Flexible workers often work in the health and welfare sector (23%) and commercial services (14%). Relatively few flex workers work in the industrial sector (15%).

Most on call workers work for a relatively long period on basis of the contract (on average 938 days), although often the number of weekly working hours is low (eleven on average).

There are between 250,000[5] and 330,000 self-employed persons without staff in the Netherlands;[6] some assessments give higher figures. For instance, the Central Statistics Office counted in the third quarter of 2009 almost 630,000 self-employed without staff. From research it appears that the large majority (95%) of the self-employed voluntarily chose this status;[7] only 1.2% appeared to be forced by their employer to become self-employed. However, it may also

4. R. Knegt et al., *Tweede evaluatie Wet flexibiliteit en zekerheid* (Amsterdam: HIS and TNO, 2007), 13.
5. See P. Vroonhof et al., *Zelfstandigen zonder personeel* (Zoetermeer: EIM and Bureau Bartels, 2008).
6. Frans Pleijster and Pim van der Valk, *Van onbemind tot onmisbaar. De economische betekenis van ZZP'ers nu en in de toekomst* (Zoetermeer: EIM, 2007).
7. See P. Vroonhof et al., *Zelfstandigen zonder personeel* (Zoetermeer: EIM and Bureau Bartels, 2008).

happen that employers appear to *encourage* their employees to become self-employed. About 3.6% chose this status as they saw no other way to earn an income; these were often persons in receipt of benefits.

2. CRITERIA FOR ADOPTING A CONTRACT OF EMPLOYMENT

Having a contract of employment is essential for an employee; it is not only itself a source of rights and duties, but it gives access to various other rights and duties in the area of individual and collective labour law and social security law. In other words, the contract of employment is the key to labour law.[8] In order to be a contract of employment, the contract must require the worker to perform work, in exchange for wages, during a certain time, in subordination of an employer, and to be done personally (i.e., he cannot have himself replaced without permission of the employer).

The subordination element is the most difficult to assess. Still, it is a very important criterion. Subordination entails that the employee has to obey instructions given by the employer, irrelevant of whether the employer actually makes use of the power to give instructions. It is often difficult to check whether the subordination criterion is satisfied, since many workers have considerable, if not a large, freedom to do their work, on which the employer has little influence. It is therefore hard to prove that there is a subordination relationship (or hard to prove that there is no such relationship).

The two other types of contracts under which work is done – the contract for services and the contract to realise a certain work – are contracts to to perform a certain task respectively and to realise a certain work respectively. Also under these contracts the principal can give instructions on how the job is done; these instructions, however, do not concern the way the person who accepted the mission runs his enterprise, but they concern the actual task to be done. It is obvious that the borderline between areas where instructions can be given can be very narrow.

An important judgment in which the *Hoge Raad* (Supreme Court) gave a set of criteria in order to determine when there is a contract of employment is the *Groen/Schoevers* judgment.[9] The case concerned a Mr Groen, who had his own company (Groen Tax Advisors) and this company made an oral agreement with a private training institute for secretaries (Schoevers Institute) by which it agreed that Mr Groen teaches at the institute. Groen Tax Advisors required payment for the working hours of Mr Groen, on a gross basis plus VAT. The institute did not apply its collective working conditions scheme on Mr Groen and no holiday allowance was paid to him.

---

8. C. Bosse, *Bewijslastverdeling in het Nederlandse en Belgische arbeidsrecht* (Deventer: Kluwer, 2003), 47.
9. *Hoge Raad* (Supreme Court) 14 Nov. 1997, *NJ* 1998/149; *JAR* 1997/263.

When the institute terminated the contract, however, Mr Groen claimed that he had a contract of employment with the institute. In his view the contract of service has to be reclassified as a contract of employment, since he worked under a subordination relationship for the institute, he had to teach at specific times and days and he had to take the holiday periods into account. In addition, he was obliged to be present at the times specified; he had to make use of the prescribed materials and he had to follow the teaching programme of the institute.

The *Hoge Raad*, however, decided that he did not have a contract of employment. It argued that the question which type of agreement was at stake had to be decided on the basis of the facts and circumstances of the case. For this purpose, the intention of the parties when they concluded the contract was decisive. The Court added, however, that the way in which the parties elaborated the agreement in practice is also relevant to this. In other words, a practice different from the terms of the contract is important for interpreting the intention of the parties.[10]

The second step in the analysis of the Court was that, after having determined the intention of the parties, the legal effects which the parties have connected with their relationship has to be considered. The Court of First Instance, whose task is to consider the facts of the case, found that the remuneration for the work was so different from what is common for contracts of employment, that this cannot be called 'wages'. For the *Hoge Raad* this finding was relevant to concluding which legal effects were connected with the contract. In addition it also took into account the fact that the working conditions rules were not applied to Mr Groen.

The third step in the reasoning of the judgment was to consider the question whether it could be said that there was still a subordination relationship of such a form and extent that, despite the earlier findings of the case, it had to be concluded that there was a contract of employment. For the answer to the question the *Hoge Raad* found it insufficient that Mr Groen had to be present at fixed times and that he had to follow the guidelines of the training institute. After all, in case of a contract of service the principal can also give instructions. The circumstances mentioned by Mr Groen, the Court continued, had more to do with work discipline and the rules of the organisation as a whole than with subordination of a person to a direct superior. Crucial is, it added, whether the position of the person concerned resembles so much that of the other workers, given the terms of the agreement and the way of functioning, that it has to be accepted that he is an employee.

Finally, the *Hoge Raad* decided that the social position of the worker is relevant. Important in this case was that the form of remuneration was proposed by Mr Groen himself. So in case of persons who can be assumed to be able to make an agreement in accordance with their will reclassification is less likely than in case a person who is highly dependent on the work provider.

---

10. In this respect also another famous judgment must be mentioned – i.e., the *Agfa* judgment (*Hoge Raad* 8 Apr. 1994, *NJ* 1994, 704). The worker in this case was given a contract as a temporary worker paid on an hourly basis, but was in fact continuously employed as a full-time worker. She performed the same activities as the other employees working in the enterprise. The Supreme Court considered that the initially agreed conditions are not decisive, but relevant is also how the parties elaborated the contract and thus have given it a different content.

Thus, in the *Groen/Schoevers* judgment, the Supreme Court considered the parties' intention as very important. At first sight this may seem remarkable, as this approach is contrary to the idea that the weaker party has to be protected against the stronger party. As a party may be forced to accept a particular contract because he is so dependent on work, in labour law the intention of the parties and the name of the contract has always been considered with caution. This is also the approach of the ILO Recommendation. The problem was, however, that Mr Groen presented himself as a self-employed person, had more than one principal and benefited from his position by having a higher net income (he was not subject to employee insurance contributions), and did not claim to be an employee until he needed labour law protection. The *Hoge Raad* appeared to be reluctant to accept such an opportunistic use of labour law.

Although the actual circumstances of Mr Groen were decisive for the decision, the relevance of the judgment is much wider: also in later judgments the *Hoge Raad* referred to the criteria of this judgment.[11]

In the application of the *Groen* criteria the position of the worker is relevant, as we saw, and since Mr Groen really acted as a self-employed person and was in an independent position he was not considered an employee. We might then expect that the court will come to a different conclusion in the case of workers in a weaker position having a contract stating that they are not an employee. This is indeed the case, as can be seen in the *Beurspromovendi* judgment. The case concerned persons writing a PhD thesis at a university who were given the status of student with a grant, instead of employee, which is the usual legal status of persons doing this work at a university in the Netherlands.[12] The Court did not confront these PhD writers with the fact that they signed a contract stating that they were not an employee.[13]

Thus many circumstances are important for deciding whether there is a contract of employment. In her PhD thesis, Claire Bosse included a checklist of relevant criteria made on the basis of an analysis of the case law.[14] This checklist has not acquired an official status nor are there other checklists with such status. In other words, deciding whether there is a contract of employment happens to a large extent on a case to case basis.

3. THE FLEXIBILITY AND SECURITY ACT

As we have seen, sometimes it is uncertain whether persons performing work have a contract of employment or not. In 1998 the Civil Code was amended in order to

11. Hoge Raad 10 Oct. 2003, *JAR* 2003/263 (*Van der Male/Den Hoedt*). See also Hoge Raad 10 Dec. 2004, *JAR* 2005/14, *NJ* 2005/239 (*Diosynth/Groot-Veen*); E. Verhulp, 'Een arbeidsovereenkomst? Dat maak ik zelf wel uit!', *Sociaal Recht* (2005), 87 et seq.; C.J. Loonstra, 'De gezagsverhouding ex artikel 7:610 BW', *Sociaal Recht* (2005), 96 et seq.
12. They may also be civil servant, but we will not discuss this here.
13. *Hoge Raad* 14 Apr. 2006, *JAR* 2006/119, *RVDW* 2006/387.
14. C. Bosse, *Bewijslastverdeling in het Nederlandse en Belgische arbeidsrecht* (Deventer: Kluwer, 2003).

improve the position of flexible workers. In this section I will describe the background of this amending law; in the following sections I will describe the changes in larger detail.

The discussion on the need of protection of those providing work under a contract other than a contract of employment dates from the 1970s if not before. In 1972 it was proposed to introduce a provision into the Civil Code containing a refutable legal presumption that work done under particular circumstances was done under a contract of employment.[15] However, this proposal was not accepted.

In the 1990s, politicians and authors became more and more aware that the labour market was to a large extent divided, that is, between persons having a permanent contract of employment, which involved good working conditions, and persons with a marginal legal position. The large difference between the legal position of persons with a permanent contract of employment and flexible workers was hard to justify and, moreover, affected in particular women negatively. Progress in addressing this issue was made when two separate discussions were linked.

The first discussion was the need for a more flexible labour market, as often heard from employers and some economists. The then Minister of Social Affairs, Ad Melkert, presented a Paper, the *Nota Flexibiliteit en Zekerheid* (White Paper on Flexibility and Security),[16] in which he argued that, in order to have the labour force better adjusted to economic needs, more flexibility was required.

The second discussion was on the (bad) legal position of flexible workers.

These two discussions were linked, in that it was argued that if the labour market required more room for employing flexible workers, their legal position has to be improved.[17]

The link which was made between these two discussions allowed the Minister to bring the old issues of a more flexible labour market and a better protection of flexible workers to a higher level. Whereas in previous discussions, proposals for more flexibilisation meant a unilateral reduction of employment protection, now the need to improve the position of flexible workers was also made part of the problem (and solution).

The Minister asked the national employers and employees' organisations to investigate the possibilities of introducing more flexibility for the persons with a permanent contract and improving the legal position of flexible workers. The negotiations led to a unanimous Advice.[18]

The Advice was adopted in the *Wet Flexibiliteit en zekerheid*[19] (Law on Flexibility and Security, which amended the Civil Code) and the *Wet allocatie*

15. E.M. Meijers, *Ontwerp van een Nieuw Burgerlijk Wetboek* ('s-Gravenhage, 1972), 1040. See also T. Koopmans, *De begrippen werkman, arbeider en werknemer* (Alphen aan de Rijn: Samsom, 1962), 337 et seq.
16. Parliamentary Papers of the Second Chamber of the Parliament 1995–1996, nr. 24 543.
17. The connection between introducing more flexibility and also more security is often referred to as *flexicurity*. See, for more on flexicurity, <www.tilburguniversity.nl/faculties/law/research/reflect/publications/papers>.
18. Advice of *Stichting van de Arbeid* of 3 Apr. 1996, *Flexibiliteit en Zekerheid*, Den Haag 1996.
19. Act of 14 May 1998, *Stb.* (Official Journal) 300.

van arbeidskrachten door intermediairs (Waadi – the Law on allocation of workers by intermediaries),[20] concerning temporary agency work.

The Civil Code was enriched by the legal presumption that if a person has been working for some time, as specified by the Act, he has a contract of employment, unless this presumption is refuted by the employer (this will be discussed in Section 4 *infra*). In addition the position of persons working for a temporary work agency was improved (discussed in Section 6).

In addition the Act introduced more flexibility by allowing a longer chain of fixed term contracts. Before the change the Act provided that if a fixed term contract was followed by another one within a period of thirty-one days, the second one was to be treated as a contract for an indefinite period. Article 668a of the Civil Code, introduced by the Flexibility and Security Act, provides that if fixed term contracts have succeeded each other with periods of interruption of less than three months and the total period taken together lasted more than three years including the periods of interruption, the last contract is considered a contract for an indefinite period. Alternatively, if after three fixed term contracts the next contract is *ex lege* a contract for an indefinite period, unless these contracts are interrupted by a period of more than three months. These rules also apply in the case of successive contracts between an employee and different employers if they reasonably have to be considered each other's successor in respect of the work that was performed. Only collective agreements can deviate from the rules of Article 668a, so deviation is not possible by means of an individual employment contract.[21]

4. LEGAL PRESUMPTIONS

4.1. The System of Legal Presumptions

The introduction of the legal presumption that there is a contract of employment if certain statutory conditions are satisfied was deemed necessary, given the uncertainty I have described in Section 2 on the existence of a contract of employment in particular circumstances. The new provision is a refutable legal presumption, by which is meant that the law connects the rights and duties of a particular legal status to a particular situation. If the other party disputes this, the burden of proof is reversed: the alleged employee can benefit from the presumption and the alleged employer has the burden of proof if he wishes to refute the presumption.

---

20. Act of 14 May 1998, *Stb.* (Official Journal) 306.
21. For example, if a person works three times under a contract for employment of six months, the following one is a contract for an indefinite period, even if it was given for six months only.
    If a person first works for three months for an agency for temporary work for enterprise X, and he is then engaged by X for the same work for six months, and then again by the agency for three months for the same work for X and then again by X for three months, the protection of 668a also applies. The same is true in case of three successive contracts with the agency to work for X and then the worker is employed by X itself.

The statutory presumption provides that a contract of employment is presumed if a person has worked during at least three months in any week or at least twenty hours a month for the same employer (Article 7:610a of the Civil Code).

It is to the employer to prove that the conditions for the presumption are not satisfied or that the conditions for the legal status that is presumed are not satisfied.

There were several objectives linked to the legal presumptions in the Flexibility and Security Act. The first one was to encourage employers to avoid uncertain provisions and fake constructions in the future. The second one was to contribute to solving disputes on whether there is a contract of employment and therefore avoiding court cases. These objectives meant to reduce the use of and problems with marginal contracts (prevention). The third objective was to improve the position of persons working under marginal contracts.

4.2. Presumptions of the Existence of the Contract

Since the legal presumption is refutable, the employer can provide proof that there is no contract of employment. The Act does not elaborate *how* the legal presumption can be refuted, but it is likely that the employer has to show that one or more criteria for the contract of employment are not satisfied, that is, he can try to prove that the worker does not do the work personally, for wages, for a certain period and under a relation of supervision. Since the statutory conditions for the presumption mention elements other than the conditions for a contract of employment, it is eminently possible that the employer succeeds in proving that there is no contract of employment.[22] Thus, the presumption did not extend the coverage of the contract of employment by loosening the conditions, but introduced a reversal of the burden of proof and therefore improved the legal position of the worker.[23]

In the *Beurspromovendi* judgment[24] – already mentioned in Section 3 – the *Hoge Raad* decided that courts only have to investigate whether the legal presumptions are refuted. If the court decides that this has not successfully been done, the existence of a contract of employment is to be assumed. In other words, the court does not have to investigate itself whether the conditions of the contract of employment are really satisfied. Thus, in case of weak arguments presented by the employer, the worker is assisted by the law.

A relevant argument of the employer for refuting the presumption can be that the parties did not have the intention to conclude a contract of employment. He can also prove that the parties in reality did not have a relationship which must be considered as one of subordination and in which the worker has to do the work

22. See also J.J.M. de Laat, 'De rechtsvermoedens van het bestaan en de omvang van de arbeidsovereenkomst', *Sociaal Recht* (2006), 266; G.C. Boot, 'Rechtsvermoedens', *Sociaal Recht* (1997), 198; G.C. Boot, 'Weerlegbare rechtsvermoedens', *Arbeidsrecht* (1998), 53.
23. See De Laat, *ibid.*, 266.
24. *Hoge Raad* 14 Apr. 2006, *JAR* 2006/119.

personally.[25] The employee for his part can try to refute the arguments of the employer.

The rules on the legal presumptions were made in favour of the employee. It is not clear yet whether an employer can also benefit from these rules. An employer may wish to rely on the legal presumptions, for instance, if he wants an on-call worker to answer the call by saying that he is obliged to do so on the basis of a contract of employment, whereas the worker prefers not to work.

4.3. Presumptions of the Number of Working Hours

Apart from the uncertainty of the qualification of marginal contracts, there may also be disputes on the number of working hours for which the contract was made. After all, if the worker can benefit from the presumption that there is a contract of employment, but the employer denies that there is any obligation to let the worker work during a particular number of hours and in fact no work is given, the worker is not really helped by the presumption that there is a contract of employment. For this purpose Article 7:610b of the Civil Code was introduced.

Article 7610b provides that if a contract of employment has lasted for at least three months, the contracted number of working hours is assumed to be the average monthly number of working hours of the preceding three months.

> For example, if a contract mentions a weekly number of twenty hours, and the worker works thirty hours in June, twenty-seven hours in July and thirty-three hours in August, he can invoke the presumption that he has a contact for thirty hours. The employer can refute this presumption, for instance by saying that this worker has to replace another worker during the summer holidays and that in the rest of the year his average number of working hours is twenty.

Article 7610b does not require that a person has worked for at least three months; relevant is only that the contract has lasted for three months. For instance, if the person has worked for two months and in one month he did not work, the average over these three months is taken.

In the *Tence Uitzendbureau*[26] judgment, the Court of First Instance decided that the legal assumption is not only relevant if the number of working hours is not or not clearly fixed, but also if the actual number of working hours has for a longer period been higher than the number initially agreed on.

Also the legal presumption on the number of working hours can be refuted. In order to be successful in doing so, the employer has to state and to prove that the average number of working hours in the months mentioned by the employee is not a representative sample of the number of hours normally worked.[27] For instance,

25. Examples of a successful refutation are Court of Amsterdam 16 Jun. 2000, *JAR* 2000/167 and Court of Appeal of the Hague 2 Jul. 2004, *JAR* 2005/20.
26. Ktr. (Court) Maastricht 22 Mar. 2006, *JAR* 2006/111.
27. Ktr. Gouda 19 Feb. 2004, *JAR* 2004/77.

the employer can take a longer period of time which shows a lower average number of working hours. In cases on the legal presumption of working hours the length of the period of reference is frequently disputed; the Act does not give criteria to determine the period of reference. So far in the case law the maximum period of reference has been one year.[28]

4.3.1. Minimum Remuneration per Call

Another improvement for on call workers was that Article 628a of the Civil Code was introduced, which provides that in case a number of working hours of less than fifteen per week was contracted and the working times at which the work had to be done was not defined or the extent of the work to be done was not or not clearly defined, the employee is entitled for each period of less than three hours of work to the wage corresponding to three working hours.

It is not possible to deviate from this article (by individual or collective agreement) to the detriment of the worker. Article 628a is relevant only if a number of working hours is agreed which is lower than fifteen and the working times are not laid down in the agreement.

4.4. Assessment of the Legal Presumptions

4.4.1. Assessment of the Objectives

The first objective of the Flexibility and Security Act was to encourage employers to avoid uncertain provisions and fake constructions in the future. The second objective was to contribute to solving disputes on whether there is a contract of employment and therefore avoiding court cases. From evaluations of the Flexibility and Security Act it appeared that the first two objectives were to a large extent met: as a result of the Act other and better formulated contracts came to be used.[29] This also appeared from a second evaluation of 2007.[30] The presumptions thus have mainly preventive effects, in the sense that employers concluded different types of contracts than before or with more precise conditions.

The following findings are from the 2007 Report. It appeared that since 2000 in particular women who took up work again after having raised their children[31] were no longer working on the basis of on-call contracts. One explanation might be that they found another, better job; it is also possible, however, that after the

28. J.P.H. Zwemmer, 'Rechtsvermoeden, omvang arbeidsduur, een updating', *ArbeidsRecht* (2005), 50.
29. Ministerie van Sociale Zaken en Werkgelegenheid, *Flexibiliteit en zekerheid, Effecten en doeltreffendheid van de Wet Flexibiliteit en Zekerheid. Eindrapport* (Den Haag, 2002), I-20.
30. R. Knegt et al., *Tweede evaluatie Wet flexibiliteit en zekerheid* (Amsterdam: HSI and TNO, 2007).
31. In the past in the Netherlands many women gave up working completely when children were born; this tradition is now changing.

introduction of the Act on Flexibility and Security employers became reluctant to make use of such contracts because of the legal presumptions. Around 2005 the use of this type of contracts was higher, but it was still less than before the introduction of the Act. In 1998 there were 200,000 on-call contracts; in 2006 there were 117,000.[32] At present mainly young persons (under 25) do this type of work; these are predominantly students.

It cannot be determined exactly, the Assessment report concluded, to what extent the decrease of number of on-call contracts was due to economic factors and to which extent to the Flexibility and Security Act. Most employers mention as reason for making use of on-call contracts that they wish to be able to respond to changes in work supply; to try out new workers or to replace ill employees. For these purposes it is not useful for them to offer these workers a higher number of working hours after three months of work.[33] They therefore prefer other types of contracts. It must be kept in mind that effects of the Act may to a large extent be dominated by the economic situation of the time.

The third objective of the Flexibility and Security Act was to improve the position of persons working under marginal contracts. It appeared, however, that the legal presumptions were hardly ever invoked before court, even though figures showed that a large group of the employees work longer than their contracted number for a period of more than three months.[34]

There seem to be three reasons for not invoking the presumptions: workers appeared to prefer some flexibility themselves, in the sense that they did not want to work more hours than offered. A second reason was that the workers did not know the regulations on the presumptions. A third reason is that they did not want to damage the relationship with the employer.

4.4.2. Self-employed

In section 1, I mentioned the situation of the self-employed without staff. Also these persons could, in some circumstances, benefit from the presumptions. Of the persons working as self-employed who were interviewed for the assessment study of 2002, 25% fulfilled the conditions for the presumptions, but hardly anyone of them has invoked the presumptions, as they were either unfamiliar with the rules or they considered their situation as satisfactory.

As regards employers' reactions, it is relevant to mention that where they foresaw that presumptions could lead to problems, they offered a contract for a definite term instead of an on-call contract. Less frequently then in the first years after the Act came into force they asked permanent workers to work more hours or employed agency workers. An effect of the Act was also that the number of home workers and freelancers was reduced.

32. R. Knegt et al., *supra* n. 29.
33. R. Knegt et al., *supra* n. 29, 31.
34. *Ibid.*, 37.

4.4.3. The Number of Working Hours

Also as regards the presumption on the number of working hours it appeared that the number of procedures is very low. Still, almost one in ten of the agencies for temporary work has been involved in a procedure in which the presumption on the number of working hours was invoked; these were most often lost by the employee. For the other employers involved in the study (900) there were twenty-two procedures (against some of these employers there was more than one); in the cases where more than one procedure against one employer was followed, they were won by the employee.[35]

4.4.4. Minimum Guarantee

Van den Toren et al.[36] claimed that the guaranteed wages per call rule meant that the organisation of the work was improved. Employers now (in 42% of the cases) applied a minimum period per call of at least three hours. Also the nature of the contracts changed: the type of contract by which it was only provided that a worker could be called to do work was replaced by fixed term contracts or contracts for an indefinite term. Contracts with a minimum and maximum number of working hours were replaced by contracts with a fixed number of working hours.

Almost half of the interviewed employers state that they always pay the guaranteed wage, most often by requiring the employees to work for more than three hours.[37] Fifty per cent of the on-call workers claim that the minimum number of working hours and the periods of work are not defined in their contract. Only 25% of the on call workers on whom the rule applies claim that they indeed receive wage for three hours per call. Thus, the act is often not applied correctly; still 60% of the employers apply contracts in which no number of working hours are mentioned. Thus in that case the legal presumption applies after three months.

5. THE OBLIGATION TO GIVE CONTRACTS OF EMPLOYMENT TO POSTMEN

A new development on the Dutch labour market concerns the position of persons delivering mail. After the (partial) liberalisation of the post market new companies entered the Dutch market and started competition with the former monopolist post company (TNT). The new companies do not offer a contract of employment to most of their staff, but instead the postmen are paid for each piece they delivered. As a result the new postmen are much cheaper than those of TNT; the other side of the coin is, of course, that their wage is much lower, often below minimum wage.

---

35. *Ibid.*, 36.
36. J.P. van den Toren et al, *Flexibiliteit en zekerheid: effecten en doeltreffendheid van de Wet flexibiliteit en zekerheid* (Doetinchem, 2002).
37. R. Knegt et al., *supra* n. 29, 56.

The postmen have to work on two days a week and are free to choose their working times between 7 a.m. and 9 p.m. Their average working time is 5.6 hours a week. They are provided with company coats and bags but are not required to do the work personally. In case one is not able or willing to work one must seek a replacement.

As a result of these conditions it can be doubted whether they have a contract of employment.

After heavy political debates in Parliament and pressure by the unions, a regulation was made on the basis of the Post Act,[38] which provides that the post companies must make use of a contract of employment for their workers, unless a collective agreement is made which satisfies the conditions mentioned in the regulation. The postmen of TNT traditionally have such a contract, so the regulation was meant to create a 'level playing field' by requiring this from the new companies.

Employers and employees' organisations made a collective agreement, in which it was provided that after forty-two months 80% of the workers would have a contract of employment. This target had to be reached gradually. However, in April 2010 the target of 14% had to be reached, but at that time only 0.5% of the workers actually had a contract of employers. Therefore the trade unions denounced the collective agreement.[39]

When the moment on which the obligation for the post companies would become effective approached, it appeared that there was high resistance against the Act by the companies. They claimed to go bankrupt. They also claimed that the postmen did not want to have a contract of employment since that would limit their freedom to work or not and to decide their working times. One of the problems was also that the unions could simply reach their target by denouncing the collective agreement.

Since he situation was not satisfactory, a labour market expert and former union president, Ruud Vreeman, was asked to investigate the situation, which led to his report of January 2011.[40] One element of the advice was that he introduced a system in which the prices for the mail can be increased, so that competition can take place without having to take recourse to too low wages. A second element is that he insists on better consultation of the employers' and employees' organisations. In fact, this is in line with the approach of the ILO Recommendation, which recommends consultation of the social partners before a particular situation is defined as an employment or self-employment relationship.

38. *Postbesluit 2009, Stb.* (2009), 418.

39. For a critical approach, see A. Veldman, 'Tijdelijk besluit arbeidsovereenkomst post: de goede weg om looncoucurrentie in een geliberaliseerde markt tegen te gaan?', *Tra* (2011), no. 3.

40. *Advies Vreeman betreffende de postmarkt.*

6. THE LEGAL POSITION OF TEMPORARY AGENCY WORKERS

6.1. Introduction

As we saw in section 3, in 1998 the *Wet allocatie arbeidskrachten door intermediairs* (Waadi – the Law on Allocation of Workers by intermediaries) was adopted, which abandoned the previously existing rule that work for agencies for temporary work could be temporary only.[41] Also the permit system for agencies for temporary work was abolished. A rule, still found in the Waadi Act, is that the agency has to pay the agency workers the same wage and compensations as those due to workers in the same or comparable jobs employed by the user company. However, this provision does not apply if in a collective agreement, applicable to an enterprise to which an agency worker has been posted, the wage rates are applicable to agency workers.

The Flexibility and Security Act regulated the legal position of the agency workers. As we will elaborate below there is a connection between these rules and the Waadi. Before the Flexibility and Security Act there was serious discussion on the question whether agency workers have a contract of employment with the agency, with the user company, or no contract at all. The problem was that the agency does not really exercise supervision of the agency workers, but supervision is actually realised by the user company. In academic publications the agreement with agency workers was mostly seen as a contract of employment,[42] but in case law the outcomes of the cases varied.[43]

Furthermore, the Flexibility and Security Act amended the Civil Code in order to apply explicitly to agency workers and to provide that their contract with the agency is a contract of employment. However, also important exceptions were introduced in the Civil Code to the general rules applicable to employed persons and further exceptions were allowed by the Code to be made by collective agreements. Still, this system improved the position of the trades unions in their negotiation on collective agreements for agency workers. Whereas the unionisation of agency workers is so low that unions hardly have the power to convince employers to start negotiations, as a result of the provisions of the Civil Code agencies cannot operate without a collective agreement. Without a collective agreement the general rules of labour law which are also applicable on agency workers would make agency work very difficult. An example is the rule that the employer has to pay wage even if there is no work and the rules on the limitation of successive fixed

41. Agency workers were allowed to work six months or 1,000 hours as a maximum for a particular third person.
42. M.G. Rood and M.J van der Ven, *Flexibele arbeidsrelaties* (Alphen aan den Rijn: Samson, 1988), 23; K.M. van Holten, 'Detachering als alternatief voor uitzendarbeid: een valkuil', *TVVS* (1994), 121.
43. In a decision of the *Hoge Raad* (18 Nov. 1988, *NJ* 1989/344) it was decided that it was presumed that the agency worker had a contract of employment. It was thus up to the agency to show that the presumption was not correct.

term contracts (see Section 3). Collective agreements can deviate from these rules, so these are necessary. As a result of the stronger negotiation powers of unions, it could to a large extent be left to the collective bargaining to regulate agency work and the position of workers in collective agreements. In Section 6.3 I will mention some of the achievements.

6.2. The Provisions on Agency Workers in the Civil Code

The Flexibility and Security Act introduced Article 7:690 of the Civil Code, which provides that: an agency agreement (an agreement between the worker and the agency for temporary work) is the contract of employment by which the employee is made available by the employer, as part of the profession or enterprise of the employer, to a third person on the basis of an order given to this employer, to work under supervision and direction of this third person.[44] Although the wording of this article is – from a grammatical point of view – not very clear, in the explanatory memorandum to the Act the legislature stated univocally that 'first of all in Article 690 the agency agreement is qualified as a contract of employment'.[45] It was indeed the aim of the legislature to terminate the discussion on whether there is a supervision relation between the agency and the agency worker: the fact that a person works for a third person is insufficient to deny that there is a contract of employment with the agency.[46]

Article 690 provides that if a person is made available for a third person or firm, the rules on the contract of employment apply, except for the deviations made in the section on agency contracts of the Civil Code. In this agency contracts section special rules for the agency agreement are given. These special rules apply only for those enterprises which really have an allocation function on the labour market; by this reservation is meant that making workers available for work for a third person or firm is part of their job or enterprise and is not done on an incidental basis only. Thus incidentally posting a worker to a third person by an employer who has completely different professional activities is not governed by the regime on the agency agreement, but by the general rules on the contract of employment. This approach restricts the possibilities of abusing the agency agreement.

Moreover, the agency agreement cannot be used for posting persons within one and the same group of enterprises. As a result, an enterprise cannot escape the provisions of the Civil Code on the contract of employment by sending employees to a daughter firm.

---

44. See, for a detailed discussion, F.B.J. Grapperhaus & M. Jansen, *De uitzendovereenkomst* (Deventer: Kluwer, 1999).
45. Parliamentary Papers (*Kamerstukken II*) 1996–1997, 25 263, nr. 3, 33. See, for critical comments, I.P. Asscher-Vonk, 'Flex en zeker: de uitzendkracht', *SMA* (1997), 376.
46. See also W.J.P.M. Fase, 'De uitzendkracht wordt een normale werknemer, al duurt het even', *Arbeid Integraal* (1997), 12; W.J.P.M. Fase, 'De gefaseerd afnemende flexibiliteit van uitzendarbeid', in F.J.L. Pennings (ed.), *Flexibilisering van het sociaal recht* (Deventer: Kluwer, 1996).

The agency agreement allows particular exemptions from the rules on the contract of employment. These exemptions, related to the special nature of agency work, are the following (Article 7:691 of the Civil Code):

- the general prohibition to distinguish between persons on a contract for a fixed term and for an indefinite period does not apply (Article 7:649(5) Civil Code);
- the limitation on successive contracts for a definite period, as provided for in Article 7:668a Civil Code) applies only after the employee has been working for twenty-six weeks for an agency for temporary work;
- during the first twenty-six weeks of work an agency contract may include a provision that the contract ends *ex lege* as the posting relationship ends on request of the third person or firm.

The periods mentioned in Article 7:691 of the Civil Code during which can be deviated to the detriment of the agency workers from the provisions of the Civil Code can be extended by collective agreement.

A collective agreement is also important for agencies in view of Article 7:628 of the Civil Code, which provides that the employee maintains the right to wages if he does not work for a reason which is in all reasonableness for the risk of the employer. Lack of work is, in general, for the risk of the employer. In Article 7:628(5) it is provided that during the first six months of a contract of employment the obligation to pay wages in case of a lack of work can be contracted out by a written contract; after this period this exemption is possible only by means of a collective agreement. This rule is not limited to agency contracts, but for agencies it is essential that the risk that they have to pay wage in case of a lack of work is also taken away after this period of six months.

As I have already remarked, the provisions allowing exemptions from the Civil Code by collective agreement (only) give unions relatively large negotiation powers, since, without a collective agreement, agency work is almost impossible. Moreover, a collective agreement is important to fix the wages for agency workers, and to allow lower wages than provided in the applicable collective agreement for the other works in the industrial section concerned.

As a result, a collective agreement on agency work was made between the employers association and the trade unions in which the legal position of agency workers was elaborated, the so-called ABU Collective Agreement. On the basis of this collective agreement also facilities for supplementary old age pensions and training were organised. It must be added that agencies can evade some of the protective rules by simply ending the relationship with an agency worker just before a threshold is reached after which the legal position would have been improved. Still, there are provisions in the collective agreement which cannot be evaded, such as those on pay.

More recently also other agency organisations and other trade unions have made agreements on agency workers, which have cheaper working conditions for temporary agency workers than the ABU Collective Agreement. Since there is no system in the Netherlands to distinguish representative from unrepresentative unions such competition is very well possible. An additional problem is that the unionisation rate is so low that it is hard to say which union is representative. This is a weak point in the Dutch system of collective bargaining.

6.3. The System of the ABU Collective Agreement

In order to give an idea of the meaning of the collective agreement for agency workers I mention some main elements of the ABU Collective Agreement (2004–2009). For the first seventy-eight weeks during which a person works for an agency (Phase A) an agency worker can be given an unrestricted number of fixed term contracts. If there is no longer work, the agency can terminate the contract without a period of notice. If the employee still works for the *same* agency after completion of Phase A, the worker receives a fixed term contract. If he is no longer needed for a particular client of the agency, this no longer means the end of the contract between the agency and the worker; and the contract and wage payment continue to exist. Thus the agency has to find new, suitable work for at least the same wage. This is Phase B, which lasts for a maximum of two years or eight contracts.

Phase C starts after the completion of Phase B or if no more than thirteen weeks have passed after the end of Phase B. In Phase C the agency agreement is for an undefined period. It can be terminated only by the application of the general rules of labour law, that is, by a permit of employment office (*Uwv werkbedrijf*), which has to assess the application for the permit on the basis of a regulation of public law. Another possibility, apart from mutual agreement, to terminate the contract is dissolution by a judge.

6.4. Health and Safety

Article 7:658 of the Civil Code concerns the liability of the employer for the damage incurred by an employee in the exercise of his activities. This is also relevant to agency workers. If the employer does not meet his obligations properly, he has to pay the damage incurred by the employee. An exception to this rule applies only if the accident at work is the result of intent or conscious recklessness of the employee. If the agency worker suffers damages in the performance of his job, he can claim damages from the agency for temporary work and also hold the third person, that is, the enterprise which made use of his work, liable on basis of Article 7:658(4) of the Civil Code.

Figures

In 2002 the legal position of the agency workers was assessed.[47] According to the researchers in 2000–2001, 80% and 85% respectively of all agency workers were in phase 1 and 2. In these years 13% and 11% respectively of all agency

47. Berenschot, *Flexibiliteit en zekerheid, effecten en doeltreffendheid van de Wet Flexibiliteit en zekerheid* (Utrecht, 2002) Report II, p. 4.

workers were in phase 3 and not more than 7% and 4% of the agency workers had a contract for an indefinite period.[48]

7. PROTECTION OF NON-EMPLOYEES

In this section I will discuss the position of persons not working under a contract of employment. I will focus on the self-employed persons without staff, as they may be in a position closely resembling that of employees and therefore need special attention.

7.1. Health and Safety

The protection in case of accidents at work and occupational diseases is not limited to employed persons. Article 7:658 BW(4), already mentioned in the previous section, provides that a person who has another person work on a contract other than a contract of employment is liable for damages.[49] This extension of employees' protection concerns assignments for work which is done professionally, provided that these are activities which the principal could also have his employees do in his enterprise or profession.

7.2. The Remuneration

Also the Act on Minimum Wages is relevant to some self-employed without staff. On basis of Article 3 of this Act it is possible to assimilate working relationships with contracts of employment for this Act. The Minister of Social Affairs issued a Decree[50] to assimilate working relationships of a person who works on the basis of a contract of employment for remuneration for at most two principals unless the work performed is done as professional or an enterprise, and the work has to be done personally or exclusively with the help of family members. This working relationship has to last at least three months and the work must take at least five hours per week. This is relevant to some self-employed persons.

The Act on collective agreements can also be applicable on categories of the self-employed and thus give even higher protection than at the minimum level; according to Article 1(2) of this Act a collective agreement can concern contracts for services or assignments. This is relevant, in particular, where (very) low rates apply for a certain kind of work. A well-known example is that of translators and

48. R. Knegt et al., *Tweede evaluatie Wet flexibiliteit en zekerheid* (Amsterdam: HSI and TNO, 2007), 85.
49. Some cases from the case law are Hoge Raad 18 Nov. 2005, JAR 2005/288 and Ktr. Utrecht 4 Feb. 2009, *Ljn* BH2287.
50. Decision of 2 Sep. 1996, *Stb.* (1996), 481.

persons making subtitles for television/films. However, from the point of competition law the question was raised whether it is allowed to fix minimum rates for self-employed persons by collective agreement, since that means, in fact, setting common rates for 'enterprises'. This question became urgent when in the Collective Agreement for persons replacing employees of orchestras, a minimum remuneration was mentioned for others than employees; the Dutch competition authority published its view that the fixed rates were inconsistent with competition law.[51]

Whether this conclusion is correct remains to be seen. In the light of the *Albany* judgment a different approach would certainly be defendable.[52] The *Albany* judgment entailed that collective agreements were not contrary to EU competition law if the collective agreements were made in negotiations and if they served to realise social purposes. It would go beyond the limits available for this contribution to discuss this issue in more detail,[53] but if self-employed persons are in a position very close to that of employees and if on average they have a low income, there are, in my view, reasons to accept social purposes justifying collective agreements also for improving their position. If a category of the self-employed is, in general, able to negotiate rates which realise a sufficient income, competition should, of course, not be hindered. However, if there are strong principals and the rates are very low, there may be a good reason for interfering, in particular if the work done by the self-employed resembles very much that done by the employees of the principal and when the average incomes of the self-employed lie below the corresponding minimum wages. On this issue consensus is still far from being reached.

7.3. Protection against Dismissal

The principal is allowed to give notice at any time, regardless of whether the assignment is for a fixed period or an indefinite period. It is, however, possible to lay down in the contract that giving notice is impossible, except when the principal is a private person. Apart from giving notice it is possible to require dissolution of the agreement when one of the parties fails in meeting the contract's requirements. This possibility cannot be excluded.

Parties can make a provision on the period of notice. Termination of a contract without assuming any notice period by a principal other than a private person can be deemed contrary to the legal principles of fairness and reasonableness.

---

51. The view of the Competition authorities is called *Cao-tariefbepalingen voor zelfstandigen en de Mededingingswet* <www.nmanet.nl/Images/Visiedocument%20zelfstandigen%20-%20DEFINITIEF_tcm16-109264.pdf>.
52. Case 67/96, [1999] ECR I-5751.
53. See also Diana de Wolff & Frans Pennings, 'Dienstbetrekking of zelfstandig ondernemerschap, de reikwijdte van de sociaalrechtelijke bescherming van de zelfstandige zonder personeel', in S.S.M. Peters & M.S. Houwerzijl (eds), *Exit: Onderneming, werknemer en het einde van de dienstbetrekking* (Deventer: Kluwer, 2009), 363–388.

Article 7:411 of the Civil Code gives to some extent protection in the case of contracts of service in case of termination before the assignment is completed. If the contract ends before the work is completed or before the time for which the contract was made has expired, and the obligation to pay a remuneration depends on these elements, the worker is entitled to part of the remuneration determined on basis of what is reasonable. The person who accepted the job is entitled to the full remuneration if the end of the agreement is to be contributed to the principal and the payment of the full wage, given all circumstances of the situation, is reasonable.

In addition also the system of the requirement of a dismissal permit by the *Uwv werkbedrijf* can be applicable to a contract for services. According to the applicable Regulation, the *Buitengewoon Besluit Arbeidsverhoudingen*, a person who performs his work personally for another person is covered, unless he does the work usually for more than two principals or if he is assisted by more than two other persons (other than spouse or members of the family) or id the work is of a subsidiary nature for the person.

8. DECLARATIONS FOR SOCIAL SECURITY AND TAX LIABILITY

In the previous sections I discussed the criteria relevant to the existence of an employment relationship. The idea underlying this discussion was that labour law protection was beneficial to these workers and thus desired by them. Self-employed persons without staff often consider their situation differently: they do not want to be an employee and be protected as an employed person by employees' insurance schemes. Coverage under such schemes would mean that they are more expensive for their principals (due to applicable social security contributions) and that they have a lower net income.

Therefore the issue of 'lifting the veil' has different dimensions. When discussing the contract of employment in the previous sections, I mentioned that a self-employed person is considered an employed person if he does the work personally in subordination to another person. If a contract of employment is assumed, the person concerned is insured under the employees' insurance schemes. The suspicion that a self-employed person is, in fact, an employee, rises, for instance, and in particular, if a person resigns from a job, but continues to work for the same employer as self-employed.

In the case of self-employed without staff there is often legal uncertainty. Since this uncertainty was found undesirable, an instrument was introduced to solve this problem, the *Verklaring arbeidsrelatie* (VAR – Declaration on the Working relationship).[54] This declaration was introduced by the legislature; it can be issued by the Tax Office on application.

By various Acts this declaration has been given important legal consequences for the principal who can show such a declaration. One is that the principal will not

54. See also M. Aarts, *De zelfstandige in het sociaal recht* (Deventer: Kluwer, 2007) 213 et seq.

be confronted later by the claim of the Tax Office that a person is not really self-employed and that therefore tax and social security contributions had to be paid by the principal. The declaration thus protects the principal, not the self-employed. For the self-employed person the declaration is attractive as it makes it easier for him to be engaged by the principal since important uncertainties are removed.

In order to be granted the declaration as a self-employed[55] the applicant must have an assignment of at least three principals per year; he must have a subordination relationship with the principal; he has to present himself as an independent company and he must work at least 1,225 hours a year for the enterprise. For the purpose of issuing the declarations, the Tax Office made policy rules.[56] According to the policy rules it is very probable that a person works in subordination to a principal (in which case the declaration is refused) if his activities constitute an essential part of the enterprise of the principal. Examples mentioned are the activities as a driver of a transport enterprise, pizza carriers working for a pizza enterprise, pickers of fruit for a fruit enterprise. These persons are part of driving, visiting or delivery schemes which have to be followed. If an applicant in such circumstances denies subordination, he has the burden of proof. If a former employee is going to work as self-employed for his former employer the Tax Office will often call this situation 'change of the front'; this is assumed if he continues to do the same type of activities as before under comparable conditions for a person he worked for in an employee relationship before.

If a declaration has been issued the principal does not have to deduct taxes and social security contributions. He does not have to do this afterwards when it appears that a person having this declaration is not really self-employed. This is different, of course, if the principal did not act in good faith. Bad faith is assumed, for instance, if an employer forces an employee to work as self-employed.

The Tax Office examines the data of the application for the Declaration. After the Declaration is issued, the Tax office can change or withdraw it if it appears that the data which were mentioned for the application appear to be incorrect. A declaration is valid for a limited period only – one year – and for a new declaration the data are re-examined in view of the conditions for the declaration.

If the Tax Office finds that a declaration is invalid or is used for different purposes then mentioned in it, the situation will be investigated. If the conclusion of that investigation is that the person was working in an employment relationship, employees' contributions have to be paid by the person claiming to be self-employed, unless the principal acted in bad faith (in the latter case the principal has to pay).

As will be clear declarations are issued on the basis of data which are not 100% certain at the time of the application: for instance, the applicant may still not know the number of principals he will have in the coming year. It may also be uncertain whether the workers are actually obliged to do the work personally or

55. Other types of declarations are also possible; these are not discussed here.

56. Policy rules for assessing a working relationship (*Beleidsregels beoordeling dienstbetrekking*), 6 Jul. 2006, *Stcrt.* (2006), 141.

whether they can be replaced in view of their specific expertise. This uncertainty will still remain for the applicant after a declaration has been issued.

In order to work as self-employed a declaration is not obligatory, so also persons whose declaration is refused may still take up such work. They take the risk, of course, that the Tax Office decides, on the basis of the actual circumstances, that they are subject to the employees' insurance schemes.[57]

From investigations it appeared that almost 40% of persons who received a declaration had one or two principals a year and 45% had between three and seven principals. Thus for a quite large part of the holders of a declaration there is doubt whether they really satisfy the conditions for being self-employed and whether they are in fact not rather an employee.[58]

A more recent development is that person without personnel are offered the possibility to make an agreement with a private company, Uniforce, which gives more protection and certainty. Under the Uniforce formula the self-employed person establishes a legal person of which he is the sole shareholder. Uniforce holds 20% of the shares and has the right to dismiss the self-employed person but only in case he does not pay the due contributions. Thus, he is fully in charge of his own work (which is one of the advantages of being self-employed), but subject to the dismissal powers of Uniforce for one issue only, but as a result he is an employee for the employees insurance schemes. The Tax Office has accepted the formula,[59] so the principal can be sure that he does not have to pay the employees contributions. Thus the formula does not give all the advantages of being self-employed – the Uniforce worker still has to pay the employees' insurance contributions (including the employers' part).

The self-employed are not covered for the employees' insurances (sickness, unemployment and disability); there is no disability insurance for the self-employed anymore in the Netherlands. Voluntary and private insurances are possible, but rather expensive.

A condition for the Voluntary Insurance under the statutory schemes is that the person was compulsorily insured for the employees' insurance in the year before he started to work as a self-employed person.[60] If a self-employed person is employed by his own company, for example, in the case of the Uniforce formula, the employer will have to continue to pay wages in case of sickness and in case of lack of work. Insurance is therefore not useful for these contingencies, as in practice the 'self-employed' thus has to pay for them. Private insurance insurers can refuse a person, among others because he has a higher chance of becoming ill or disabled.

---

57. Two-thirds of the applicants are considered to be self-employed, J.P. Vendrig et al., *Evaluatie Wet uitbreiding rechtsgevolgen verklaring arbeidsrelatie* (Zoetermeer: EIM, 2007), 26.
58. J.P. Vendrig et al., *Evaluatie Wet uitbreiding rechtsgevolgen verklaring arbeidsrelatie* (Zoetermeer: EIM, 2007), 6.
59. Not to be confused with the Declaration.
60. The contributions for the Voluntary Insurance are relatively high: for 2008, for the disability law it is 6.37%, for unemployment insurance 4.58%, sickness benefit contribution 6.54%.

In July 2008 a statutory scheme was introduced to protect self-employed persons in case of pregnancy and maternity leave.[61] According to the scheme a pregnant self-employed person is entitled to benefit for a period of sixteen weeks around the delivery; its amount depends on the income during the year before the benefit is claimed, subject to a maximum of EUR 1,317 (gross income) a month.

9. CONCLUSIONS

The Employment Relationship Recommendation 198 did not lead itself to much change in the Dutch system. However, the problems addressed in the Recommendation have been addressed by the legislator and various approaches recommended in Recommendation 198 can be found in the previous sections.

The Recommendation requires (Article 2) that the nature and extent of protection given to workers in an employment relationship should be defined by national law or practice, or both, taking into account relevant international labour standards. In the previous sections we saw that the most important criteria and their interpretation were developed in the case law. The legislature has a quite modest role, although he was active by introducing the legal presumptions and the law on the agency workers.

In addition the legislature provided guidance for the parties concerned, in particular employers and workers, on effectively establishing the existence of an employment relationship and on the distinction between employed and self-employed workers (Section 4). The legal presumptions and the law on agency workers were examples of such guidance. Also the declaration for the self-employed can be mentioned.

Interesting are also the more specific provisions on the determination of an employment relationship. Article 9 provides that for the purposes of the national policy of protection for workers in an employment relationship, the determination of the existence of such a relationship should be guided primarily by the facts relating to the performance of work and the remuneration of the worker, notwithstanding how the relationship is characterised in any contrary arrangement, contractual or otherwise, that may have been agreed between the parties.

As we saw in the description of the case law, the Dutch approach is to take all circumstances of the case into account. The name of the contract is not decisive. Remarkable is the case law which took the intention of the parties as a main point of departure. However, since the court takes also the position of the parties into account, the case law may still be consistent with the spirit and objective of the Recommendation. The case law shows also, interesting enough, that in a developed post-industrial economy there may be situations where persons try to make an opportunistic use of labour law.

The Declaration system for the self-employed may be more problematic in the light of the objectives of the Recommendation. The problem here is that, primarily,

61. Act of 29 May 2008, *Stb.* (2008), 192.

it is the self-employed person himself/herself who does not want to be covered by labour law, although we have to remain cautious in respect of situations where the person is very strongly encouraged by the principal to be(come) self-employed. Given the fact that persons with a declaration did not satisfy the conditions after all it is important that the practice of awarding them becomes stricter, or in any case the renewal of the declaration after it has expired.

Article 11(b) of the Recommendation– providing for a legal assumption that an employment relationship exists where one or more indicators are present – is followed in the Dutch system by the legal presumptions of the Civil Code. This is an interesting innovation of labour law. However, it is good to look at the side effects. They entailed that other types of employment contracts became more used, which can indeed be seen as a good development. However, it can mean that particular groups of workers who used to work on such contracts were substituted by others.

The need for flexibility and economic developments entail that employers keep looking for constructions which are less expensive. It can be seen that changes in the laws – like the legal presumptions – do not mean that from now on particular contracts – such as the classic contract of employment – are used but that alternatives are tried. Furthermore, many of the improvements have left escape routes open: for example, by defining on-call contracts more specifically and/or terminating agency contracts before a threshold is reached the statutory improvements can be escaped. Monitoring the developments, as required by the Recommendation, remains therefore very important.

Chapter 8
The Protection of Working Relationships in Poland

Andrzej Marian Świątkowski

1. INTRODUCTION

The International Labour Organisation holds as its main priority the protection of working and social rights which should give all employees decent working conditions and remuneration.[1] One of the essential elements for achieving this goal is to encourage its Member States to establish the principle that any work carried out by an employee under supervision of an employer and for remuneration is protected by labour law.[2] ILO Recommendation 198 is meant to support this goal by requiring Member States to introduce transparent criteria distinguishing between freely commissioned rendering of services and an employment relationship. Further, the Recommendation encourages Member States to assure that the protection of workers' rights should be accessible to all, particularly vulnerable workers, and this should be based on law that is efficient, effective and comprehensive, with expeditious outcomes, and that encourages voluntary compliance.

---

1. See A.M. Świątkowski, *Międzynarodowe prawo pracy (International Labour Law)*, vol. I *Międzynarodowe publiczne prawo pracy (International Public Labour Law)* (Warszawa: C.H. Beck, 2008), vols 1–3.
2. A.M. Świątkowski, *Międzynarodowa polityka społeczna wobec świadczących pracę w niezorganizowanej gospodarce (International social policies for workers working in unorganized markets)*, Polityka Społeczna (*Social Policies*) (Warszawa, 2003), vol. 4, 1 et seq.

Frans Pennings & Claire Bosse, *The Protection of Working Relationships*, pp. 109–125.
© 2011 Kluwer Law International BV, The Netherlands.

This chapter analyses the present Polish regulations and how they are applied. It will also discuss the proposals of the Codification Commission in 2006 for a new Labour Code as well as the Code on Collective Working Relations.[3]

2. THE PRESENT LAW

2.1. Freedom of Work

The Labour Code in Poland came into force on 26 June 1974.[4] In accordance with Article 10 § 1 of the Code, which establishes the freedom of work,[5] every person is at liberty to choose his employment. This principle is confirmed by Article 65(1) of the Polish Constitution (passed on 2 April 1977[6]), which upholds the freedom to choose a place of work and the freedom to carry out one's profession.

Work may be carried out under a contract of employment for an indefinite period of time or for a fixed term. Fixed term contracts include probationary contracts of employment, contracts for the duration of a specific job and contracts of employment in order to replace another worker, for example a pregnant worker.

Article 25 of the Labour Code outlines the various types of contract of employment. Furthermore it provides that work carried out in a working relationship may be done on the following basis: commission, choice, appointment, as well as on the basis of a co-op working agreement. According to Article 2 of the Labour Code every person who works on such a basis is considered an employee. The principle of freedom to work grants parties to decide on the contents of the contract and on the contents of the work to be carried out.

Apart from a contract of employment, work may also be carried out on the basis of a contract drafted according to the principles of civil law. Such type of contracts include sub-contracts (including the 'order contract' which is specific to Polish civil law), agency contracts, managerial contracts, leasing contracts and other types of contracts, generally termed 'non-specified' contracts. Work may also be done as a self-employed person.

Employment under a contract of civil law widely occurs, as it decreases the costs for an employer who would otherwise be obliged to pay social security contributions for the worker (which is obliged for all employees working on a contract of employment). Further, sub-contractors neither have a legal right to advantages such as paid holidays nor to any rights assured by collective labour

3. The draft Labour Code was submitted by the Codification Commission to the Minister of Labour and Social Policy, who presented it to the social partners. At present the draft is under discussion of the interested parties.
4. *Official Journal* of 1998, No. 21, item 94, often amended since.
5. See A. Patulski, *Wolność pracy – próba ujęcia wielopłaszczyznowego* (*Freedom of Work – An Attempt at a Multi-level Analysis*) (Warszawa: Warsaw University, 1992), 164 et seq. Z. Górlal, *Prawo do pracy. Studium prawa polskiego w świetle porównawczym* (*The Right to Work. A Study of Comparative Polish Law*) (Lodz: Lodz University, 1994), 137 et seq., 203 et seq.
6. *Official Journal*, No. 78, item 483.

agreements. The rules of the Labour Code on trade unions, on negotiations on collective work conditions and on collective actions (strikes) do not apply to the sub-contractors.

Persons who are not covered by a contract of employment or by a sub-contract agreement, or who are not self-employed may render civil or public services (e.g., public servants, judges, prosecutors, civil workers) or render work based on administrative agreements (e.g., professional soldiers, the police and other State officials working in uniform). Currently, labour law does not regulate the legal relations in which persons render services (soldiers and the police force), but it is clear that they do not hold the legal status of employee, as is provided by Article 2 of the Labour Code. Nor does the Labour Code regulate the position of persons holding State service positions, including the President, the Premier, parliamentarians, ministers and regional government officials. The current labour regulations do not view such high positioned functionaries and administrators on a State or regional level (either elected or appointed) as employees, as they carry out their duties and state obligations as representatives of State bodies.

This legal analysis concentrates on those who are not employed on the basis of a contract of employment. This is to compare the situation with ILO Recommendation 198, which obligates Member States to undertake measures in order to guarantee effective protection for workers who perform work in the context of an employment relationship.

2.2. The Presumption of Employment Relationship

Since the Labour Code Amendment of 2 February 1996,[7] Article 22 of the Labour Code includes the principle that all work carried out in Poland for an employer and under supervision (including the situation that working times are specified by the employer) for remuneration should, regardless of the legal contract entered into, be regarded as employment based on a contract of employment (Article 22 § 1^1).[8] The Supreme Court specified that all employment that is voluntarily entered into, which is done personally for remuneration and carried out under the supervision of an employer is regarded by law as an employment relationship, regardless of the name of the contract.

By introducing the presumption of Article 22 § 1^1 of the Labour Code, the legislature did not prohibit parties to enter into a civil law contract instead of a contract of employment. The contract entered into, however, cannot be of a mixed nature. Thus it cannot contain both work agreement elements and sub-contracting clauses.[9] Therefore, for the purpose of deciding which type of contract is involved,

7. Since then amended again by the Amendment Act enforced on 26 Jul. 2002.
8. See A.M. Świątkowski, *Kodeks pracy. Komentarz* (*Labour Code Commentary*) (Warszawa: C.H. Beck, 2006), 95.
9. Supreme Court ruling on 23 Jan. 2002, I PKN 786/00, Supreme Court Jurisdiction – Labour Law Chamber, 2004, No. 2, pos. 30, first thesis.

it has to be determined whether civil law sub-contract elements or contracts of employment elements prevail.[10]

Given this framework and the legal presumption of Article 22, decisive for adopting a contract of employment is whether the work has to be done personally. If this is not the case, there is no legal framework which provides that the work is done on the basis of a contract of employment.[11] Consequently, it is impossible to include a clause in a contract of employment requiring or allowing that work is done by a third party in lieu of the employee. Such a clause, however, is permissible in a civil law sub-contract, such as an 'order' contract.[12]

All work carried out within a work relationship is done in subordination to the employer. The subordination of the employee appears from the time frame for the work to be carried out, the definition of his duties, as well as the description of the method by which and the order in which the work is to be done. Only some categories of workers responsible for specific jobs (e.g., in creative sectors) have a certain degree of freedom in doing their work.[13] Contracts of employment are not limited to certain types of work; instead, the criteria for such a contract are that the work is done for remuneration, must be done personally, in subordination by the employer and must be carried out for the employer who is liable for all the risks.[14]

2.3. Limiting the Freedom to Choose the Type of Contract

From this description of the legal rules and case law it follows that parties have the freedom to choose the type of contract they use for performing the work: a contract of employment or a sub-contract of civil law. However, if work is done for an employer and under supervision for remuneration it is under a contract of employment.

In 1996 there was one panel of the Supreme Court that ruled that it cannot be presumed that parties having full legal capacity have in fact entered into a contract of a character different from that they decided to conclude, that is, that they have made a contract of employment instead of a contract of civil law.[15] This seems to have been a misjudgment. Currently, it is an established presumption that if

10. Supreme Court ruling on 14 Sep. 1998, I PKN 334/98, Supreme Court Jurisdiction – Labour Law Chamber, 1999, No. 20, pos. 646.
11. Supreme Court ruling on 28 Oct. 1998, I PKN 416/98, Supreme Court Jurisdiction – Labour Law Chamber, 1999, No. 24, pos. 775.
12. Supreme Court ruling on 12 Feb. 1998, I PKN 458/98, Supreme Court Jurisdiction – Labour Law Chamber, 2000, No. 3, pos. 94.
13. Supreme Court ruling of 7 Sep. 1999, I PKN 277/99, Supreme Court Jurisdiction – Labour Law Chamber 2001, No. 1, pos. 18.
14. A.M. Świątkowski, *Polskie prawo pracy* (*Polish Labour Law*) (Warszawa: LexisNexis 2003), 25 et seq.
15. Supreme Court ruling of 5 Sep. 1997 r., I PKN 229/97, Supreme Court Jurisdiction – Labour Law Chamber 1998, No. 11, pos. 329.

personal work is performed under supervision for wage there is a contract of employment. If a civil law contract is used for this work it is converted, regardless of its official title, into a contract of employment.

Neither the Polish law nor the judiciary treat employment, regardless of the type of the agreement or the legal relationship in which the work is rendered, as done on the basis of a contract of employment. If the parties claim and prove that the employed person can be substituted or aided by a third person, that he may carry out the work independently and is not supervised by an employer or another worker, there is no legal basis upon which the contract should be treated as a contract of employment. It would therefore be impossible to define the worker with the use of Article 2 of the Labour Code.

The Labour Code thus does not promote the concept of employment performed within an employment relationship; it does not mean that work rendered on other legal foundations (other than those stipulated under Article 2 of the Labour Code or under a civil law contract) may be regarded as an employment relationship. Whether the national legal system in Poland can become more adjusted to Recommendation 198 of the ILO is to be viewed in light of the recently published draft Labour Code (Section 3).

Analysing the actions of the Polish authorities in the light of ILO Recommendations 198, we can conclude that the amendments introduced in 1996 on the presumption of a contract of employment (i.e., ten years before the Recommendation was passed) to some extent fit in with the objectives of this Recommendation. All work carried out personally under subordination to an employer for remuneration (regardless of the official name of the contract) is considered as employment on the basis of a contract of employment.

2.4. Contracts for an Indefinite Period and Fixed-Term Contracts

The Polish legislature has undertaken actions to reduce a too liberal use of fixed-term contracts. An amendment of Article 25 § 1 involved that a fixed-term contract following two prior ones (with the subsequent third contract of employment coming into effect within a month of the expiration of the last one) is considered by law as a contract of employment for an indefinite period. This provision limits the freedom of the parties to make a third contract for a fixed period. Regardless of the will of both parties within the work relationship to make another contract for a fixed period, the legislation dictates that such a subsequent work contract is considered as a contract of employment for an indefinite period.[16]

This provision shows the determined stance of the government to regulate the individual work relationship. Until recently there was more freedom in this area, but this limitation was made in order to protect the interests of the worker and in order to implement Directive 1999/70/EC of 28 June 1999 concerning the

16. This provision was introduced by the Act of 14 Nov. 2003.

framework agreement on fixed-term work concluded by *European Trade Union Confederation* (ETUC), UNICE and CEEP. This rule became effective from the day Poland became a EU Member (1 May 2004).

The legal restriction of the choice of parties can, however, have the effect that parties evade the rules. At the end of the day the worker is worse off. Parties may enter into agreements that by-pass the statutory prohibition of successive fixed-term contracts of employment. It indeed appeared that, in order to bypass the prohibition of the Law, parties do not make contracts of employment, but instead extended the existing contract for a fixed term by the use of an annex. The courts were thus confronted by the fact that parties to a fixed-term contract attempted to avoid the prohibition of several successive agreements by means of an annex.[17] If such avoidance (by the use of the extension annex) can be proven, Article 58 § 1, Article 300 and Article 18 § 1 of the Labour Code provide that the agreement is deemed void as in breach of Article 25 § 1. The new contract is *ex lege* a contract for an indefinite period. Also a third subsequent contract of employment transforms *ex lege* into a contract of employment for an indefinite period of time.[18]

2.5. Legal Sanctions

A contract under which a person renders services personally, under subordination of an employer, for remuneration and at the risk of the employer, has to be treated by the parties as a contract of employment. If a civil law contract is made instead, the employer infringes the rights of the worker and may be imposed a fine, ranging between one thousand zloty (EUR 246) and thirty thousand zloty (EUR 7,380) (Article 281 § 1 of the Labour Code). A worker who has entered into a civil law contract with an employer instead of a contract of employment is not imposed a fine.

The system of legal protection has been construed in a particular manner. A worker who has consented to conclude a contract other than a contract of employment can without hesitation file a complaint to a Labour Court without the risk of being imposed an administrative sanction. On the basis of Article 199 of the Polish Civil Procedure Code such a worker can demand the recognition of a contract of employment.

An employee, a trade union and a State labour inspector have the right to file such a complaint. The Civil Procedure Code (Article 63 § 1) permits State labour inspectors to appear independently on behalf of the interested party that is employed on the basis of a civil law contract. Such a civil law contract must have the effects of a contract of employment and should be treated as such by the parties. The claim filed should seek the recognition of a legal relationship in

17. Supreme Court ruling on 17 Nov. 1997, I PKN 370/97, Supreme Court Jurisdiction – Labour Law Chamber, 1999, No. 17, pos. 506.
18. Supreme Court ruling of 21 Nov. 2000, I PKN 93/00, Supreme Court Jurisdiction – Labour Law Chamber 2002, No. 11, pos. 270.

order to allow the labour court to conclude whether the civil relationship as defined by the parties is indeed a work relationship.[19]

3. THE DRAFT LABOUR CODE

3.1. Freedom to work

Recently a draft was published for a new Labour Code.[20] It did not bring any changes to the concept of freedom to work. Article 17 § 1 of the proposal assures all persons the right to work. This includes the freedom to choose work and profession. The concept of the freedom to work is completed by Article 19 of the proposal in which it is stated that it is necessary to specify the conditions of the work relationship regardless of the legal basis in accordance with the will of the parties. The proposal further redefines the concept of work. It does not give a formal legal definition of employee, although it gives a definition of employer.

It is difficult to know what brought the drafters of the proposal to limit themselves to defining an employee as a person of age (Article 4 § 1). From this provision it follows that an employee is a person of age and employed within a legal relationship under the rules of the Labour Code.

The proposal does not define the employment relationship. It limits itself to expressing that when an employment relationship is established, 'an employee is obliged to render work personally under supervision, the work is to be of a specific nature for the employer and for the latter's risk'. If these conditions are fulfilled remuneration is due (Article 43 § 1). Work which is personally done, paid for and carried out under supervision that fulfils the abovementioned requirements is an indication that this is a contract of employment regardless of the agreement that both parties entered into (Article 43 § 2).

The proposal does not differentiate work relationships on basis of the type of contract under which the work is done.

The draft Labour Code also deals with specific contracts. These are contracts that establish non-typical work relationships, which are defined in the third volume of the Labour Code proposal. Because the project does not define non-typical work relationships, we have to look how the authors of the project have described them. This description does not give criteria for these contracts, such as that work is rendered for fixed periods of time, is a contract for telework, a work experience contract, a managerial work contract, a cottage work contract, a contract for work carried out by family members of an employer or work in a co-op. Even though

19. Supreme Court ruling of 29 Dec. 1998, I PKN 494/98, Supreme Court Jurisdiction – the Labour Law Chamber, 2000, No. 4, pos. 149. A suit filed by the work inspector or trade organisation on behalf of the worker, to establish the existence of a work relationship may be filed in any court proceeding under Art. 56 § 1 Civil Process Code. See: Supreme Court ruling of 28 Jun. 2001, I PKN 508/00, Supreme Court Jurisdiction – the Labour Law Chamber, 2003, No. 9, pos. 224.
20. See *supra* n. 3.

Volumes 2 and 3 do not provide that typical and non-typical work agreements represent the basic or exclusive forms of establishing employment relationships, it is possible to conclude that the authors of the project were of the view that the main relations of the future Labour Code are employment relationships and employment as non-employee.

The sixth Volume of the draft Labour Code regulating employment by others than employees expresses for the first time the dichotomy between non-employees on the basis of a civil law contract (first title) and those not working on the basis of a contract (second title). We may assume that in case of non-employee employment outside a formal contract, an employee relationship will in the future be regulated by Labour Code regulations. These rules will be appropriately applied to any work carried out that is not based on a legal relationship. This type of division supports the hope that the objectives of ILO Recommendation 198 will be fulfilled, that is, that hidden employment contracts will be protected under labour law.

The authors of the Labour Code Project suggest the possibility of introducing changes to the criteria that until now have been used to describe the scope of labour law. Until now the definition of a legal relationship was regulated by labour laws, which included in various degrees elements of civil and administrative law and divided a work relationship into categories of work and service relationships. Instead of such an approach, the authors of the Labour Code Project introduce criteria which will separate labour law regulations from other branches of law.

Chapter 2 of the sixth Volume of the Labour Code Project explains that employment of non-employees outside a contract contains the category of workers outside the general category of persons working under a contract of employment.[21]

The provisions of the proposal dealing with employment outside a formal contract of employment do not allow lawyers or other institutions to monitor whether employers who make use of these abide the labour laws.

3.2. Working Relationships

3.2.1. Contracts of Employment (Volume II, Chapter 1)

Work relationships are legally based on contracts of employment. The Labour Code Proposal describes two types of contracts of employment. The difference between these two types is based on the definition of the duration of the contract, namely whether it is for a permanent or a temporary period (Article 70 § 1 of the Labour Code Proposal). The Proposal has moved away from the approach initiated

21. These are persons fulfilling the most important of State functions, including the president and the prime minister (Art. 446), parliamentarians (Art. 447), professional soldiers, other military organisations and other uniformed services such as fire fighters and border control (Art. 448). It also covers persons in special positions as the imprisoned and juveniles in detention centres (Art. 449).

in 1996 of restricting the use of temporary contracts of employment. Instead, it substitutes the rule in which a third subsequent contract of employment (entered into within a month of the last) is treated by law as a permanent work agreement. Without limiting the number of work agreements entered into, the Labour Code Project stipulates that employment based on subsequent work agreements for an indeterminate period of time by the same employer cannot exceed three years (Article 71 § 1). On the basis of this rule the following will be considered as being in accordance with the law:

- one contract of employment entered into for a period of three years;
- two contracts for indeterminate periods of time, one of which is entered into within the first month of a three year taxation period and the second entered into the last thirty-fifth month of the said period.

3.2.2. Temporary Work Agreements (Volume III, Chapter 1)

A temporary work agreement is compiled of three parties, namely a temporary work agency, an employer who is the 'user' and a temporary worker. Labour law legislation does not regulate the legal relationship of parties who do not have a work relationship. When the proposal for the Labour Code will regulate all work relationships, Division II of the Code will be amended in order to regulate the contract between the work agency and the 'user' employer (Article 148). Such an agreement must be in writing. The Labour Code does not indicate what the legal consequences may be if this rule is not abided by.

A temporary work agreement should stipulate the following: the type of work performed by the temporary employee, the qualifications required for the position, the specification of the agency and the 'user' employer, the presumed expected time of work, the place of work and the working hours, the remuneration, as well as the duties allocated by the employer (the temporary work agency).

In Article 148(7) of the Labour Code proposal, two requirements have been added (considered by the legislature to be the most fundamental), namely the obligation to pay temporary workers and the obligation to grant paid holidays. In another article, Article 149, it is deemed invalid to establish a contract between a temporary worker and an employer who is the user of the worker, if this leads to an extension of such employment on the given conditions. The parties then remain in a factual relationship of temporary work although they are not formally bound by a contract of employment.

If a temporary work agency and the user employer adopt a contract prohibiting to employ a temporary worker by a user employer after the work agreement has ceased to exist, this invalidates the agreement between the two parties who divided between themselves the responsibility for the temporary worker. The rules regulating temporary work provide that an agreement between a temporary work agency and a 'user' employer must be entered into before a temporary work agreement can be made.

The Labour Code Project allows the employment of workers by one 'user' employer on the basis of a temporary work agreement within a twenty-four month period for a period that does not exceed twelve months (Article 161 § 1). If this period is exceeded the Labour Code Project proposes to accept the presumption of employment based on an employment agreement for a permanent period of time (Article 161 § 2). The presumption of Article 25^1 § 1 of the Labour Code is that the third employment agreement shall be contracted for a permanent period of time. So far this has not been accepted by the Supreme Court.

The Labour Code project replaces the above with the presumption stating that the employment contract with a temporary employee shall be contracted for a permanent period of time when his total employment time within the last twenty-four months exceeds twelve months. The legal concept of the analysed regulation of the labour law is reflected in Article 25^1 § 1 of the Labour Code.

The following conclusion can be drawn from the proposed regulation of temporary employment exceeding twelve months in a period of twenty-four months: all temporary employment agreements giving the basis for temporary employment of over twelve months transform by law into permanent work agreements, if a temporary employee works for one employer in the twenty-four consecutive months. Article 161 § 2 of the Labour Code introduces a further rule on employment agreements involving employment agencies. In case of a prolonged employment period a work relationship entered into between an employment agency changes by law into a work relationship between employee and employer (previously institutional and individual clients of the employment agency).

A contract between an employment agency and a worker is called a 'temporary employment agreement'. Article 150 of the Labour Code does, however, not attempt to classify the new type of contract into one of the existing categories of employment contracts, namely for a permanent and non-permanent period of time. From the perspective of a 'user' employer, the employment based on a temporary employment agreement will be considered as contracted work, regulated and described by an agreement between the temporary employment agency and the employer. Such agreements do not impose on employers the obligation of determining the period of temporary employment. Article 148 pt. 3 of the Labour Code Proposal requires only to determine the foreseen period of work. In a temporary employment agreement with a temporary worker the employment agency has to specify the following elements: parties to the agreement, type of work, commencement date, the name of the 'user' employer, the period of work agreed between the agency and the employer, as well as the conditions of the temporary employment during the period of work (Article 150 § 2).

These important rules on temporary work contracts show that this type of employment agreement now concludes the *essentialia negotii*. Therefore, in order to change the type of temporary employment agreement, a notice for change will be required.

In addition, temporary work agreements can be concluded for a permanent or non-permanent period of time. It is also possible to conclude a temporary employment agreement for the same period during which the employer is bound by the employment agency within their mutual general contract. Such an agreement is regulated by Chapter II of the Labour Code project, which specifies the conditions of temporary employment.

Therefore the question arises for what reason the Labour Code project regulates the relationship between a temporary employee and the two bodies which partially have the role of employer of the temporary worker. A temporary employment agency acts as an intermediating body in the work placement process. In comparison with other work placement institutions, it may be considered as a body specialising in intermediation between employers and particular groups of workers. 'User' employers with their temporary employees are not bound by work agreements. However, they have duties and rights as far as necessary in order to organise work for a temporary worker (Article 154 § 1).

Although the proposed new Labour Code aims to regulate all work regardless of the type of employment agreements, the relationship between temporary employees and their 'user' employers remains unregulated. The Labour Code project does not answer the question why this relationship does not have the status of employment relationships. Article 43 of this document provides the criteria to describe the features of work which qualify it as work performed within an employment relationship. These criteria include remuneration, work carried out personally, under subordination and at the risk of the employer. Assuming that all these conditions are to be fulfilled at the same time in order to qualify work as performed within an employment relationship, the conclusion can be that a relationship between a temporary employee and an employer contracting via an employment agency can be regarded as an employment relationship in the light of the Labour Code Project. This is because the employer does not take the risks for the activities or lack of activities of a temporary employee. The characteristics of work performed under a temporary work agreement allow it to be qualified as conducted 'for the benefit of employer', although the work is not done for the temporary employment agency itself. The agency merely benefits from the work being done. The draft Labour Code does not give rules on agency service charges in its part regulating the relations between temporary employment agencies and their employer clients.

It can be concluded that the Labour Code project forbids further employment of a temporary employee after the agreement between the agency and the employer has terminated, while it does not forbid the employers, parties to a work hire agreement, to establish rules of payment for services rendered by their temporary workers. Such an agreement cannot be regarded as an agreement establishing a work relationship, although it directly regulates work as a focal element of labour law. Work relationship cannot be established between two employers only. The effect of such agreements is that a legal relationship is established which is regulated by the Labour Code, by which employers divide the duties and entitlements of temporary employees. This special employment relationship with two bodies on the employers' side legally bound to one employee sets an aim for the Labour Code Project to regulate this situation by labour law regulations. Otherwise, not all legal relationships of temporary employment could be classified as employment relationships, regulated by Chapter II of the drafted Labour Code, and would not achieve the objectives recommended by Recommendation No. 198 of the ILO.

3.2.3. Telework (Volume III, Chapter 2)

In the second Title of the Labour Code project, the legal concepts of Chapter IIb of the Labour Code (Articles 67^5–67^{17})[22] are duplicated (Article 163 of the Labour Code project). Telework as a form of work organisation assumes mutual agreements of the parties within an employment relationship in terms of the place of work (any place chosen by the worker apart from the workplace of his employer) and the way of work (via IT machines). Telework is employment within an employment relationship.

3.2.4. Managers (Volume III, Chapter 3)

Employment of managers can have different forms. It may either be a traditional employment agreement or a managerial contract. Title 4 of the Labour Code project regulates workplace managerial work according to the regulations of labour law. This applies to the situation in which the parties enter into a general (unnamed) contract (Article 172 § 1). The drafters of the proposal for the Labour Code are not precise in this area. The regulation involved in the Labour Code Project includes a management contract in labour law regulations only in cases when the employer, according to the entitlement of Article 172 § 1, enters into such an agreement with his manager. Lack of consent to conduct a work agreement for workplace management can lead to a situation that workplace management is not regulated by labour law. This means that the legislator has left the concept that every work should be regulated by labour law. When parties make an agreement describing the type of work as 'workplace management', such an agreement will significantly differ from an agreement where the employment risk is taken by the employer. Management contracts establishing a work relationship can obligate a manager to achieve particular goals (Article 173) and guarantee his remuneration on a higher level, exceeding an agreed amount, depending on the results. One of the fundamental elements of a employment relationship is that the risk is taken by an employer. It has to be noted that a workplace management agreement regulated by Chapter IV of the drafted Labour Code cannot be regarded as an employment agreement. The above does not change, even though such an agreement qualifies a manager as an employee entitled to minimal remuneration for work and paid holidays.

22. See A.M. Swiatkowski, 'Poland', in R. Blanpain (ed.), *European Framework Agreement and Telework: Law and Practice, A European and Comparative Study*, Bulletin of Comparative Labour Relations, Vol. 62 (The Hague: Kluwer Law International, 2007), 205 et seq.

3.2.5. Commissioned Work (Volume III, Chapter 5)

The Labour Code Project could not come to a decision whether a person carrying out commissioned work from home is an employee or whether he benefits only from the rights described in Chapter 5 of the Labour Code Project. In case of commissioning work to a worker for the party who gave the order, the Labour Code Proposal also uses the terms 'a person who carries out the commissioned work' (the worker) and the 'commissioning party' (the employer). The project avoids the use of descriptions that could involve that the parties to the commissioned work are not part of an employment relationship.

The authors of the Labour Code Project attempt to cover all types of work under labour law regulations, regardless of the type of agreement that was entered into by the parties. Therefore it is possible to conclude that 'one who carries out the commissioned work' has the rights and duties as employees within an employment relationship. In that case the 'commissioning party' has the status of an employer.

3.2.6. Home Workers (Volume III, Chapter 6)

The Labour Code Project brings home workers under the regulations of labour law. Chapter 6 of the draft Labour Code contains a definition of a home worker. Article 190 states that a person who works in a household in order to satisfy his family needs or in order to satisfy the needs connected with running a household has a legal status. Does this mean that home work is done on the basis of a contract of employment? A characteristic that is specific to home work is that home workers work for the sake of other household members or the household and not for the sake of unidentified receivers. However, the definition between an employment relationship and other forms of employment does not include the beneficiary of the work as a distinguishing criterion. From this point of view, there is no difference between fulfilling the needs of employers and the needs of other persons. Therefore a person working in a household can be regarded as person employed on the basis of an employment agreement. However, Article 190 of the Labour Code Project does not give an answer as to who the employer of such a person is, namely whether it is a particular member of the family (the head of the family) or the family (the household) represented by particular members of a family. The clear advantage of Article 190 of the Labour Code Project is that it classifies work done by non-family members in households as work carried out under a contract of employment. Therefore the regulations of Chapter 6 of the draft Labour Code realise the objective to protect dependent work.

3.2.7. Family Members of the Employer (Vol. III Chapter 7)

The Labour Code project also regards members of the family of an employer as employees if they work in the same workplace (Article 198 § 1). Article 199 of the drafted Labour Code allows husband and wife to establish an employment relationship where one spouse acts as an employer and the other as an employee.

The Code, however, makes an exception of the workplace of a joint property of husband and wife. This means that family members of an employer cannot be home workers. In some cases there are doubts how to distinguish family members of an employer working in a family workplace. Article 198 § 3 of the draft Labour Code includes individual family farms in the group of family workplaces. As far as work for family members is concerned, the legislator complies with the intention of ILO Recommendation No. 198, namely to protect dependent workers by giving legal ground under which an employment relationship exists where at least one relevant indicator listed in this Recommendation (subordination) is present.

4. EMPLOYMENT OF NON-EMPLOYEES (VOL. VI)

An aim of the Labour Code project is to include work carried out other than on the basis of an employment contract into labour law. This is the first time in the history of Polish labour law that a draft Labour Code regulates work carried out by persons for other persons outside a traditional employment relationship. Employment of non-employees may be with or without an agreement. Regardless of whether there is an agreement, the work is regulated by Volume VI of the Labour Code project

4.1. NON-EMPLOYEES WITH AN AGREEMENT (VOLUME VI, CHAPTER 1)

An agreement establishing a legal relationship between the employer and a person who is not an employee is not regarded as an employment agreement. The main difference between such an agreement and an employment contract is that a non-employee can obtain help for his work from his family members if they live in the same household. The possibility mentioned above of taking advantage of other people's help does not clash with the personal nature of carrying out this work (Article 432 § 3). The legislature uses a legal fiction of personal work, despite the real possibility that the work is carried out by third parties. However, the circle of potential helpers is limited.

The main distinguishing criteria of the work relationship (i.e., that the work is of a personal nature) is problematic. This very criterion allows the possibility to link the following acts, the Civil Code, the Commercial Law or Labour Code, with a particular work relationship and its agreement. The necessary condition for a person to be regarded as non-employee and for the employing party not to be regarded as an employer is that they carry out continuous and repeatable actions for the sake of the employing party or 'for the sake of others' in return of a remuneration of more than half of the minimal remuneration regulated by Article 432 § 1 and 2. Non-employees employed on the basis of a general (unnamed) agreement are protected by the draft Labour Code in the parts concerning collective work agreements, fair remuneration for work, and conditions of work with a special attention to health and safety regulations (Article 434).

What distinguishes employees and non-employees is the level of wages. Only persons earning at least 50% of the official minimum wage may be considered non-employees.

4.2. Non-employees Without an Agreement (Vol. VI, Chapter 2)

A significant new element to the Labour Code project is the protection of work of non-employees. Under the Labour Code there was no regulation for these groups. The group of non-employees include the President of Poland, the Prime Minister, other ministers, professional soldiers, policemen, secret intelligence services, custom officers, prison officers and firemen. The legislature suggests that the tenure of post or service work should be included into periodical work – the basis of all employee entitlements (Article 446 § 2, Article 448 § 2). As far as the President, the Prime Minister and other ministers are concerned, the Labour Code can be applied in its parts concerning the protection of remuneration, paid vacation, maternity leave as well as the other provisions of Volume 4 of the Labour Code Project dedicated to the rights and duties of parties to an employment relationship (Article 446 § 1). All controversies on non-employees employment are subject to the jurisdiction of labour courts.

An obligation of both institutions and private businesses employing persons under agreements other than employment agreements or non-workers without an agreement is to ensure health and safety conditions of work (Article 450). The obligation of ensuring healthy and safe work conditions is of a common nature. It concerns students, pupils, social workers, soldiers in active service, members of agricultural co-operatives and members of their families, members of different agricultural associations and self-employed persons.

Persons employed as non-employees with or without an agreement are excluded from the law on employment relationships. This means that they do not receive the protection of labour law, apart from the protection of healthy and safe working conditions. Therefore they do not receive adequate protection, even if they work in person, for remuneration, under supervision, for the sake of and at the risk of their employer. Here, we can see a problem with Recommendation 168. The Recommendation also encourages introducing clear distinguishing criteria between work regulated by labour law and work regulated by civil, commercial and administrative law. Introducing a volume regulating non-employees' employment into the draft Labour Code blurs the borders between the different types of legal relations under which work is carried out. Recommendation No. 198 of the ILO employs traditional criteria as how to draw borders between particular fields of law. In the regulations of Volume 6 of the drafted Labour Code the borders between constitutional, administrative, commercial fields of law have become vague. This phenomenon cannot be explained by methodological reasons, since work is the main criterion for the application of labour law. It cannot be explained either through the aim of ensuring healthy and safe conditions of work for all employees.

5. CONCLUSION

Globalisation, a phenomenon of our time, leads to decreasing the national standards of workers' protection and social protection. This can be defined as the globalisation of workers' rights and of social rights. The essence of this phenomenon involves establishing high standards of workers' rights and introducing these standards into national systems of labour law. ILO Recommendation No. 198 recommends clarifying the conditions for contracts of employment and propagates clear distinguishing criteria between an employment relationship and self-employment. The latter is simply a business activity run on the self-employed person's own account and does not grant him legal protection based on labour law.

In line with the current Polish Labour Code, parties to a legal work relationship can choose the basis of employment between an employment agreement, a civil contract and a sub-contracting agreement. The Code sets distinguishing criteria which allow defining different work relationships into different jurisdictions (civil and commercial) regardless of the arrangements made by the parties. Remuneration, the obligation of carrying out work in person and subordination of the worker to his employer are of crucial importance in classifying a work relationship as subordinate to labour law.

A weak point of the present Polish Labour Code, despite its numerous amendments, is that it still allows dependent work to be carried out outside an employment relationship (Article 22^1 of the Labour Code). *De lege lata* jurisdiction has been focusing on the interpretation of Article 25^1 of the Labour Code – a norm describing the conditions of an automatic transition from non-permanent work agreements into permanent work contracts. Avoiding the extension of fixed-term work contracts was considered by the legislative authorities and judicial bodies as a response to the attempt of introducing flexible forms of employment.[23] To summarise, it has to be expressed that neither the Polish legislature nor the courts have so far entirely fulfilled the international concept to realise *decent employment.*

Evaluating the Labour Code project it can be concluded that the legislature did not fully respond to the guidelines of Recommendation No. 198. The essence of this recommendation is to realise clear criteria for the employment relationship. The legislature did not wish to bring all forms of dependent work under the Labour Code. According to the draft Labour Code not every work carried out in person, for remuneration, under compliance, under supervision and for the employer and on behalf of the employers' risk, can be regarded as an employment relationship. It is sufficient for the legislature that every form of work is to some extent regulated by

23. A.M. Świątkowski, *Ograniczenie swobody zawierania umów o pracę na czas określony jako alternatywa koncepcji flex-security* (*Limiting the Freedom to Enter into a Work Agreement for a Non-permanent Period of Time, as an Alternative to the Flex-Security Concept)* (Warswaza: Monitor Prawa Pracy, 2008), No. 11, 565 et seq.; *id.*, 'Poland', in R. Blanpain and C. Gramt (eds), *Fixed-Term Employment Contracts. A Comparative Study* (Bruges: Vanden Broele Publishers 2009), 377 et seq.

labour law. The above situation blurs the borders between the different forms of work and employment. According to the freedom of work rule included in the drafted Labour Code, work can be carried out within an employment relationship under labour law regulations or outside an employment relationship. In the latter case, however, although directly regulated by other fields of law, it will still have to remain in compliance with labour law regulations.

Nowadays legislatures should take into consideration the real situation as well as expectations of international standards in a given field. Labour law is a field of law where the interdependence of national and international law is strong and visible.[24] The draft of the Labour Code has not been entirely adjusted to the recommendations formulated by the ILO in its Recommendation No. 198 according to which:

- protection offered by national laws ought to be linked to the existence of employment relationship;
- such protection should be accessible to all working individuals;
- the legal presumption that an employment relationship exists has to be recognised.

According to ILO Declaration on Social Justice for a Fair Globalisation adopted by the International Labour Conference at its ninety-seventh Session on 10th June, 2008 in Geneva full and productive employment and decent work are placed at the centre of economic and social policies of all Member States and the International Labour Organisation. The best way for protection of working relationships is to make labour law and its legal institutions effective. The safest method to achieve that goal is recognition of the very fact of life that paid work carried out personally by the worker, according to the instructions and under the control of another party, within specific working hours, at the work place specified or agreed by the party requesting the work ought to be performed under an employment relationship.

The draft Labour Code blurs the boundaries between employees and non-employees. Perhaps it is the very reason why that project is challenged by labour unions and other organisations representing workers' interests.

24. See A.M. Świątkowski, 'Ochrona praw człowieka w świetle przepisów prawa pracy i zabezpieczenia społecznego' (Human Rights Protection in Light of Labour Law and Social Security), in A.M. Świątkowski (ed.), *Każdy ma prawo do...* (Everyone Has a Right To . . .) (Warszawa: C.H. Beck, 2009), 3 et seq.

Chapter 9

Protection of Working Relationships in Germany

Wolfgang Däubler

1. INTRODUCTION

During the last twenty years, labour law had to defend its position. Its field of application became narrower, whereas the share of service relationships governed by civil law increased. ILO Recommendation 198 is an interesting reaction to this phenomenon. Unfortunately, it is more or less unknown in Germany. Courts and lawyers have made great progress in recognising the existence and the practical impact of European Union law, but international conventions still remain outside their field of interest. As to ILO Conventions, there are some very rare exceptions in the case law of the Federal Labour Court. Recommendations, however, are totally beyond the horizon; good wishes may come from different parts of the world, but in serious lawyers' lives they do not play any role. Even an article published in a law journal would be of a higher importance, because it may indicate how courts will decide a conflict. ILO recommendations cannot fulfil a comparable function since they are deprived of any real influence on decision-making in Germany.

Is it not inappropriate or impolite to assert this in such a harsh way? Of course, the mainstream in legal literature would not do it and assert that these ILO rules are 'not yet' taken into account. Can we, however, detect elements that could justify the hope for a better situation in the future? An expert would know that the form of recommendation was probably chosen because of the fact that a convention about

Frans Pennings & Claire Bosse, *The Protection of Working Relationships*, pp. 127–142.
© 2011 Kluwer Law International BV, The Netherlands.

'contract labour' would not be accepted by the Labour Conference.[1] Even in the ILO, there was no political will to change the existent situation and to impose legal obligations on the Member States. Under these conditions, it is up to the national legislator to deal with the problem of hidden employments. It is, therefore, a reasonable project to collect national solutions which have been developed over the last twenty years.

What can the outcome be of a project searching for hidden employment relationships? We can include them in the rules of labour law and provide the workers concerned with some protection. What we cannot do, is remove two structural obstacles for an efficient protection for all those who deserve it.

The first is that a hidden employment relationship does not exist in cases in which the working person is not obliged to follow the instructions of another person while doing his or her work. The pure fact of depending economically on one major 'customer' is not sufficient to create an employment relationship. Like other legal orders, German law requires a personal subordination.[2]

The second is that the existence of a labour relationship does not guarantee sufficient protection of basic interests of workers. Labour law is helpless if the owner of an enterprise sells it to a buyer who will not behave like a traditional employer. What can labour law do if the buyer takes measures to dissolve the enterprise and eliminate an unwelcome competitor in this way? What can labour law do if the buyer closes down some important parts of the enterprise in order to sell the remaining parts for a better price because of their high profitability? What can labour law do if the buyer does not make the necessary investments and goes bankrupt after some years? Will workers have a right of veto if the enterprise has to take over the debts the purchaser has made in order to finance the deal?

This list of examples could easily be supplemented. In all these cases, labour law plays a passive role, reducing in a modest way the disadvantages, especially the loss of working places suffered by the workers affected by these transactions. Shareholder-value capitalism has shown these problems in a massive way. Even labour lawyers who discuss these evils are difficult to find.[3] Is it not up to company law to find a solution in such cases?

2. DISGUISED EMPLOYMENT RELATIONSHIPS

As in other countries, the development of labour law was concentrated on the standard employment relationship: full-time work for an indefinite period within a plant where a representation of workers' interests is at least possible; the salary will normally be sufficient for a decent life of the worker and his family.

1. See Ch. 3.
2. Details in W. Däubler, *Arbeitsrecht 1*, 16th edn (Hamburg: Rowolt 2006), 69 et seq.
3. An exception is Wolter, 'Die Finanzmärkte, das Arbeitsrecht und die freie Unternehmerentscheidung', *AuR* (2008), 325 et seq.

This kind of labour relationship does not only give the worker social protection, but also in most cases, it serves the interest of the employer: the longer they stay with the enterprise the more productive employees become. They tend to identify themselves with their tasks. This is considered to be the best condition for innovative initiatives.

The standard labour relationship still has a dominant position in all western countries, but its importance has decreased over the last twenty years. 'Atypical' labour relationships have grown considerably and comprise one-thirds of the whole workforce – in Great Britain even more. In the following, we shall describe the main features of these 'new' forms of employment. Four different patterns seem to be the most important ones:

- Part-time contracts. The number of weekly working hours agreed upon is lower than that which is normal in the enterprise or in the branch;
- Fixed-term contracts. This form comprises employment relationships which expire at a certain date as well as those which end after a task has been fulfilled;
- Temporary agency work. The employer is an agency sending its employees to different firms on the request of those firms;
- Work in small enterprises where numerous labour law rules do not apply and where joining a union is difficult.

Self-employed workers are not covered by labour law, even if they depend on one major customer.

In most of the above-mentioned cases, the existence of an employment relationship is clear. There is no doubt that a saleswoman in a supermarket or a worker operating a machine belongs to the category of 'employee'. Uncertainties arise especially in four specific constellations:

- Workers on call may have a 'framework agreement' with an entrepreneur. The latter may ask them to come for a day, a week or three months, in each case concluding a new employment contract. The framework agreement as such may not be governed by labour law. The 'employer' remains free to ask the 'partner' or not to ask him to work. The persons concerned have no protection against dismissal; their working life becomes unpredictable.
- Employees are defined to be independent workers. A journalist working freelance for one newspaper only may serve as an example. The advantages for the entrepreneur are considerable: there is no paid annual leave and no continued payment of wages during six weeks of illness (both being legal rights of employees), there is no protection against dismissal. In German law, the most important effect is that self-employed persons work outside the social security system. Some 43% of the wage costs no longer has to be paid (normally by both sides). As a result the self-employed are extremely inexpensive workers. Why should an employer not use this possibility and claim that his field staff does independent work?

- Certain persons are stated to be 'volunteers'. They just collaborate to qualify themselves, to get work experience which will be useful for their position on the labour market. They either get no money or just receive a symbolic sum. After leaving the university, a lot of people find themselves in such a situation. A special case is an 'assimilation period' of one or two weeks in which the 'candidate' gets acquainted with the way of working in the firm – of course without any salary.
- One could finally mention work in the informal sector. An agreement exists between 'owner' and 'working person'; subordination may be quite clear as well as a salary paid every month, but social security and state agencies need not be informed. No taxes and no social security contributions are paid, no labour permit is asked for migrant workers from outside the EU. It is an employment relationship without labour law and social security – just governed by informal social rules. What would happen if such an informal worker would go to court and ask for holidays or for adequate payment?

Before looking for solutions and transforming the hidden factors in an open employment relationship, we should clarify two conditions. To which body or authority can a worker address himself or herself and ask for help? Could other persons instead of the employee ask for assistance for him? And second: which are the concrete requirements a legal relationship has to fulfil in order to be considered an 'employment' relationship?

3. INSTITUTIONS

3.1. Courts

In Germany, the most important authorities to realise labour law rules are the labour courts. A worker whose rights have been violated (or allegedly violated) can go to court and ask for compensation or for damages. Every year, about 600,000 workers (among 35 million workers) use this possibility.[4] In most of the cases, the legal action is introduced after the end of the labour relationship, especially after dismissal. As a rule, only public employees (and civil servants) go to court during an 'existing' labour relationship. Exceptions are people who accept running a high risk to be dismissed some time after the lawsuit has ended; others may be very convinced of being right or of being supported by many collaborators of the firm. Courts can, therefore, help in individual cases, but cannot offer a general solution.

3.2. Labour Inspection

The Labour inspection has a very narrow field of action in Germany. It can control only whether the rules about health protection including legal working hours have

4. See <www.bmas.de>.

been observed. It has no competence to verify if labour contracts and collective agreements have been observed. Theoretically, they could ask whether a certain person is an employee because the Act on Working Time applies only to employees. In practice, nobody has ever raised this question; it would, incidentally, only be important if the limit of forty-eight hours weekly (on an average of six months) had not been respected by the person concerned. As the capacities of the labour inspection are not sufficient to monitor the majority of enterprises during the year, they concentrate their activities on subjects which seem to be of higher importance.

3.3. Social Security Authorities

The social security system is not so much based on the liberal idea of individuals going to court, but it provides special authorities with investigative powers which can check whether the necessary contributions have been paid or not. The obligation of the employer depends on the amount of money the worker has to receive, not on the real money paid. If an independent worker is considered to be an employee by the authority, the employer has to pay the contributions for both sides, even four years back. That is a very severe sanction that can, however, be inflicted only if the person has performed in reality subordinate work. If he is a real independent worker, organising the activity on his own, no social security contributions have to be paid and no sanctions are possible.

3.4. Works Councils and Unions

It is difficult to conceive that work councils or unions would intervene in cases of a hidden employment relationship. Unlike the situation in France, they have no right to go to court in order to ask the employer to observe the laws, the collective agreements and labour contracts. The works councils have the task to control whether 'protective rules for employees' have been observed within the enterprise, but they have no means to change the situation: they can just ask the employer to comply with the rules but if he has a different view or if he follows another interpretation, he will not change his behaviour. All the union can do is to send a letter asking the employer to act in a correct way. It depends on his free will whether he will comply or not. To go on strike would be quite unusual for the union and is feasible only in enterprises with high union density; under such circumstances the fact of being an employee is normally uncontested.

If there is a case of grave misconduct – for instance if employees are exposed to hidden cameras even in toilets – work councils and unions can tell journalists or protest publicly against such a situation. The starting point for a possible campaign can, however, only be obvious violations of the law. To find such a case in our field of research would be quite difficult because of the vagueness which characterises the notion of 'employee'.

4. THE NOTION OF EMPLOYEE

To detect a hidden employment relationship requires an adequate definition of the phenomenon looked for.

4.1. Definition or Description?

There is no legal definition of the terms employee and employment relationship (*Arbeitsverhältnis*) in German labour law. Statutes use the term without giving any indication as to its contents. The independent worker as such is not defined in statute law either. It is therefore up to the labour courts to give a definition and thus decide the field of application of labour law.

According to the Federal Labour Court, the term employee has the same meaning in all parts of labour law,[5] but some statutes provide for exceptions.

Social security law requires an 'occupation relationship' (*Beschäftigungsverhältnis*) for integration into the social insurance scheme. Section 7, § 1 of the Social Security Code, Book IV, defines this as 'dependent labour especially as an employee'. The wording makes clear that even here the notion of employee is not defined and that a non-employee may be included in social security (which is the case for some small categories, e.g., artists).

According to case law in labour cases, the borderline between employees and self-employed persons depends on the 'degree of personal dependence'. An employee has to perform his services in a work organisation which structure has been determined by another person. This 'integration' becomes obvious if the employee has to follow instructions with regard to time, length, location and contents of the services. The courts often refer to section 84, § 1 of the Commercial Code, which defines a self-employed commercial representative as a person who is able to organise his activity and to determine his working hours. Despite its narrow area of application, the provision expresses a general principle in the sense that people unable to organise their work and spend their time as they want are considered to be employees.[6]

The obligation to follow instructions with regard to time, length, location and contents of the service is not required to be 'universal' in the sense that all aspects of the work must be covered. The critical requirement is that one must be at the disposal of the employer during a certain period of time. So, for example, a medical director of a hospital is considered to be an employee despite the fact that he freely decides about the measures to be taken in his job.[7] Similarly, a person in charge of controlling whether people pay their fees to public radio stations can have such a heavy workload that the lack of express working time limitation is of no

5. BAG AP Nr. 48 zu § 5 BetrVG 1972.
6. W. Däubler, *Arbeitsrecht 1*, 16th edn (Hamburg: Rowolt 2006), 72 et seq.
7. BAG AP Nr. 24 zu § 611 BGB *Ärzte, Gehaltsansprüche*.

importance; he is also an employee.[8] The judge has to give a general evaluation of the situation using all sorts of reasonable criteria.[9] The fact that the individual has to perform the services personally is indicative of the existence of an employment relationship, but the right to send another person is not automatically incompatible with the status of a worker.[10] Nor do certain economic criteria play a role: the manner of payment, the risk taken by the employee or the lack of personal economic dependence on the partner is without any importance. For example, a very wealthy person would be treated as an employee if his activity fulfils the abovementioned criteria. On the other hand, as a practical matter in the vast majority of cases, the employee loses his economic existence by losing his job.

According to case law, the concept of employee is what we call a '*Typus*' (type), not an exact notion. It is sufficient if some of the criteria are satisfied; the non-satisfaction of others is of no importance, if – seen as a whole – the activity to be done is characteristic for an employee. The Federal Labour Court has clearly declared that there are no abstract criteria applicable to *all* employment relationships.[11]

What is the basis for judging whether a person has to follow instructions or fulfils other conditions of an employment relationship? The courts generally agree that the name of the contract has no bearing on it. A worker cannot become a self-employed person merely by changing the heading of his contract.[12] Moreover, if there is a contradiction between the contract and the way services are actually being performed, the practice prevails. Thus, a clause providing for 'voluntary performance' has to be put aside if the circumstances show that the worker may not refuse to come without the risk of losing the job.[13]

In its methodology of describing the employee, the Federal Social Security Court follows the Federal Labour Court; the results are more or less identical.

4.2. Problems of Application

The lack of a clear definition makes it difficult to use the abovementioned instruments in order to integrate certain persons into labour law. The number of court decisions dealing with the question whether a person is an employee has increased considerably over the last fifteen years. The problem has been raised in very different fields; we can give only a short overview.

The most controversial area concerns journalists who work for newspapers and radio stations. The Federal Labour Court, in some cases, has tried to find a rather easy solution. If the same activity is also performed by employees, the

8. BAG AP Nr. 104 zu § 611 BGB *Abhängigkeit.*
9. See *supra* n. 8.
10. BAG AP Nr. 90 zu § 611 BGB *Abhängigkeit.*
11. BAG AP Nr. 48 zu § 5 BetrVG; BAG AP Nr. 90 to § 611 BGB *Abhängigkeit.*
12. BAG AP Nr. 48 zu § 5 BetrVG 1972; BAG AP Nr. 90 and 103 to § 611 BGB *Abhängigkeit.*
13. BAG AP Nr. 90 zu § 611 BGB *Abhängigkeit.*

journalist can ask to be considered as an employee, because it would infringe the general principle of equality to make such a distinction in status without any obvious justification.[14] If that approach was not available, the Court has examined whether or not the person was free in organising his or her work. On the one hand, a photographer who is only obliged to deliver a certain number of photos a month without being obliged to be present at certain moments was considered not to be an employee, but a freelancer.[15] On the other hand, a journalist who is entitled to refuse certain shifts was considered to be an employee, because he was expected to accept the shift proposal by the director.[16] The same approach was taken with a contributor to the radio show *Deutsche Welle*, which is broadcast world-wide with introductions in several languages. He had to collect information, draft a text and read it at 6 p.m. Despite the fact that he was free to start working at his own discretion – at, say, 9:00 or 11:00 a.m. – the actual constraint of working intensively was considered to be decisive.[17] Newspaper men are normally employees,[18] but a different result is possible if their workload is so heavy that it can only be done by several persons.[19]

Another important group are teachers. The Federal Labour Court classifies teachers at general State schools as employees, whereas teachers at adult educational centres are considered to be self-employed persons.[20] The reasoning does not seem to be very convincing. The activity in adult educational centres is deemed to be essentially schematic since the owner of the school gives no additional instructions in 'completing' the contract. In addition, the teacher normally has the freedom to choose the time of the courses which he offers two times a week. In a more recent decision, however, teachers in vocational education were considered to be employees because the owner of the school determined the objects of the training, as well as the time and place of the teacher's activity.[21] For the same reason teachers in evening schools (where one can study for *die Abitur*) are employees.[22] However, a person who has to analyse social science publications and provide a short summary with some headwords was a freelancer because the contents of his work was carefully established in the labour contract as 'directives' and because he was not obliged to be present at any specified times. The fact that a certain quantity of work had to be done during a fixed period of time was of minor importance as self-employed persons have to be on time as well.[23] This decision was criticised, however, because 'subordination' can be evidenced

---

14. BAG AP Nr. 10, 16, 17 and 20 on § 611 BGB *Abhängigkeit.*
15. BAG DB (= Der Betrieb) 1992, 1781.
16. BAG AP Nr. 74 zu § 611 BGB *Abhängigkeit.*
17. BAG AP Nr. 15 zu § 611 BGB *Abhängigkeit.*
18. BAG DB 1992 p.1429.
19. BAG AP Nr. 4 zu § 611 BGB *Zeitungsausträger.*
20. BAG AP Nr. 61 zu § 611 BGB *Abhängigkeit.*
21. BAG AP Nr. 133 zu § 611 BGB *Lehrer, Dozenten.*
22. BAG AP Nr. 122 zu § 611 BGB *Lehrer, Dozenten.*
23. BAG AP Nr. 48 zu § 5 BetrVG 1972.

not only by concrete instructions, but also by meticulous redaction of a labour contract.[24]

In the transport sector, lorry drivers, who had worked under labour contracts, were transferred to self-employed persons as 'common carriers'. The Federal Labour Court accepted that contract if the driver had the right, in practice and not only in theory, to secure work from other customers.[25] Obviously, this was not the case when he was obliged to telephone the employer every hour, from morning to night, to learn whether there was a job to be done.[26] However, the fact that a driver worked only for one entrepreneur is not of essential importance because, in another case, his freedom to organise the work was judged sufficient to render him as a freelancer.[27] The Federal Supreme Court (*Bundesgerichtshof*) came to the same conclusion when the driver had two lorries and employed a worker whom he could send in his place.[28] A customer service man was considered to be an employee because he had to work under general instructions of the owner and at a time and a place the customers wanted.[29]

Some cases concern the question of whether franchisees were self-employed persons or employees. Applying the general criteria, the regional labour courts came to different results;[30] the Federal Courts have never had to take a clear position.[31]

It is relatively easy to criticise the Courts' approach. One rarely knows in which cases the 'evaluation of all the circumstances' will lead the judge to conclude that the person is an employee or self-employed. This kind of legal uncertainty vexes, as it concerns the crucial question whether labour law is or is not applicable.

For employers, this situation is rather comfortable, for two reasons. First, they can intentionally conclude contracts in the grey area of uncertain classification. Realistically, they can expect the dependant person not to sue and risk a loss of employment. Second, they can change the organisation of the work in such a way that the 'dependant' will nevertheless, in his own interest, 'function' according to his partner's desires. In this way, the costs of the employer can be reduced considerably.

5. TRANSFORMING HIDDEN EMPLOYMENT INTO RECOGNISED EMPLOYMENT RELATIONSHIPS?

Let us come back to the four cases described in section 2. Is there a way to bring persons who are considered to be self-employed into the field of application of labour law? If a worker has a framework agreement that he can possibly do

24. Otto, note to BAG, *supra* n. 22.
25. BAG DB 1998, 624; BAG DB 1999, 436.
26. BAG see *supra* n. 24.
27. BAG AP Nr. 103 zu § 611 BGB *Abhängigkeit*.
28. BGH (Bundesgerichtshof) DB 1999, 151.
29. BAG AP Nr. 102 zu § 611 BGB *Abhängigkeit*.
30. LAG (Landesarbeitsgericht) Düsseldorf DB 1988, 293; LAG Rheinland-Pfalz LAGE (*Sammlung von Entscheidungen der Landesarbeitsgerichte*) § 611 BGB *Arbeitnehmerbegriff* Nr. 32.
31. See BGH DB 1999, 152.

short-time jobs but which is not obliged to accept, the chances to come under labour law are limited. The Federal Labour Court has clearly decided that the framework agreement is not an employment contract.[32] The arguments are, in a certain way, formalistic, stressing the fact that the individual may refuse at any time to conclude a new contract. The economic constraint that will often oblige the person to accept the offer of the employer is not really taken into account.

In some cases there may be another way out. Fixed-term contracts require a 'just ground' which cannot be found if the employee is always asked to do the same job. An intelligent employer will, however, get good advice from lawyers in order to prevent such a situation. Even a less intelligent one would run no big risk: the only way for the worker to get the normal protection of labour law would be to sue the employer at the labour court. He would run the risk that after some time the employment relationship would find its end 'for other reasons'. To go to the social security authority would not be helpful; during the short jobs the employer will normally pay social security contributions or use an exception rule for casual work.[33] The fact of being deprived of paid holidays and protection against dismissal is not a matter of interest for social security bodies.

Freelancers were the second case. As the references to the court decisions show, many people have tried to find a solution with the help of the labour jurisdiction. It would be wrong, however, to look only at those cases that went to court. Works councils and unions in this sector normally give a lot of examples of people not going to court, not even in the public sector, because the outcome of the lawsuit is unpredictable. If the employee fails to win, his situation becomes difficult. Labour courts are helpful in specific cases, but not as a general remedy. The intervention of the social security authority may be much more effective, but here is the same problem of vagueness: how can it possibly be proved that a person was not employed, according to his contract, as a freelancer but as an employee? How to prove that there were instructions and strict time limits? Will other people in the enterprise tell the social security officer that the person concerned had to follow instructions or that he did exactly the same job as employees? Will they do that even if the employer has told them that he will be forced to pay all social security contributions for the last four years and that this enormous sum could endanger his whole activity?

In 1998, the legislature intervened exactly where this point was concerned. The notion of the 'occupation relationship' in Article 7 of the Social Security Code Book IV was changed. The legislature established four criteria which could more easily be proved than the traditional 'employment' or 'occupation' relationship; if two of them were fulfilled there was a presumption of the person concerned being an employee. The 'employer' had to prove that the presumption was wrong and that the person was working as a self-employed person.[34]

---

32. BAG DB 2003, 96 = AuR 2003, 307.
33. Article 8 § 1 of the Social Security Code Book IV.
34. Gesetz zu Korrekturen in der Sozialversicherung und zur Sicherung der Arbeitnehmerrechte of. 17 Dec. 1999, BGBl I S. 3843 et seq., which changed Art. 7 § 4 of Social Security Code Book IV.

The four criteria were:

- The person does not employ other persons as employees;
- The person works essentially for one single customer;
- The person is performing work which is typically done by employees;
- The person does not offer his services or his products on the general market.

The resistance of small employers was considerable. The mass media launched a campaign against this 'stupid way' of forcing people into social security. The chancellor himself, member of a law firm, was quite furious because his firm had to pay social security contributions for three lawyers they had employed as 'freelancers'. The idea behind the law was a good one, but the concrete rules were sometimes too strict: an employer runs a considerable risk if he made a mistake in qualifying a person as self-employed. The decisions of the social security bodies can be controlled by the Social Security Courts, of course, but it may take several years, as is usual in court cases, before the employer gets a decision. In the meantime, he has to pay. The law was changed in 2000:[35] from the original five criteria three had now to be fulfilled. The main point was, however, that the employer could ask the administration whether a person was self-employed or employee. Contributions had to be paid only for the time after the statement of the authority that the person was an employee. Afterwards, the situation rapidly calmed down. The problem of 'fictitious self-employment' disappeared. One may presume that in some cases contributions are paid that were not paid before, and that in some other cases the work is organised in such a way that nobody can pretend that the person concerned is in fact an employee. In the following years the demand for a low-paid workforce was met by temporary agency workers earning about 40% less than comparative workers in other sectors of the economy. They took over the function the supposed freelancers had to fulfil in the nineties.

The problem of 'volunteers' who are in reality employees at the beginning of their career still exists. Unions and several political parties ask for an amendment of the law in order to integrate these people into labour law. There is, however, no political will which is sufficiently strong to realise such a demand. Moreover the problem is not so much a legal one: the persons concerned normally fulfil the same tasks as employees except that they need some useful instructions from colleagues – a situation typical for all beginners, but never an argument not to consider them as employees. The proof that they are employees would not be very difficult, but nobody goes to court: they want to continue working with the firm or at least obtain a certificate declaring their excellent capacity for doing a job with high responsibilities. The labour inspection has no possibility to intervene (because health protection and the forty-eight-hours-week are observed), the social security authorities could, but they still see problems of proving the correct nature of the activity. Work councils and unions may protest, but the problem is not 'broad' enough for triggering a general pressure against the employer, much less a strikes. So business goes on as usual.

---

35. *Gesetz zur Förderung der Selbständigkeit*, BGBl 2000 I, 2.

Work in the informal sector may not be gainful employment (activities within the family, in associations, churches, political parties, unions,etc.) which is outside the scope of this study. Gainful work which is not declared to state or social security authorities remains important: There are serious estimations that 14.7% of the gross domestic product is produced in this way.[36] There may be a lot of small businesses doing (real) self-employed work but salaried activities are also well-known in this sector. Many households practice it (the cleaning lady being paid in cash), the construction sector has the same reputation, as well as restaurants and hotels. Many citizens from non-EU countries without any permit will be found in these sectors. Normally, the legal situation does not create any doubts. State authorities fight against these phenomena and have some success, especially in the construction sector, but this does not result in a fundamental change. The employees are usually interested in conserving the situation, because the alternative would be unemployment; in the case of foreigners the obligation to leave the country can be added. As to the work within households, it may be a second or a third activity; there is no need to pay contributions to the social security scheme because the integration is guaranteed by the first job. A cleaning lady informing the social security authorities would, by the way, be considered as a very unfair person who broke rules that are generally accepted.

6. PERSPECTIVES

6.1. A New Notion of Employee?

One solution could be to create a new notion of employee which would comprise all kinds of activities, except those which are typical for an entrepreneur: going voluntarily to the market for goods and services having at the same time a chance for profit as well as running economic risks.

There is a scientific study putting such a notion at the place of the traditional vague concept of employment relationship,[37] which even received the support of two regional labour courts.[38] The main argument is that the 'notion' of an employee is not linked to the purpose of labour law: expressed in a simplified manner, the protection by labour law rules should be given to all those who need it, not to a group which is characterised (in a certain way by chance) by a personal subordination. If employees are paid during six weeks in case of illness, why should a freelancer depending (more or less) on one enterprise be deprived of such right? If employees are protected against unfair dismissal, why should a

36. Vogler & Ludwig, *Undeclared work* (Munich: European Employment Observatory, 2007), <www.eu-employment-observatory.net>.
37. R. Wank, *Arbeitnehmer und Selbständige* (München: C.H. Beck, 1988).
38. LAG Niedersachsen LAGE § 611 BGB Arbeitnehmerbegriff Nr. 24; LAG Köln LAGE § 611 BGB Arbeitnehmerbegriff Nr. 27.

freelancer lose his job all of a sudden without having any legal rights? Why are only employees covered by social security?

The Federal Labour Court did not follow these arguments and did not change its case law. After the bad experience with the reform of the Social Security Code, the legislature does not want to enter into new experiments.

6.2. The Employee-Like Person

There is one possible way out which has to be mentioned here. Beside the concept of employee, German law has developed the so-called employee-like person (*arbeitnehmerähnliche Person*). These persons are formally independent contractors without any personal subordination, but are characterised by a position of economic dependence; they are regarded as needing protection similar to that of employees.

To be a worker-like person does not automatically mean that a definite set of legal norms apply. Specific legislation exists for home-workers and commercial representatives. All other employee-like persons are subject to some labour law statutes and principles, how much of it is, however, not always clear.

6.3. Home-Workers as a Special Group

The oldest group, whose social problem became notorious by the end of the nineteenth century, are home-workers.[39] Their actual situation is regulated in the Home-working Act[40] and in a number of specific Labour Law Acts in which they are expressly included. The number of home-workers nowadays is approximately 150,000.[41] They do not benefit from the expansion of telework; teleworkers are usually employees because of their integration into the employer's organisation.[42]A home-worker is a person who, in a workplace of his own choosing, normally the home, undertakes paid work for traders who sell the products afterwards. Home-workers have no direct contact with the market for goods, and they are not 'employees' because they organise their work themselves. Up to 1974, only typical blue-collar work could be the object of home-working. This was changed, but until now it is still not quite clear whether all white-collar work is included or not. The customer has to be a 'trader', which excludes the state and other public organs.

---

39. Historical development described by Hromadka, *NZA* (*Neue Zeitschrift für Arbeitsrecht*), 1997, 1249.
40. Heimarbeitsgesetz vom 14 Mar. 1951 (BGBl I 191), last modification 31 Oct. 2006 (BGBl I 2407).
41. M. Kittner, *Arbeits- und Sozialordnung*, 35th edn (Frankfurt am Main: Bund-Verlag 2010), 818.
42. For more details see P. Wedde, *Telearbeit*, 3rd edn (München: C.H. Beck 2002), 17 et seq.

The main rules governing the status of a home-worker are the following:

- Collective agreements for home-workers are possible, but virtually non-existent. Consequently, the legislature has provided for home-working committees organised by the labour administration. These are normally composed of two union and two employers' representatives (a civil servant being the chairperson) and can determine minimum wages and other working conditions for the branches where such work exists.[43] Section 25 of the Act gives the labour administration the right to sue the customer without any special authorisation; the judgment is valid for the home-worker.
- The periods of notice which have to be respected by employers if they dismiss an employee also apply to home-workers if they work mainly for one person. If a homework relationship is to be terminated, there is a danger that the employing person will allocate less work and so reduce the home-worker's income in the interim. The law provides that a certain minimum calculated on the basis of the last twenty-five weeks has to be paid automatically.
- Home-workers are integrated in the works constitution of the enterprise they predominantly work for.[44]
- Home-workers have a right to annual paid leave and are included in all social security systems.
- The only remaining difference of importance concerns the protection against dismissal. Under German law, the employer can only dismiss an employee if there is a 'just ground' making the dismissal 'socially acceptable'. This rule does not apply to home-workers. There may be a certain minimum protection excluding arbitrary dismissals,[45] but there is no real case law about it.

6.4. Commercial Representatives

Commercial representatives are persons arranging or concluding transactions for one or more entrepreneurs. They are not employees; indeed, their legal status is far removed from labour law rules, even if they depend economically on another enterprise. They are governed by Section 84 et seq. of the Commercial Code; only very few labour law rules are applied by analogy. The Commercial Code contains the following salient features:

- Definition of the circumstances under which the representative earns a commission.
- Periods of notice which are different of those of employees.

43. Sections 17–22 of the Home-Working Act.
44. Section 5 § 1 of the Works Constitution Act.
45. BAG NZA 1998, 1003.

- After the end of their job, representatives have a right to a compensation payment because the customers they won for the enterprise will continue their contracts.[46] This is the only case in which German law provides for an automatic compensation at the end of a 'labour relationship'.
- Collective agreements cannot be concluded for commercial representatives. It is expressly excluded in section 12a, § 4 of the Act on Collective Agreements.
- Unlike other employee-like persons, representatives can go to the labour courts only if they do not earn more than EUR 1,000 per month. In practice, this means that normally the ordinary courts will have jurisdiction.

6.5. Employee-Like Persons in General

If an employee-like person is neither a home-worker nor a commercial representative, a set of labour law rules applies because of an explicit inclusion by certain laws:

- Employee-like persons have the same legal right as employees to four weeks of annual paid leave.[47]
- Employee-like persons are explicitly included in the general rules of health protection at the workplace.[48]
- The Antidiscrimination Act explicitly includes employee-like persons.[49]
- The new law on nursing care at home for family members (*Pflegezeitgesetz*)[50] also includes employee-like persons.
- Section 12a of the Act on Collective Agreements permits the conclusion of collective agreements for employee-like persons. This is of considerable importance in state-owned radio and television stations where a lot of 'free-lancers' are covered by collective agreements. In the private sector, almost no agreements can be found.
- Section 5, § 1, phrase 2 of the Act on Labour Courts[51] extends the jurisdiction of the labour courts to all employee-like persons. This is of practical importance to the application of other rules of labour law because ordinary courts would be much more inclined to use civil code provisions exclusively.

In two important fields the application of labour law rules to persons who are not legally 'employees' does not exist. Employee-like persons do not participate in the Works Constitution; nearly all authors agree that the express inclusion of home-workers operates to exclude other employee-like persons from integration

46. Section 89b of the Commercial Code.
47. Section 2 of the Act on Annual Paid Leave (*Bundesurlaubsgesetz*).
48. Section 2, § 2, Nr. 3 of the Act on Health Protection (*Arbeitsschutzgesetz*).
49. Section 6, § 1, Nr.3 of the Act on Equal Treatment (*Allgemeines Gleichbehandlungsgesetz*).
50. 28 May 2008 (BGBl I 874), s. 7, § 1, Nr. 3.
51. Arbeitsgerichtsgesetz of 3 Sep. 1953 BGBl I, 1267), last modification by Act of 21 Dec. 2008 (BGBl I, 2940).

into the system of the Works Constitution. Further, the Act on Protection against Dismissals is limited to employees.[52]

As to other rules of labour law, the situation is more or less unclear. The right to organise would probably be accepted by the courts, because it is a precondition for concluding collective agreements. It would be the same for the right to strike, but there are no court decisions on the subject. In a ruling, the Federal Labour Court has applied labour law rules governing covenants not to compete, which means that after the conclusion of the contract, such a restraint is permissible only if the person receives compensation of at least 50% of the salary he had as an employee and which restraint must not last more than two years.[53] The reasoning of the court was quite strict in stressing that a similar need of protection exists related to employee-like persons. Whether this is a new approach or not cannot be determined yet at the moment. As to the maximum working hours regulated by the Act on Working Time,[54] employee-like persons are generally excluded. This is taken for granted because of the pure fact that the Act uses the term *employee*. The discussion is underdeveloped in the field of maternity protection as well. The inclusion of most of the home-workers is considered to be a sufficient reason not to apply the Act to all other employee-like persons. As to youth employment protection, the relevant Act[55] includes workers, home-workers and persons rendering services which are similar to those of workers and home-workers. The decisive point is, therefore, the nature of the activity and not the economic dependence and the need for social protection. This is in contradiction to all the other rules on employee-like persons; some authors try to assimilate both concepts by including those young people who, by direct or indirect economic need, are constrained to provide certain services.

7. CONCLUSION

Theoretically, one could apply all labour law rules to employee-like persons except those which presuppose the employer's right to give instructions. Until now, the Courts have not been willing to go that far. Some legal authors are more inclined to extend labour law rules but it does not seem very probable that the Courts will share this view. On the other hand, such a solution would make most of the discussions about the complicated concept of 'employee' superfluous. If we would add the right of the union to sue the employer or if we would enlarge the control capacity of the labour inspection we would approach more and more a situation where all people working under an employment relationship are really treated as employees. Despite all the difficulties, let us keep some feelings of optimism.

52. See Rost in *Kommentar zum Kündigungsschutzrecht (KR)*, 7th edn (2005), *Arbeitnehmerähnliche Personen*, No 34 et seq. with further references.
53. BAG DB 1997, 1979.
54. *Arbeitszeitgesetz*, dated 6 Jun. 1994 (BGBl I, 1170), last modified by Ordinance 31 Oct. 2006 (BGBl I, 2407).
55. *Jugendarbeitsschutzgesetz* dated 12 Apr. 1976, last modification by Ordinance 31 Oct. 2008.

Chapter 10

The Protection of Working Relationships under United Kingdom Law

Alan C. Neal

1. INTRODUCTION

This chapter offers a brief consideration of the historical Common Law traditions for considering relationships between employers (until recently designated 'masters') and those who perform work for them (formerly characterised as 'servants') in the United Kingdom. It notes relatively modern moves towards focusing upon 'the contract' as the key element in employment relationships, and highlights the significance of this trend in the context of increasing use being made of 'hard law' statutory provisions to establish and deliver 'employment protection' in the form of individual rights at work. Problems with the relevant statutory definitions since the middle of the twentieth century are discussed, and the prospects of a more 'continental-style' analytical approach to the work relationship are canvassed in the context of recent Supreme Court observations. The chapter concludes that an uneasy reliance upon traditional contractual analytical tools has hampered judges in their search for the limits of protective coverage under modern Labour Law statutes, and that significant shortcomings remain in the legislative draughtsmanship of the relevant provisions. A move towards clearer demarcation of the scope of protection under employment legislation is called for, with more general enjoyment of protective rights by the category now described as 'workers', and with a

Frans Pennings & Claire Bosse, *The Protection of Working Relationships*, pp. 143–172.
© 2011 Kluwer Law International BV, The Netherlands.

limiting of instances where only a small privileged group (currently described as 'employees') are granted particular protections. The author expresses pessimism that any such moves are unlikely to be brought about in the near future – notwithstanding a clear recognition on the parts of senior judges that the changing face of modern work and employment relationships has given rise to an urgent need for reconsideration and reform.

2. HISTORICAL BACKGROUND

The background to the United Kingdom's approaches to 'employment relationships' within the modern world of work is firmly rooted in the traditions of the Common Law and the values which those traditions have carried with them through the pronouncements and attitudes of the judiciary over more than six centuries.[1] When United Kingdom labour law research was developing under the influential eye of the late Sir Otto Kahn-Freund, in the three decades after the ending of World War II in Europe, attention was commonly drawn to what was described as the shift 'from status to contract' – reflecting the rise of the contractual paradigm as the framework for nineteenth and early twentieth century analyses of working relationships.[2] While numerous politico-legal critiques of this development have been used to challenge the orthodox view of historical progression in this field of regulation,[3] the emergence of the 'contract of employment' as the point of reference for analysing the relationships of persons performing work for others

1. The evolution of the notion of 'master and servant' which developed in the fourteenth century has been the subject of remarkably concentrated discourse in recent years, as the underlying elements of the modern 'contract of employment' have come increasingly into focus for legal historians, labour market historians, and social policy commentators. For the historical background, see, *inter alia*, D. Hay & P. Craven (eds), *Masters, Servants, and Magistrates in Britain and the Empire, 1562–1955* (Chapel Hill, NC, 2004), and the interesting comments by Bruce Smith, in his 'Imperial Borrowing: The Law of Master and Servant', *Comparative Labor Law and Policy Journal* (2005), 447, and for a broad overview, with helpful further references, see J. Fudge, E. Tucker & L. Vosko, *The Legal Concept of Employment: Marginalizing Workers* (Report for the Law Commission of Canada, 2002).
2. See the important work, *inter alia*, of Kahn-Freund himself, including his short 'Servants and Independent Contractors', *Modern Law Review* 14 (1951), 504, and the later 'Blackstone's Neglected Child: The Contract of Employment', *Law Quarterly Review* 93 (1977), 508; Brian Napier, on the basis of the material presented in his 1975 D. Phil., produced under the supervision of Kahn-Freund in the University of Cambridge: *The Contract of Service: The Concept and its Application*; Mark Freedland, over nearly half a century in the wake of his seminal doctoral thesis, published as *The Contract of Employment* (Oxford, 1976), including his most recent contributions in the form of his *The Personal Employment Contract* (Oxford, 2005) and in the context of presenting recent joint research to be published in 2011 under the title of *The Legal Construction of Personal Work Relations*; and more recent considerations by Simon Deakin, including his early 'The Contract of Employment: A Study in Legal Evolution', *Historical Studies in Industrial Relations* 11 (2001), 1 and the later unfolding picture painted in successive editions of S. Deakin and G. Morris, *Labour Law*, 5th edn, most recent edition (Oxford, 2009).
3. See, for example, the wide-ranging overview offered (from a Canadian perspective) in the report prepared by J. Fudge, E. Tucker and L. Vosko *supra* n. 1.

and, increasingly, for identifying which members of the world of work should qualify for various forms of 'employment protections' under modern labour legislation cannot be denied.

During the 'post-Beveridge era',[4] with the establishment of the so-called 'Welfare State' in the United Kingdom, there has been a steady flow of legislative initiatives bringing with them specific protections or 'rights' for particularly designated persons at work, while the regulatory arrangements for taxation, social insurance (what in the United Kingdom is described as 'National Insurance'), and benefit entitlement have endeavoured to differentiate between various groups in the active labour market along with those for the time being out of work.

Against this background, it has been suggested that something of a 'reverse trend' was taking place, with a move back to 'status' as the key point of reference.[5] Whether or not that alleged characterisation of a 'reverse trend' can be made out, however, the extent to which statutory normative provisions have taken precedence in recent years over Common Law regulation of personal work relationships (and, indeed, across the whole spectrum of Labour Law regulations) has been highlighted by the important report of the European Commission on *The Evolution of Labour Law 1992–2003*, which, having pointed out that:[6]

> in relation to individual labour law, the advent of the regime introduced by the Industrial Relations Act 1971 – and particularly the introduction of a statutory protection against 'unfair dismissal' – was to constitute a watershed. Certainly, by 1974, the presence and hugely influential role of legislation

---

4. See the highly influential report *Social Insurance and Allied Services* (report by Sir William Beveridge), (Cmnd 6404, HMSO, London, 1942). The report laid down (in paras 7–9) 'three principles' for building its 'Plan for Social Security', namely:

   > 7. The first principle is that any proposals for the future, while they should use to the full the experience gathered in the past, should not be restricted by consideration of sectional interests established in the obtaining of that experience. Now, when the war is abolishing landmarks of every kind, is the opportunity for using experience in a clear field. A revolutionary moment in the world's history is a time for revolutions, not for patching.
   > 8. The second principle is that organisation of social insurance should be treated as one part only of a comprehensive policy of social progress. Social insurance fully developed may provide income security; it is an attack upon Want. But Want is one only of five giants on the road of reconstruction and in some ways the easiest to attack. The others are Disease, Ignorance, Squalor and Idleness.
   > 9. The third principle is that social security must be achieved by co-operation between the State and the individual. The State should offer security for service and contribution. The State in organising security should not stifle incentive, opportunity, responsibility; in establishing a national minimum, it should leave room and encouragement for voluntary action by each individual to provide more than that minimum for himself and his family.

5. See, for example, the approach adopted by S. Simitis, 'The Case of the Employment Relationship: Elements of a Comparison', in W. Steinmetz (ed.), *Private Law and Social Inequality in the Industrial Age: Comparing Legal Cultures in Britain, France, Germany, and the United States* (Oxford, 2000), at 181 et seq.
6. See this author's contribution to the report prepared for the European Commission, *The Evolution of Labour Law (1992–2003), Volume 2, National Reports* (Luxembourg, 2005), at 495.

> ('hard law') had been confirmed at the expense of traditional 'legal abstentionism.

went on to observe that:

> A succession of statutory provisions between 1979 and 1989 ensured that the role of 'voluntary industrial relations' as the regulatory framework for labour relationships was continuously being pushed to the background, while the role for labour law in its 'hardest' form of statutory provisions was moving inexorably into the ascendancy. This continued through the successor administration under Prime Minister John Major, until a change of government in 1997, and the return for the first time for nearly two decades of a Labour government under the leadership of Prime Minister Tony Blair.

Nor can there be any doubt that the period since 1997 has contributed still further to this process, with a continuous down-pouring of normative measures relating to the regulation of the world of work and its participants.[7]

- Within this context, the nature of employment relationships has come in for close scrutiny, primarily for the purposes of determining who should be the recipients and beneficiaries of the various rights and protections introduced by the legislator – whether directly, in the form of domestic provisions such as the National Minimum Wage, or indirectly, as the conduit for the introduction of protective measures deriving from legislation created at the level of the European Union (EU).
- Although there has been a good volume of interesting academic musing over the nature of the working relationship,[8] and the 'political realities' of modern United Kingdom practice in determining the standing of any given individual in his or her labour market setting,[9] the practical reason for this concentration upon the scope of coverage for modern labour law protections arises out of an unsatisfactory legislative drafting approach to the definitional issue of 'who is the protected party?', to which detailed reference is made below.
- For current purposes, however, this picture of an increasingly normatively regulated framework for determining the scope of modern labour law

7. In the period from 1997 until 2010, when the Labour Party lost office at a general election, a substantial raft of what might broadly be termed 'Labour Law' legislation was brought into effect. For comment during this period, see, *inter alia*, C. Kilpatrick, 'Has New Labour Reconfigured Employment Legislation?', *Industrial Law Journal* 32 (2003), 135. See, for a wider treatment, P. Davies & M. Freedland, *Towards a Flexible Labour Market: Labour Legislation and Regulation since the 1990s* (Oxford, 2007).
8. See, for example, the important recent series of contributions by Mark Freedland and Nicola Countouris, consideration by scholars such as Brian Napier, Douglas Brodie and Keith Ewing, and, in particular, the group of articles contained in a special edition of the *Industrial Law Journal*, 36, no. 1 (2007).
9. As, for example, in the interesting observations contained in the 2002 report prepared for the Canadian Law Commission (*supra* n. 1). More 'nakedly' political evaluations can be found *inter alia* in the stimulating work of Hugh Collins, Keith Ewing, and the late Brian Bercusson.

> protections in the United Kingdom serves to underline not only the huge significance of enjoying that 'safety net' of protection but also, in consequence, the need for clarity and certainty in that process, such that those participating in the world of work, social policy-makers, advisers in the field of labour relations, and, by no means least, judges and others charged with making determinations as to whether particular individuals qualify for protection in given circumstances are able to reach their judgments and assessments in an open and consistent manner.

Yet, as will be seen in the following presentation, that basic clarity and certainty is notoriously absent when it comes to administrative or judicial practice in the United Kingdom. Indeed, even as between varying functions designed to determine qualification for 'Welfare State' protection at work, there is remarkable inconsistency between, for example, the exercise when undertaken for the purposes of liability to particular taxation treatment,[10] or when done to decide what contributions should be made by a working citizen to the welfare benefit arrangements operating at large within the United Kingdom (the system of 'National Insurance'),[11] or when approached with a view to determining whether specific individual employment protection rights (such as the right not to be 'unfairly dismissed' or the right to 'equal treatment' in the context of non-standard working arrangements) apply to a given employment relationship,[12] or, even, when conducted in order to ascertain whether the relevant 'employer' might be held liable for the consequences of contraventions under health, safety and hygiene legislation, including liability for fatal incidents occurring during the course of the working day.[13]

10. See the Income and Corporation Taxes Act 1988. In particular, there is an important division into different taxation categories for 'employed' ('Schedule E', as set out in s. 19 of the 1988 Act) and 'self-employed' ('Schedule D', as set out in s. 18 of the 1988 Act) members of the labour market.
11. See the arrangements set out in the Social Security Contributions and Benefits Act 1992. The system of compulsory contributions to the United Kingdom system of 'national insurance' distinguishes – much in the manner of the differential treatment for taxation purposes – between 'earnings related' contributions ('Class 1', as provided for by s. 1(2)(a) of the 1992 Act – generally regarded as being due from 'employed' persons) and contributions 'in respect of the profits or gains of a trade, profession or vocation' ('Class 4', as provided for by s. 1(2)(e) of the 1992 Act – normally associated with 'self-employed' persons) contributions.
12. See the key definitions of 'employee' and 'worker' set out in the Trade Union and Labour Relations (Consolidation) Act 1992 and the Employment Rights Act 1996. By and large, until very recently there has not been an approach focusing upon any notion of an 'employment relationship' in the United Kingdom – although this now needs to be seen in the context of comments made by Their Lordships during the course of referring specific questions for consideration by the European Court of Justice in the Supreme Court case of *O'Brien v. Ministry of Justice*, [2010] UKSC 34. See further *infra*.
13. See the definitions of 'employee' (defined as 'an individual who works under a contract of employment') and 'self-employed person' (defined as 'an individual who works for gain or reward otherwise than under a contract of employment, whether or not he himself employs others'), in s. 53 of the Health and Safety at Work Act 1974. Section 51 of the 1974 Act also provides that 'Nothing in this Part shall apply in relation to a person by reason only that he employs another, or is himself employed, as a domestic servant in a private household'.

Before considering some of the detail relating to the 'classification exercises' which have come to dominate modern employment law practice, a few words will be said about the purposes of undertaking such classification exercises in relation to arrangements in the modern United Kingdom world of work.

3. THE INCREASING SIGNIFICANCE OF 'CLASSIFICATION'

The shift to a predominance of statutory normative provisions in the regulation of United Kingdom workplace relationships has already been identified as perhaps the most significant development in the past quarter of a century.[14] Accompanying that shift in regulatory method, there has also been witnessed a veritable explosion of statutorily-based individual employment rights being introduced with remarkable regularity.[15] These individual employment rights – adjudicated, for the most part, by a judicial dispute resolution system through the Employment Tribunals[16] – currently give rise to something in excess of 200,000 claims per year, of which the majority relate to complaints of 'unfair dismissal' or alleged non-payment of wages due.[17] Where such rights and protections are introduced, there has been a phenomenon whereby certain of the benefits are enjoyed generally by individuals satisfying a broad definition of 'workers', while other benefits are only enjoyed by a more limited group of persons who satisfy a statutory definition of 'employees'. While a broad pattern for the choice of whether a particular right is to be enjoyed by 'workers' or 'employees' can arguably be identified in certain circumstances,[18] there appears to be no formal policy behind the allocation process. Indeed, the whole approach to drawing such a distinction has been the subject of a discussion document issued by the United Kingdom government in 2002.[19] The consequence of this development has been that the issue of 'who is covered within the scope of

14. European Commission, *The Evolution of Labour Law (1992–2003)* (Luxembourg, 2005).
15. Indeed, so concerned have the authorities been at the profusion of new rights and regulations, and the associated problems for (in particular) employers, that a process now exists whereby changes to employment legislation are introduced on two fixed dates each year – 6 April and 1 October. See the report of the Better Regulation Task Force (2002), which was then followed by a consultation document produced by the United Kingdom government: *Better Regulation: Consultation on Commencement Dates for Employment Regulation* (URN 02/286).
16. The Employment Tribunals – first established as 'Industrial Tribunals' by the Industrial Training Act 1964 – are currently established and regulated under provisions contained in the Employment Tribunals Act 1996.
17. The number of claims presented to the Employment Tribunals was 189,300 in 2007–2008, 151,000 in 2008–2009, and 236,100 in 2009–2010. See *Annual Statistics for the Tribunals Service, 2009–10* (Tribunals Service, London, June 2010).
18. In particular, note may be taken of the broad scope of coverage granted by the legislator when the rights in question have their origins in provisions introduced at the level of the European Union.
19. See Department of Trade and Industry, *Discussion Document on Employment Status in Relation to Statutory Employment Rights* (URN 02/1058) (HMSO, London, July 2002).

protection of United Kingdom labour law?' features every day that courts and tribunals are dealing with employment protection rights, with an inevitable focus upon the underlying definitions and identification of those falling within the protective net. This pragmatic need to clarify and provide some measure of certainty to the notion of the protected species under modern United Kingdom labour law stands as the most urgent requirement when considering the issue for the purposes of this presentation.[20]

Before turning to the current analytical approaches to resolving this issue, however, a few words need to be said about where the United Kingdom situation differs from other legal systems (particularly within the Civil Law tradition to be found across so much of Continental Europe), and where certain assumptions or common frames of reference may play a less significant role when considering the position in the context of modern United Kingdom labour market regulation.

An initial 'parochial' point for Common Law commentators is that the United Kingdom does not historically utilise the distinction, known to many North American commentators, between 'Labour law' and 'Employment Law' to denote, respectively, collective regulatory arrangements and individual regulation for working relationships. Instead, the use of 'Labour Law' and 'Employment Law' has been broadly interchangeable in the literature, something which can also be seen reflected in the titles of courses and syllabus content at university degree level in this field. On the other hand, there is a very clear division between approaches to 'individual labour law rights' and 'collective labour law' – not least in the reality that the former tend to be dealt with by a specialised system of 'Employment Tribunals', whereas most collective matters are either left to be dealt with through the residual contract and tort jurisdictions of the Supreme Court of Judicature (for these purposes, meaning that cases will commence before, in the main, the High Court, rather than before the system of tribunals) or are regulated through legislative arrangements which seek consciously to segregate matters of 'individual rights' and issues of 'collective industrial relations' significance.[21]

Mention of the relevant forum for the resolution of disputes in the area of United Kingdom labour law further requires mention of the position whereby there has not been a historical division of 'causes of action' along divisions such as 'Commercial Code' treatment (e.g., commercial travellers in certain

20. A United Kingdom government consultative document included a useful overview (in tabular form) of the individual employment rights which were, at the time of its writing, enjoyed by respectively 'employees' and 'workers', see *Discussion Document on Employment Status in Relation to Statutory Employment Rights* (London: HMSO, 2002), 15–16.
21. A division which presents particular problems in the context of individual employment protections being applied against a background of collective industrial action. See, for example, the efforts of the legislator in relation to Sch. 1, para. 8(2) of the Trade Union and Labour Relations Act 1974 – subsequently consolidated and modified until reaching its current formulation as s. 238 of the Trade Union and Labour Relations (Consolidation) Act 1992. For a more contemporaneous commentary on this provision, see the wonderfully provocative annotations to s. 62 of the Employment Protection (Consolidation) Act 1978, penned by the late Brian Bercusson, for *Current Law Statutes Annotated 1978* (Volume 2, London, 1978).

countries).[22] While older litigation relating to the world of employment tended to find matters being brought before Magistrates within the general penal arrangements, the modern position is that issues arising out of relationships at work are broadly categorised as 'civil matters'. A consequence of this modern situation is that questions of jurisdiction play a significant role in the context of working persons seeking to enforce their alleged rights before judicial instances, given that the Employment Tribunals are 'creatures of statute', endowed only with the scope of jurisdiction which has been granted upon them by the legislator through legislative fiat.[23]

When it comes to the express exclusion of particular groups from the scope of labour law, it may be noted that – notwithstanding historical divisions between Crown Servants and others, with associated 'public law' connotations – there is no equivalent under modern United Kingdom arrangements relating to any group akin to the German *Beamte*.[24] Here, a modern trend towards a common scope of protection has been evident in the last half century – including exercise of statutory powers to promote this unitary approach, as well as specific concession of jurisdiction to the normal Employment Tribunals in cases relating to the working conditions of what are now described as Crown servants.[25] In consequence, the

22. See, by way of example, the situations addressed in the *Thematic Report 2009: Characteristics of the Employment Relationship*, produced by the group known as the European Labour Law Network (Leiden, 2009), s. 5.6.
23. Issues relating to 'time limits' are particularly common in litigation before the Employment Tribunals, while other areas of problem relate to State immunity, service qualification periods, and territorial jurisdiction matters.
24. Note the separate treatment afforded to such groups – often those falling within the category described by Johannes Schregle (in his contribution 'Labour Relations in the Public Sector', *International Labour Review* 113 (1974), 381) as 'employees engaged, primarily as officials or civil servants, in central, regional or local government administration, including Municipalities' – discussed in Alan C. Neal, 'Public Sector Industrial Relations – Some Developing Trends', *The International Journal of Comparative Labour Law and Industrial Relations* 17 (2001), 233, see especially at 242.
25. See the powers contained in s. 191 of the Employment Rights Act 1996. For those purposes, the expression 'Crown employment' means 'employment under or for the purposes of a government department or any officer or body exercising on behalf of the Crown functions conferred by a statutory provision'.

    It may also be noted that The Employment Act 1988 introduced, in what was s. 30, provisions to the effect that, where a person holding office under the Crown on terms which do not constitute a contract of employment between that person and the crown, those terms were to be deemed to constitute a contract for the purposes of the law relating to the economic torts, in respect of inducement to breach of contract or interference with a contract or intimidation to effect the same. The intention behind this section was to bring industrial action by civil servants within the framework of the balloting requirements of the 1984 Trade Union Act. If civil servants did not have contracts of employment there could be no liability in tort for their breach and the relevant unions would have no incentive to hold a ballot on proposed industrial action. This special provision is now contained in s. 235 of the Trade Union and Labour Relations (Consolidation) Act 1992, which operates to modify the 'standard' definition of 'contract of employment', by virtue of s. 295(2) of the Trade Union and Labour Relations (Consolidation) Act 1992.

old approaches to what have traditionally been classified as Office-holders, subject to 'public law' analysis and treatment, are arguably of diminishing significance – although there remain questions in this regard pertaining to groups such as judicial office-holders.[26]

In practical terms, however, the key phenomenon for modern purposes has been the 'watershed' of the legislative intervention undertaken through the 1971 Industrial Relations Act, which provided the launch-pad for modern definitions and analytical classifications of individuals undertaking work in the modern United Kingdom labour market. This has resulted in the most significant context for approaching analysis of 'employment status' being in relation to the issue of whether a particular person is or is not within the protective scope of modern individual employment rights, such as the right not to suffer 'unfair dismissal',[27] the right not to be subjected to discrimination at the workplace,[28] or the right to time off work for designated purposes.[29] This leaves untouched the approach to classification of the same persons for other purposes – such as in relation to their

---

The statutory approach to 'Crown employment' – extending employment protection rights beyond the traditional narrow scope recognised by the Common Law – is also to be found (subject to limitations) in relation to the Armed Forces (see s. 192 of the Employment Rights Act 1996).

26. See, for example, the matters raised by S. Deakin, *Interpreting Employment Contracts: Judges, Employers, Workers*, ESRC Centre for Business Research, University of Cambridge, Working Paper No. 267 (June 2003).
27. By reference to the basic protection in this regard, contained in s. 94 of the Employment Rights Act 1996.
28. Originally, under a broad range of protective legislation which for many years has gone beyond the limited 'six grounds' commonly noted as the scope for EU protective measures. See, in particular, the Sex Discrimination (Gender Reassignment) Regulations 1999, enacted in the wake of the decision of the European Court of Justice in Case C-13/94, *P v. S and Cornwall County Council*. The whole framework for protection against discrimination at work has been subjected to re-casting, within the provisions of the Equality Act 2010, which begins to come into force from October 2010 onwards. Under the new provisions, protection is given in relation to what are designated as being 'protected characteristics' – extending to age, disability, gender reassignment, marriage and civil partnership, pregnancy and maternity, race, religion or belief, sex and sexual orientation.
29. For example, in relation to trade union duties (see ss 168–170 of the Trade Union and Labour Relations (Consolidation) Act 1992), for the discharge of duties as a health and safety workplace representative (as provided for in the Safety Representatives and Safety Committees Regulations 1977 and the Health and Safety (Consultation with Employees) Regulations 1996), to receive ante-natal care (see s. 55 of the Employment Rights Act 1996), for other reasons relating to pregnancy, in respect of parental leave, or adoption leave (following reforms introduced by the Work and Families Act 2006), or to seek employment in the context of 'redundancy' (the United Kingdom expression used in respect of a termination of employment on economic grounds) (see s. 52 of the Employment Rights Act 1996). Further provisions are to be found, for example, in relation to time off work to perform public duties (see s. 50 of the Employment Rights Act 1996), and, in certain circumstances, for the purposes of study or training (see s. 63D of the Employment Rights Act 1996, and, for 'union learning representatives', s. 43 of the Employment Act 2002), while there is also protection against dismissal or detriment on account of taking time off to perform jury service (see ss 43M and 98B of the Employment Rights Act 1996).

treatment by the authorities responsible for taxation or for national insurance contributions, or as regards their enjoyment of protection in relation to their health, safety and hygiene at work.[30] Against that background, there can also be seen some development in the direction of introducing 'new categories' of protected persons[31] for specific purposes in limited circumstances – as, for example, with 'agency workers'[32] or with 'home workers'.[33]

This basic issue in Labour Law has relatively recently – as has already been noted – been the subject of government consultation against the background of a DTI document issued in July 2002.[34] The matters arising in this area are of huge significance for both United Kingdom domestic Labour Law and in relation to the application of EU social policy rights at work. Indeed, although no direct legislative activity followed the DTI consultation, debate over 'employment status' continues to dominate both academic and policy concerns, not least in the aftermath of the adoption by the International Labour Organisation of their 2006 Recommendation 198, concerning the employment relationship.[35] Indeed, most recently, the issue has regained particular judicial prominence with the reference, by the United Kingdom Supreme Court in the case of *O'Brien v. Ministry of Justice*,[36] of key questions for clarification before the European Court of Justice.

---

30. Leaving aside contractual and other distinctions between 'employment' and 'self-employment' (or other like terms). Note may also be taken of the move from use of the expression 'master and servant' to that of 'employment' – as, for example, reflected in the titles used in the Law Reports and in contemporary monographs and reports.
31. See, in particular, the power set out in s. 23(1) of the Employment Relations Act 1999, which provides that '(1) This section applies to any right conferred on an individual against an employer (however defined) under or by virtue of any of the following – (a) the Trade Union and Labour Relations (Consolidation) Act 1992; (b) the Employment Rights Act 1996; (c) this Act; (d) any instrument made under section 2(2) of the European Communities Act 1972. (2) The Secretary of State may by order make provision which has the effect of conferring any such right on individuals who are of a specified description. (3) The reference in subsection (2) to individuals includes a reference to individuals expressly excluded from exercising the right. (4) An order under this section may – (a) provide that individuals are to be treated as parties to workers' contracts or contracts of employment; (b) make provision as to who are to be regarded as the employers of individuals; (c) make provision which has the effect of modifying the operation of any right as conferred on individuals by the order; (d) include such consequential, incidental or supplementary provisions as the Secretary of State thinks fit.'
32. Initially, as a matter of domestic legislative initiative – see s. 34 of the National Minimum Wage Act 1998 and Regulation 36 of the Working Time Regulations 1998 (S.I. 1998 No. 1833) – and, more recently with a view to implementation of Directive 2008/104/EC of the European Parliament and of the Council of 19 Nov. 2008 on temporary agency work, as contained in the Agency Workers Regulations 2010 (S.I. 2010 No. 93), due to come into force from 1 Oct. 2011.
33. See s. 35 of the National Minimum Wage Act 1998. The operation of the legislation on the minimum national wage has also given rise to reconsideration of the protective net as regards 'voluntary workers' in the United Kingdom (defined in s. 44 of the 1998 Act) – see DTI, *Consultation Document: National Minimum Wage and Voluntary Workers* (HMSO, London, June 2007).
34. See DTI, *Discussion Document on Employment Status in Relation to Statutory Employment Rights* (HMSO, London, 2002).
35. ILO, *Employment Relationship Recommendation, 2006* (R198), adopted on 15 Jun. 2006.
36. [2010] UKSC 34. See s. 5 *infra*.

How the challenges surrounding the issue have been addressed from a technical legal perspective is the subject of the following section.

4. THE FORMAL ANALYTICAL FRAMEWORK UNDER STATUTORY PROVISIONS

We begin by asking the basic question: Who is the recipient of labour law protection under modern United Kingdom arrangements? However, before attempting to answer this question, a warning should be sounded about the use of various terms in relation to the employment relationship. In particular, there has been a modern application by statute of very specific notions associated with particular terms. The most significant of these are the terms 'employee' and 'worker', which for the last four decades have reflected the legislative scope of modern United Kingdom employment protections at work.

The term 'employee' is defined in s.295(1) of the Trade Union and Labour Relations (Consolidation) Act 1992 and in section 230 of the Employment Rights Act 1996, such that 'employee' means an individual who has entered into or works under (or, where the employment has ceased, worked under) a contract of employment.

The 1996 Act, broadly speaking, deals with a range of individual employment protections (such as the right not to be unfairly dismissed, rights not to have unlawful deductions made from wages, or rights to 'redundancy pay' in the event of termination of employment for economic reasons), while the 1992 Act is generally concerned with collective labour law regulation (including arrangements for recognition of trade unions, collective bargaining and collective agreements, or the scope of liability in the event of industrial action).

The legislator's definition of 'employee' should be compared with the rather broader statutory definition of 'worker', which is set out in section 296(1) of the Trade Union and Labour Relations (Consolidation) Act 1992 in terms that:

> 'worker' (subject to the following provisions of this section) means an individual regarded in whichever (if any) of the following capacities is applicable to him, that is to say, as a person who works or normally works or seeks to work – (a) under a contract of employment, or (b) under any other contract (whether express or implied, and, if express, whether oral or in writing) whereby he undertakes to do or perform personally any work or services for another party to the contract who is not a professional client of his; or (c) in employment under or for the purposes of a government department (otherwise than as a member of the naval, military or air forces of the Crown) in so far as any such employment does not fall within paragraph (a) or (b) above

and should also be put alongside the definition included as section 230(3) of the Employment Rights Act 1996 (which is in the same terms).

Certain categories are given particular attention in the statutory arrangements, so that, for example, it may be noted that, as regards health service practitioners, section 279 of the Trade Union and Labour Relations (Consolidation) Act 1992 provides that:

> 'worker' includes an individual regarded in his capacity as one who works or normally works or seeks to work as a person providing general medical services, general dental services, general ophthalmic services or pharmaceutical services in accordance with arrangements made – (a) by a Family Health Services Authority under section 29, 35, 38 or 41 of the National Health Service Act 1977, or (b) by a Health Board under sections 19, 25, 26 or 27 of the National Health Service (Scotland) Act 1978.

a provision to be found repeated in section 43K of the Employment Rights Act 1996,[37] which also extends the statutory scope of the meaning of 'worker' to persons introduced or supplied by third parties, home workers, and work experience trainees.[38]

Having discovered the statutory definitional distinction between 'employees' and 'workers', however, serves little more than to constitute the 'starting line' for a remarkably convoluted marathon to flesh out each of those labels with some substance which might serve to assist employers, employed persons, and judges charged with determination of the formal 'employment status' of those active and providing their labour in the world of work. Thus, 'just for starters', the definition of 'employee' normally requires the person concerned to be working under what is described in the legislation as a 'contract of employment'. This term is itself defined in section 230(2) of the Employment Rights Act 1996 such that 'contract of employment' means a contract of service or apprenticeship, whether express or implied, and (if it is express) whether oral or in writing.

The relevant related definition contained in section 295(1) of the Trade Union and Labour Relations (Consolidation) Act 1992, however, merely provides that 'contract of employment' means a contract of service or of apprenticeship.

Apart from the case of apprenticeship, therefore, the requirement comes down to a need to be working under a 'contract of service'.[39] Yet, no further definition is given to assist with the task of identifying what is a 'contract of service'.

---

37. Inserted by the Public Interest Disclosure Act 1998.
38. Mention should also be made of an enabling provision contained in s. 41 of the National Minimum Wage Act 1998 (reflected in similar terms across a variety of statutes), which allows the Secretary of State (the relevant Minister) to make provision to apply that Act to individuals who are not otherwise 'workers'.
39. It should also be noted that, for certain 'special cases', the particular employment relationship is deemed by statute to constitute employment under a contract of employment. For one example of this device, see s. 134A of the Employment Rights Act 1996 – inserted by the Police (Health and Safety) Act 1997 – which treats the officers concerned as employed under contracts of employment for the purpose of conferring protection against unfair dismissal on certain grounds relating to health and safety. Elsewhere, specified situations are deemed to give rise to a relationship of 'worker' and 'employer' for statutory protective purposes, as can be seen, for example, in s. 42 of the Working Time Regulations 1998, in relation to 'non-employed trainees'.

In summary, therefore, as regards the 'basic state of play' for the 'employee' concept under the various modern United Kingdom employment law statutes, we find a good example – and it is one of many – where the legislator has made an assumption about the clarity of the law upon which the statutory definitions have been constructed. Thus, it has been assumed by the formulators of the statutory definitions that the development of case law and the statements of judges over the years have led to a situation where it is not necessary to define specifically what is meant by a 'contract of service'. Instead, it is assumed that reference to the relevant case law will resolve that problem, and thereby clarify the requirement which forms part of the statutory definition of 'contract of employment', and, in turn, the vital issue of who is an 'employee' under that statutory definition.[40] Whether that state of affairs is the result of a conscious decision on the part of the Parliamentary draftsman (the 'charitable' view), or (the 'unintended consequences' view) simply reflects sloppy draughtsmanship at the time of the introduction of the relevant modern terms,[41] has been the subject of differing opinions both amongst judges and academic commentators.[42] Given that the terms 'employee' and 'worker' had apparently – at least up until 1972 – been utilised

40. By way of example as to how it is assumed that the scope of the term 'employee' is taken to be virtually self-evident see *The Fixed-term Employees (Prevention of Less Favourable Treatment) Regulations 2002*, whose Part I defines pretty much every actor dealt with by the Regulations except for the 'employee'.

41. With the modern 'employee'/'worker' distinction to be found in s. 167 of the Industrial Relations Act 1971, then in s. 30(1) of the Trade Union and Labour Relations Act 1974, and thereafter in subsequent legislation.

For the earlier definition of 'employee' in modern United Kingdom legislation – without a 'worker' definition – see, *inter alia*, s. 8 of the Contracts of Employment Act 1963, s. 25(1) of the Redundancy Payments Act 1965, and s. 11(1) of the Contracts of Employment Act 1972.

On a longer historical perspective, it may also be mentioned that the phrase 'a contract personally to execute any work or labour', forming an important element of the 'worker' definition in s. 296(1)(b) of the Trade Union and Labour Relations (Consolidation) Act 1992, is to be found, for example, in s. 10 of the Employers and Workmen Act 1875.

42. In *Brook Street Bureau (UK) Ltd v. Dacas (UK) Ltd*, [2004] EWCA Civ 217, Mummery LJ opined (at para. 5 of his judgment) that 'There is no definition or further description of a "contract of service" in the legislation. The omission is deliberate. For better or for worse, Parliament decided to leave in the hands of the courts and tribunals the responsibility for defining the limits of a contract of service on a case by case approach. The general principles of the law of contract are applied and, in dealing with cases brought under the employment rights legislation, the courts take into account the object and scheme of the relevant statutory provisions. In that way the courts and tribunals decide who is within the category of employees, on whom it is intended to confer employment rights, such as the right not to be unfairly dismissed. The courts have to address general, as well as technical, questions: who is Parliament legislating for? If not for an individual in the position of the applicant, why not? What is meant by "a contract of service" in this context?'

However, no direct authority or evidence is provided for that view, and, as is illustrated *supra* n. 41, there is no clear evidence as to the rationale (if there was one) for the change from a situation in which the terms 'employee' and 'worker' were used interchangeably, to a situation where the distinction has become crucial to the scope of protection provided by United Kingdom labour law.

interchangeably,[43] the failure of the legislator, dealing in 1971 with a novel definitional distinction in primary legislation,[44] to furnish a complete self-contained definition for the new statutory 'employee' concept would appear more probably to be a consequence of incompletely thought-through drafting technique, with inappropriate reliance upon assumed assistance from accumulated judicial pronouncements within the English Common Law tradition.

Before turning to consider the problems to which that absence of adequate statutory definitions give rise, it should be noted that recent statutes have also introduced two particular new notions into this area of terminology – namely, persons referred to as 'agency workers' and others referred to as 'home workers'. To some extent, this reflects the need to recognise explicitly the presence in the labour market of various categories of 'atypical' workers.[45] Thus, section 34 of the National Minimum Wage Act 1998 and Regulation 36 of the Working Time Regulations 1998 both contain a definition of 'agency worker' in terms of an individual who:

> (a) is supplied by a person ('the agent') to do work for another ('the principal') under a contract or other arrangements made between the agent and principal; but (b) is not, as respects that work, a worker, because of the absence of a worker's contract between the individual and the agent or the principal; and (c) is not a party to a contract under which he undertakes to do the work for another party to the contract whose status is, by virtue of the contract, that of a client or customer of any profession or business undertaking carried on by the individual.

Meanwhile, section 35 of the National Minimum Wage Act 1998 contains a provision intended to bring 'home workers' within the scope of the statutory protections, and defines the protected category of worker in subsection (2) such that:

> (2) In this section 'home worker' means an individual who contracts with a person, for the purposes of that person's business, for the execution of work to be done in a place not under the control or management of that person.

43. See this author's United Kingdom report, forming part of European Commission, *The Evolution of Labour Law (1992–2003), Volume 2, National Reports* (Luxembourg 2005), at Part 9, 505. As pointed out there, 'It may be noted that this 2-category distinction is of relatively recent origin. Indeed, as recently as in the second edition of Wedderburn's *The Worker and the Law* (1971) one can find the terms "employee" and "worker" being used almost interchangeably'. A particularly vivid example of this terminological interchangability can be found in the speech of the then Minister of Labour (Mr John Hare) when introducing the Contracts of Employment Bill into Parliament in 1963, reported at *Hansard*, HC Deb, 14 Feb. 1963, vol. 671, cc 1503-618 – where the expressions appear (with no apparent distinguishing quality as between them) not only in the same paragraph but even in the same sentence.
44. Eventually to be set out in s. 167 of the Industrial Relations Act of that year.
45. See, for an early consideration of the problem of what is 'atypical' in the modern context of globalised labour markets, Alan C. Neal, 'Atypical Workforms and European Labour Law', *Recht der Arbeit* 45 (1992) 115.

In this context, by way of illustration as to how modern legislative draughtsmanship has begun to take a more particularised approach to the actors in the modern world of work, it may be observed that the National Minimum Wage Act 1998 also deals with the notion of what are described as 'superior employers', by establishing a particular definition in section 48 to the effect that:

> Where – (a) the immediate employer of a worker is himself in the employment of some other person, and (b) the worker is employed on the premises of that other person, that other person shall be deemed for the purposes of this Act to be the employer of the worker jointly with the immediate employer.

In the absence of adequate guidance from the 'employee'-linked statutory provisions themselves, therefore, it is necessary to turn to the relevant case law on this matter. Unfortunately, however, it quickly emerges that the situation is far from clear, since there have been developed a wide variety of approaches (along with a variety of so-called 'tests') to determine who works under a 'contract of service' – the exact content of each of which depends upon the context in which and the purpose for which that question is being posed.[46] No clear answer emerges in response to the question 'Am I an employee?' – with the situation effectively only becoming evident in hindsight, once a judge or other authority has pronounced on the issue, and when the consequences of the *ex post facto* classification are already established by reference to that classification.

This poses particular problems for judicial decision-makers – normally, in the United Kingdom, Employment Judges sitting in the specialised system of Employment Tribunals, or other civil judges (County Court or High Court judges, together with judges sitting at appellate levels) exercising general jurisdictional powers. Nevertheless, an important modern consideration of the judicial approach which should be adopted to identifying 'who is an employee?' in proceedings at first instance was provided by the House of Lords in 2000 – albeit that a related focus of the relevant observations was directed towards whether a finding of 'employee status' should be regarded as a finding of law or a finding of fact.[47]

---

46. The position appears to be variable (and inconsistently so) depending upon whether the purpose of the exercise is, *inter alia*, to determine liability to tax as an 'employee or office holder', to determine the appropriate rate of national insurance contributions which should be made by the individual, to identify whether the individual can be brought within the scope of employment protections as a matter of labour law, to establish whether the individual enjoys protection in relation to their health, safety and hygiene at work, or whether there is protection against unlawful discrimination by reference to a group of 'prohibited grounds'.
47. See *per* Lord Hoffman, in *Carmichael and Another v. National Power Plc.*, [2000] I.R.L.R. 43. The approach set out in the Opinion of His Lordship reflected the refinement of a presentation which had earlier been given by Lord Hoffman to an annual congress of the Council of Industrial Tribunal Chairmen, held in Cambridge.

    The issue of whether such a finding is one of 'law' or 'fact' is particularly significant in the context of United Kingdom statutory employment protection rights, since appeals from Employment Tribunals (to the Employment Appeal Tribunal, and thence, potentially, to the Court of Appeal (Civil Division) and thereafter to the United Kingdom Supreme Court) are only

The following offers a broad indication of the way in which the case law on the meaning of 'employee' has developed.

The characterisation of the contract of employment has, by and large, been approached in terms of the attempt to divide workers into those who work under (1) 'contracts of service', and (2) 'contracts for services'. In taking this approach, the courts have adopted a variety of 'tests'. Amongst these are numbered (a) the 'control' test;[48] (b) the 'organisational' or 'integration' test;[49] (c) the 'multiple' test;[50] (d) the

---

possible if it is alleged that there has been an 'error of law' on the part of the first instance tribunal. See s. 21 of the Employment Tribunals Act 1996.

Note that the House of Lords (the final appeal instance in the United Kingdom legal system) has recently had its final appellate duties taken on by the United Kingdom Supreme Court, which commenced its activities on 1 Oct. 2009.

48. Amongst the earliest approaches, the strongly 'subservient' nature of the service relationship tended to be emphasised: particularly through looking at the element of 'control' exercised by the employer (the 'Master'). Thus, in the case of *Yewens v. Noakes*, (1880) 6 Q.B.D. 530, Bramwell LJ stated that 'A servant is a person subject to the command of his master as to the manner in which he shall do his work.'

    As has been forcefully pointed out by Simon Deakin, this oft-cited authority was actually not concerned with 'the modern distinction between employment and self-employment for which it is still, even today, being cited. Rather, it was concerned with a completely different status-based divide, that between "servants" and labourers in manual employment, on the one hand, and those employed in higher-level occupations and managerial and clerical work, on the other'. See *Evolution for Our Time: A Theory of Legal Memetics*, ESRC Centre for Business Research, University of Cambridge, Working Paper No. 242 (September 2002), at 11–12.

49. Something of a shift away from the individualised 'control' test (depending substantially upon a consideration limited to the 'master/servant' relationship of the employer and the worker), to something which reflected more the nature of work within organisations, can be seen during the 1950s and 1960s. Thus, for example, in the Court of Appeal case of *Stevenson, Jordan and Harrison Ltd v. MacDonald and Evans*, [1952] 1 T.L.R. 101, Denning LJ suggested that 'One feature which seems to run through the instances is that, under a contract of service, a man is employed as part of a business, and his work done as an integral part of the business; whereas, under a contract for services, his work, although done for the business, is not integrated into it but is only accessory to it.'

50. The so-called 'organisational' test, although applied in a small number of cases, caused MacKenna J, in the case of *Ready Mixed Concrete (South East) Ltd v. Minister of Pensions and National Insurance*, [1968] 2 Q.B. 497, to say that: 'This raises more questions than I know how to answer. What is meant by being "part and parcel of an organisation"? Are all persons who answer this description servants? If only some are servants, what distinguishes them from the others if it is not their submission to orders?' Having made clear his unease, MacKenna J then went on, in the same case, to make a number of statements which are generally regarded as developing the 'organisational' test into a 'multiple' test, such that 'A contract of service exists if these three conditions are fulfilled. (i) The servant agrees that, in consideration of a wage or other remuneration, he will provide his own work and skill in the performance of some service for his master. (ii) He agrees, expressly or impliedly, that in the performance of that service he will be subject to the other's control in a sufficient degree to make that other master. (iii) The other provisions of the contract are consistent with its being a contract of service.' He continued: 'As to (ii) Control includes the power of deciding the thing to be done, the way in which it shall be done, the means to be employed in doing it, the time when and the place where it shall be done. All these aspects of control must be considered in deciding whether the right exists in a sufficient degree to make one party the master and the other his servant. The right need not be unrestricted.' Later, he went on: 'An obligation to do work subject to the other

'business on one's own account' test;[51] and (e) what is sometimes described (somewhat tongue in cheek) as the 'you know one when you see one' test.[52,53]

From the most recent case law developments, it may be suggested that the influence of these 'classical tests' remains significant – although there must be some scepticism as to how 'useful' they have proved to be from a practical judicial or legal advisory viewpoint. However that may be, it is also suggested that a pair of 'key' issues now play a particularly important role for anybody seeking to determine whether a particular context for the performance of work gives rise to a 'contract of service', such as to give rise to statutory 'employee' status. Those 'key features' involve an evaluation of 'control' – much along the lines developed since *Yewens v. Noakes*[54] – and what has been expressed as being a necessary 'irreducible minimum of mutuality of obligation'.[55]

---

party's control is a necessary, though not always a sufficient, condition of a contract of service. If the provisions of the contract as a whole are inconsistent with its being a contract of service, it will be some other kind of contract, and the person doing the work will not be a servant. The judge's task is to classify the contract (a task like that of distinguishing a contract of sale from one of work and labour). He may, in performing it, take into account other matters besides control.'

51. The approach laid down in *Ready Mixed Concrete* was applied by Cooke J in the case of *Market Investigations Ltd v. Minister of Social Security*, [1969] 2 Q.B. 173, a case which is noteworthy for a statement, which was approved by Stephenson LJ in the Court of Appeal case of *Young* and *Woods Ltd v. West*, [1980] I.R.L.R. 201, to the effect that 'the fundamental test to be applied is this: "Is the person who has engaged himself to perform the services performing them as a person in business on his own account?" If the answer is "yes" then the contract is a contract for services. If the answer is "no" then the contract is a contract of service.' This test of 'in business on his own account' has been widely applied. In the case of *O'Kelly v. Trusthouse Forte plc*, [1983] I.C.R. 728, there is a comprehensive run-through of many of the authorities on the issue. Furthermore, Ackner LJ is anxious to stress that 'the question is a question of law on which we must make up our own minds on the basis of the facts found by the Industrial Tribunal whether the relationship between the parties is or is not a contract of employment.'
52. In a number of the cases in which the issue 'contract of service' or 'contract for services' is addressed, there seems to be a rather less than methodical approach by the courts. The decisions considered in *O'Kelly v. Trusthouse Forte* offer several examples where this appears to be the case. Whether, though, these amount to an abandonment, in practice, of reliance upon 'tests' is open to question. – However, on occasion, the characterisation does look very much like Lord Denning's much-loved elephant: 'very difficult to define, but you know one when you *see* one', see (for example) [1983] 2 Lloyd's Rep. 453 !! – The practical question which has to be addressed in all of these cases, however, is how meaningful, or workable, are tests of this kind?
53. A practical example of the courts wrestling with this problem of 'tests' can be seen in the Privy Council case of *Lee v. Chung* and *Shun Shing Construction* and *Engineering Co. Ltd*, [1990] I.R.L.R. 236, where emphasis was placed upon the approach of 'weighing up' a spectrum of (contrasting and conflicting) 'factors'. However, the House of Lords, in the case of *Carmichael v. National Power Plc., supra* n. 47, eventually provided a more up-to-date view as to how this issue should be approached. This important case is also significant, in particular, for the indications provided by Lord Irvine and Lord Hoffmann as to how the terms of the contract (where found) are to be determined.
54. See *supra* n. 48.
55. A requisite feature emphasised sharply in *Carmichael and Another v. National Power Plc., supra* n. 47.

The emphasis upon 'mutuality of obligation', underlining (unsurprisingly) the centrality of traditional 'contract' analysis techniques, has given rise in the last three decades to continuing examples of what might be considered as being 'limited horizons' in terms of judicial application (or, more normally, non-application) of particular statutory employment rights.

Thus, for example, an important issue going to the 'personal' nature of the 'classical' contract of employment was raised by a Court of Appeal case in 1999,[56] where a provision for substitutability of the personal performance was held to deprive the relationship of its qualifying 'employee' status.[57] Following on from that decision, the Court of Appeal has also expressed concern about attempts by employers to draft contracts which contain terms inconsistent with the other party being an 'employee'.[58]

By the same token, developing case law in relation to so-called 'triangular relationships' (especially involving situations where a person is provided through an employment agency to perform work for an 'end-user') has also served to illustrate many of the problems which follow from the application of 'classical'

---

56. *Express and Echo Ltd v. Tanton*, [1999] I.C.R. 693.
57. The *Tanton* case was, however, distinguished by the Scottish EAT in *MacFarland v. Glasgow City Council*, [2001] I.R.L.R. 7, although the importance of 'personal service' was not disputed in that context.
58. See *Consistent Group v. Kalwak*, [2007] I.R.L.R. 560 (EAT) and [2008] I.R.L.R. 505 (CA), which has now been revisited in *Protectacoat Firthglow Ltd v. Szilagyi*, [2009] I.R.L.R. 365.

    In the course of her judgment in the *Protectacoat* case, Lady Justice Smith dealt with what she described as 'the principle or test for determining whether a written contract is a sham'. She observed that 'The question is always what the true legal relationship is between the parties. If there is a contractual document, that is ordinarily where the answer is to be found. But, if it is asserted by either party, or in some cases by a third party, that the document does not represent or describe the true relationship, the court or tribunal has to decide what the true relationship is.' She then pointed out that 'Tribunals will be well aware that contracts may be partly written and partly oral and that they can also be constituted or evidenced by conduct. While a document which can be shown to be a sham designed to deceive others will be wholly disregarded in deciding what is the true relationship between the parties, it is not only in such a case that its contents cease to be definitive. If the evidence establishes that the true relationship was, and was intended to be, different from what is described in the document, then it is that relationship and not the document or the document alone which defines the contract.' Finally, she stressed that 'In a case involving a written contract, the tribunal will ordinarily regard the documents as the starting point and will ask itself what legal rights and obligations the written agreement creates. But it may then have to ask whether the parties ever realistically intended or envisaged that its terms, particularly the essential terms, would be carried out as written. By the essential terms, I mean those terms which are central to the nature of the relationship, namely mutuality of obligation . . . and the obligation of personal performance of the work.'

    In particular, Lady Justice Smith expressed the view that 'I share the view expressed by Elias J in *Consistent* when he said: "The concern to which tribunals must be alive is that armies of lawyers will simply place substitution clauses or clauses denying any obligation to accept or provide work in employment contracts, as a matter of form, even where such terms do not begin to reflect the real relationship."'

approaches of contractual analysis to the individual employment relationship.[59] In particular, the Court of Appeal cases of *Dacas v. Brook Street Bureau (UK) Ltd*, in 2004,[60] and *James v. London Borough of Greenwich*, four years later,[61] illustrate vividly the conundrum facing even experienced judges in this respect. Thus, in *Dacas*, Mummery LJ, having drawn upon the evaluation of Mark Freedland that:[62]

> Our analysis of the current state of the law of personal employment contracts showed that there was a complex of serious functional problems with regard to employment arrangements or relations involving an end-user of services and an intermediary entity such as an employment agency having some kind of employing role between that end-user and the worker. The problems were firstly, that there is great resistance to the construction of triangular personal employment contracts, secondly, that there may be great difficulty in deciding whether the worker's bilateral personal employment contract is with the end-user or the intermediary, but thirdly and most fundamentally that the triangular nature of the arrangement may have the effect that the worker fails to qualify as having a contract of employment or even as having a personal work or employment contract of any kind.

expressed the view that:

> I approach the question posed by this kind of case on the basis that the outcome, which would accord with practical reality and common sense, would be that, if it is legally and factually permissible to do so, the applicant has a contract, which is not a contract of service, with the employment agency, and that the applicant works under an implied contract, which is a contract of service, with the end-user and is therefore an employee of the end-user with a right not to be unfairly dismissed;

and went on to find (for technical reasons relating to the way in which the appeal proceedings had been brought) in favour of the arguments put forward by the agency. In the course of his judgment, Mummery LJ noted 'a natural reluctance at this level of decision to add to the extent of the disagreement and to risk injecting yet more uncertainty and unpredictability into the contract of service question than already exists'. He then went on to offer a detailed consideration of existing authorities touching the problem – including reiteration of the need for an 'irreducible minimum of mutual obligation necessary for a contract of service',[63] and confirming the need to resist 'the temptation to conclude that an individual is an employee simply because he is not a self-employed person carrying on a business of his own'.[64]

59. See the important and fast-expanding body of reported cases which have emerged in this area over recent years, both at the level of the Employment Appeal Tribunal and at the level of the Court of Appeal.
60. [2004] EWCA Civ 217. See *supra*, n. 42.
61. [2008] I.R.L.R. 302.
62. See M. Freedland, *The Personal Contract of Employment*, 2nd edn (Oxford, 2003), at 55.
63. In line with the guidance given in *Carmichael and Another v. National Power Plc.*, *supra* n. 47.
64. As established by the earlier case of *Wickens v. Champion Employment*, [1984] ECR 365.

By the time he came to consider similar issues in *James*, however, Mummery LJ, having set out the challenge for the judiciary in this area in terms that:

(1) Of course, the correct legal question is not whether the claimant was 'an agency worker' (whether working for an employment agency or for an end-user under an employment agency agreement) but whether the claimant was employed by the respondent end-user under a contract of employment. The two types of contract – agency agreement and contract of employment – are not necessarily mutually exclusive. It is legally possible for a worker to have one kind of contract with an employment agency and another kind of contract with the end user to whom he renders services. This is an exercise in legal classification. It requires the fact-finding tribunal to examine and assess carefully all the relevant evidence placed before it by the parties in the particular case for the purpose of determining whether the claimant fits the description of an 'employee', as defined in the 1996 Act.
(2) In the absence of an express contract of employment, which may be written or oral, the ET is faced with the question whether it is necessary to imply a contract of employment between the claimant and the respondent. It is not always possible to predict with certainty how this question will be answered by the tribunal.
(3) The distinction between workers who are employees and those who are not is crucial for the determination of statutory rights, principally the right not to be unfairly dismissed. The legal problem confronting the tribunals and courts is to identify and apply to the facts of each case clear, comprehensible and correct criteria for determining who is an employee and who is not. This is the only way to achieve the consistency necessary for the fair administration of the law. It is, however, unrealistic to expect perfect predictability. The very nature of the judgment that has to be made allows for a degree of latitude without falling into legal error. Sometimes the tribunal has to reach a judgment on unsatisfactory and incomplete evidence of the facts relevant to the legal analysis of the relationships between the worker, the employment agency and the end-user of the worker's services.

found himself driven almost to the point of despair at the formal inability of the judiciary to achieve appropriate practical results through the legal analysis of the employment status of persons working within the increasing temporary agency work sector. Nevertheless, at the same time, his judgment reveals an encouraging appreciation on the part of the senior judiciary of some of the pragmatic issues facing the actors on the modern United Kingdom labour market stage:

(1) The courts and tribunals are fully aware of the current controversy about the absence of job protection for agency workers, who do not have an express or implied contract of employment. While this appeal and this judgment were pending, articles appeared in the newspapers under such

headlines as 'The slow death of the Real Job is pulling society apart', 'Agency Workers could get full-time rights' and 'Temps may get full work rights under EU Law.' A Private Members' Bill was introduced to reform the law. It was doomed to failure for lack of support from the Government and failed to get a reading. There is no current government proposal to introduce legislation giving agency workers similar rights to those enjoyed by employees. There are negotiations about the possible regulation of agency workers through the medium of an EC Directive to Member States on agency/temporary workers.

(2) The courts and tribunals are also well aware of the nature of the arguments for and against a change in the law, but it is not for them to express views about a change or to initiate change. This is a matter of controversial social and economic policy for debate in and decision by Parliament informed by discussions between the interested parties – the Department for Business and Enterprise, the TUC, the CBI and other employers' organisations and the European institutions and governments of Member States. The questions for discussion, negotiation and decision are not legal questions susceptible to adjudication or appropriate for comment by a court or tribunal. The questions are outside their province and competence.

(3) On the one hand, there are arguments for a flexible labour market in the interests of a competitive economy and of full employment. There is a real need to hire temporary workers from agencies at short notice for extra busy periods or special projects. If this is made less attractive or more costly, job losses may follow and more work may be added to the burden borne by long term employees.

(4) On the other hand, a significant move in the direction of the casualisation of labour and the growth of a two tier workforce, one tier enjoying significant statutory protection, the other tier in a legal no man's land being neither employed nor self-employed, vulnerable, but enjoying little or no protection, may create social injustice and a festering sense of grievance which would not be satisfactory in the interests of an efficient workforce, a competitive economy, a healthy society or anything else. There is, however, nothing to prevent wise employers from recognising that their long term interests may be better served by treating their entire workforce in a responsible and considerate way than by insisting on the strict letter of the law.

(5) Policy decisions have to be taken by others about what changes (if any) to make, what rights to confer on whom, what qualifying periods to set and so on. The increasing amounts of money, time and effort spent on litigating this issue in tribunals and on appeals might in some cases be invested more productively in making representations to and through bodies which can pursue the debate on policy or even reform the law.

While this phenomenon of 'triangular' working relationships forms part of an area in relation to which recent regulatory activity at the level of the EU is likely to have a significant impact,[65] it has to be recognised that the changes due to be made at the end of 2011 do not directly deal with the analytical problem raised by the Court of Appeal in relation to the treatment of 'triangular relationships'.

A variety of other groups, in relation to which there has been particular consideration, may also be mentioned here. Thus, the position of directors (under provisions of Company Law) has been considered in the Privy Council case of *Lee v. Lee's Air Farming Ltd* [1961] A.C. 12, where Lord Morris observed that:

> It is well established that the mere fact that someone is a director of a company is no impediment to his entering into a contract to serve the company.[66]

Meanwhile, recent guidance has been provided by the Court of Appeal, in relation to the context of a 'controlling shareholder',[67] while the special position of 'partners' has also been considered in the case of *Tunstall v. Condon*.[68]

Finally, mention has already been made of 'Office-holders', a status which places the individual in a separate (and very privileged) position as compared with workers under contracts of employment. In particular, so-called 'public law remedies' are available to the 'office holder', which are not normally considered to be available to other workers. However, major difficulties exist in determining where the limits of 'office' stop and the category of 'employment contract' takes over.[69]

65. In particular, on 19 Nov. 2008 the European Parliament and the Council of the European Union adopted Directive 2008/104/EC on temporary agency work. Art. 3 of that Directive (which has to be implemented by 6 Dec. 2011) contains important definitions for use in this context. The response of the United Kingdom legislator to the obligation to implement the Directive into domestic law has been to enact the Agency Workers Regulations 2010 (S.I. 2010 No. 93), containing core definitions (in Regulation 3) which are due to come into effect on 1 Oct. 2011.
66. For apparent limits to this principle, see *(1) Buchan and (2) Ivey v. Secretary of State for Employment*, [1997] I.R.L.R. 80 (EAT). However, this issue was revisited by the Court of Appeal in *Secretary of State for Trade and Industry v. Bottrill*, [1999] I.R.L.R. 327, where the earlier EAT approach in *Buchan* was not agreed with.
67. See *Secretary of State for Business, Enterprise and Regulatory Reform v. Neufeld*, [2009] I.R.L.R. 475.
68. [1980] I.C.R. 786, in which the EAT looked with favour upon the following proposition contained in C. Grunfeld, *The Law of Redundancy*, 1st edn (London, 1971): 'A partnership is dissolved if a partner dies or retires. But, contracts of employment of the partnership's employees do not automatically end with the technical dissolution of the partnership. Essentially, it is a question of the scope and meaning of the particular contract of employment.'
69. Furthermore, some controversy has been stirred by particular judicial pronouncements – as, for example, in the High Court case of *R. v. BBC*, ex parte *Lavelle*, [1982] I.R.L.R. 404. where Woolf J (as he was then) expressed the view that: '. . . the employment protection legislation has substantially changed the position at common law so far as dismissal is concerned. In appropriate circumstances the statute now provides that an industrial tribunal can order the re-instatement of an employee. It is true that the order cannot be specifically enforced. However, the existence of that power does indicate that even the ordinary contract of master and servant now has many of the attributes of an office, and the distinction which previously existed between pure cases of master and servant and cases where a person holds an office are no longer clear . . . '. The more general problem concerning the divide between 'public law' and 'private law' rights, and the appropriate procedures for dealing with these, is addressed in the House of Lords opinions in *Roy v. Kensington and Chelsea and Westminster Family Practitioner Committee*, [1992] I.R.L.R. 233.

5. TOWARDS A UK APPROACH TO 'THE EMPLOYMENT RELATIONSHIP'?

Having briefly surveyed the established approaches to identifying 'who is an employee' for the purposes of allocating employment protection rights and benefits, the superficial picture which emerges is of a traditional 'contractual analysis' framework, in which judges are called upon to 'flesh out' *lacunae* in the basic statutory definitions through the development of Common Law case law, but as regards which the judiciary entertains a marked reluctance to enter 'creatively' into fields which are properly to be considered as the area of political and legislative reform or adjustment.

This pessimistic view of the prospects for United Kingdom law in this area to respond sensitively or adequately to the rapidly changing pressures of 'the world of work' in a globalised economy may, however, be in the process of being addressed at the highest level of the judiciary. The impetus for this fresh consideration lies in the way in which certain employment rights have been established at the level of the EU, and the scope of application to be granted to those 'European' rights.

The basis for re-addressing the domestic United Kingdom paradigm within which employment protection is or is not extended to particular groups of persons performing work in the open labour market rests upon provisions to be found in a series of EU instruments, covering matters such as protective rights in the context of transfers of ownership of enterprises,[70] collective redundancy regulation,[71] as regards fixed-term or part-time employment,[72] and, most recently, the position of work performed through the arrangements operated by temporary work agencies.[73]

Generally speaking, those EU level instruments contain a provision spelling out the scope of application of the measure, and relating this to the range of beneficiaries in each Member State. This formulation has, over time, undergone change. Thus, whereas the English-language version of the 1975 Directive on collective redundancies spoke of 'workers', but without providing any particular definition of the term,[74] the 1977 Directive on transfers of undertakings concerned

70. Council Directive 77/187/EEC of 14 Feb. 1977 on the approximation of the laws of the Member States relating to the safeguarding of employees' rights in the event of transfers of undertakings, businesses or parts of businesses (as revised and amended).
71. Council Directive 75/129/EEC of 17 Feb. 1975 on the approximation of the laws of the Member States relating to collective redundancies (as subsequently amended).
72. Council Directive 97/81/EC of 15 Dec. 1997 concerning the Framework Agreement on part-time work concluded by UNICE, CEEP and the ETUC, together with Council Directive 1999/70/EC of 28 Jun. 1999 concerning the Framework Agreement on fixed-term work concluded by ETUC, UNICE and CEEP.
73. Directive 2008/104/EC of the European Parliament and of the Council of 19 Nov. 2008 on temporary agency work.
74. Council Directive 75/129/EEC of 17 Feb. 1975 on the approximation of the laws of the Member States relating to collective redundancies. It may be noted that the subsequent amending Directive 92/56/EEC makes mention in its Preamble of 'other forms of termination of *employment contracts* on the initiative of the employer' being equated to 'redundancies' – a situation maintained by the current version following enactment of Directive 98/59/EC.

itself with 'employees', but, again, without providing any particular definition for that term.[75] Meanwhile, the 1980 insolvency Directive provided in Article 2(2) that 'This Directive is without prejudice to national law as regards the definition of the terms "employee"'.[76] Thereafter, one finds the judicial pronouncements of the European Court of Justice beginning to have a role in this area, so that, by 1991, one finds provision that 'This Directive shall apply to every paid employee having a contract or employment relationship defined by the law in force in a Member State and/or governed by the law in force in a Member State',[77] and, by the time of the enactment of Directive 98/50/EC amending the arrangements concerning transfers of undertakings, this recognition finds express form in the Preamble to the Directive.[78] As the European-level legislative process then moved, following the Treaty of Maastricht in 1992, into an era of 'social partners' involvement,[79] the quality of draughtsmanship arguably lost some of its technical sharpness – not just in relation to the issue of defining the beneficiaries of particular rights enacted through this route. By way of example, the Framework Agreement on Parental Leave, given effect through a 1996 Directive,[80] stated that:

> This agreement applies to all workers, men and women, who have an employment contract or employment relationship as defined by the law, collective agreements or practices in force in each Member State,

75. Council Directive 77/187/EEC of 14 Feb. 1977 on the approximation of the laws of the Member States relating to the safeguarding of employees' rights in the event of transfers of undertakings, businesses or parts of businesses. However, by the time of the amending Directive 98/50/EC in 1998, the Preamble to the new Directive was speaking of the necessity 'to clarify the concept of "employee" in the light of the case law of the Court of Justice' – in consequence of which a new Art. 2(1)(d) provided that '"employee" shall mean any person who, in the Member State concerned, is protected as an employee under national employment law' – a formulation retained in the subsequent amending Directive 2001/23/EC. Interesting, too, Art. 2(2) of Directive 98/50/EC provided that 'This Directive shall be without prejudice to national law as regards the definition of contract of employment or employment relationship' – notions which then appear, in particular, in Art. 4(2).
76. Council Directive 80/987/EEC of 20 Oct. 1980 on the approximation of the laws of the Member States relating to the protection of employees in the event of the insolvency of their employer.
77. See Art. 1(1) of Council Directive 91/533/EEC of 14 Oct. 1991 on an employer's obligation to inform employees of the conditions applicable to the contract or employment relationship. That formulation is then utilised to constitute the definition of 'employee' by virtue of Art. 2(1) of the Directive.
78. See *supra* n. 75.
79. For consideration of some of the problems arising in this context, see Alan C. Neal, 'We Love You Social Dialogue – But Who Exactly Are You?', in Fondazione Giulio Pastore (ed.), *La contrattazione collettive europea: Profili giuridici ed economici* (FrancoAngeli, Milan, 2001), 113.
80. Council Directive 96/34/EC of 3 Jun. 1996 on the framework agreement on parental leave concluded by UNICE, CEEP and the ETUC. Note that this measure did not extend to the United Kingdom, by reason of that Member State's 'opt-out' from the social policy arrangements following the Treaty of Maastricht, but was eventually given coverage to that effect by way of Directive 97/75/EC.

while the 1997 Framework Agreement on Part-Time Work, given effect by Directive 97/81/EC,[81] similarly provided, in Clause 2(1), that:

> This agreement applies to part-time workers who have an employment contract or employment relationship as defined by the law, collective agreement or practice in force in each Member State.

The later 1999 Framework Agreement on Fixed-Term Work, given effect by Directive 1999/70/EC,[82] took broadly the same approach as the part-time work Directive, in providing, by way of its Clause 2(1), that:

> This agreement applies to fixed-term workers who have an employment contract or employment relationship as defined in law, collective agreements or practice in each Member State.

The relevance of these developments lies in the background to the most recent challenge to the established orthodoxy of the Common Law approach to identifying the recipients of employment protections in the modern United Kingdom labour market. In particular, the whole issue of whether it is now accepted in United Kingdom labour law that the 'employment relationship' has a special role to play in determining the scope of protections has been raised by a series of cases brought in relation to entitlement to judicial pensions,[83] by reference to the

---

81. Council Directive 97/81/EC of 15 Dec. 1997 concerning the Framework Agreement on part-time work concluded by UNICE, CEEP and the ETUC.
82. Council Directive 1999/70/EC of 28 Jun. 1999 concerning the Framework Agreement on fixed-term work concluded by ETUC, UNICE and CEEP.
83. The United Kingdom gave effect to Directive 97/81/EC (as extended by Directive 98/23/EC) and the Framework Agreement on Part-Time Work by enacting the Part-time Workers (Prevention of Less Favourable Treatment) Regulations 2000 (S.I. 2000 No. 1551) which came into force on 1 Jul. 2000. Regulation 1(2) contains definitions, including the familiar provisions that '*contract of employment*' means a contract of service or of apprenticeship, whether express or implied, and (if it is express) whether oral or in writing; '*worker*' means an individual who has entered into or works under or (except where a provision of these Regulations otherwise requires) where the employment has ceased, worked under – (a) a contract of employment; or (b) any other contract, whether express or implied and (if it is express) whether oral or in writing, whereby the individual undertakes to do or perform personally any work or services for another party to the contract whose status is not by virtue of the contract that of a client or customer of any profession or business undertaking carried on by the individual.' However, nowhere in those definitions was there any reference to *employment relationship*. However, by means of Regulation 17, the United Kingdom legislator disapplied the Regulations in relation to part-time judges, providing that: 'These Regulations do not apply to any individual in his capacity as the holder of a judicial office if he is remunerated on a daily fee-paid basis'. For comment on this approach, see this author's observations in EC, *The Evolution of Labour Law (1992-2003), Volume 2, National Reports* (Luxembourg 2005), at 506 (fn. 54), where, having pointed out that the description '*any individual in his capacity as the holder of a judicial office if he is remunerated on a daily fee-paid basis*' appeared to constitute a category never previously identified as subject to particular treatment in United Kingdom law, it was suggested that 'This naked move to "invent" a new class of non-protected member of the working citizenry raises interesting questions in the context both of the loose definitions provided in Clause 3 of the Framework Agreement on Part-Time Work whose transformation into

part-time work Directive 97/81/EC, of which the 'lead case' has been *O'Brien v. Ministry of Justice*, before the United Kingdom Supreme Court.[84]

The approach adopted by Their Lordships in the *O'Brien* case is important for a number of reasons, amongst which is the detailed consideration of case law emanating from the European Court of Justice in relation to the concept of 'the worker' for the purposes of domestic application of employment protections introduced at the level of the EU. Thus, in the course of referring questions to the Court of Justice for clarification, the Supreme Court addressed the established approach deriving from the case of *Lawrie-Blum v. Land Baden-Wurttenberg*,[85] and, in evaluating the current 'state of play' in relation to the EU concept of 'the worker', gave consideration to a wide range of related recent case law of the Court of Justice.[86]

The upshot of this litigation has been that the United Kingdom Supreme Court has concluded that it is necessary to refer the following questions to the European Court of Justice:

(1) Is it for national law to determine whether or not judges as a whole are 'workers who have an employment contract or employment relationship' within the meaning of clause 2.1 of the Framework Agreement, or is there a Community norm by which this matter must be determined?
(2) If judges as a whole are workers who have an employment contract or employment relationship within the meaning of clause 2.1 of the Framework Agreement, is it permissible for national law to discriminate (a) between full-time and part-time judges, or (b) between different kinds of part-time judges in the provision of pensions?

---

legislative form Directive 97/81/EC purports to deliver, and as regards the traditional formula used by the European Court of Justice to delimit the scope of protected workers under EU Law (identification "in accordance with national law, collective agreements or practice" in the Member State) – particularly when one bears in mind the concern of the ECJ in *Unger* C-75/63, that (speaking of the term "worker" in the context of former Articles 48–51), the relevant Community provisions would be *deprived of all effect and the above-mentioned objectives of the Treaty would be frustrated if the meaning of such a term could be unilaterally fixed and modified by national law*'.

84. *O'Brien v. Ministry of Justice*, [2010] UKSC 34.
85. Case C-66/85, *Lawrie-Blum v. Land Baden-Wurttenberg*, [1986] ECR 2121. 'That concept ["worker"] must be defined in accordance with objective criteria which distinguish the employment relationship by reference to the rights and duties of the persons concerned. The essential feature of an employment relationship, however, is that for a certain period of time a person performs services for and under the direction of another person in return for which he receives remuneration' (see at para. 17).
86. Including Case C-85/96, *Martínez Sala v. Freistaat Bayern*, [1998] ECR I-2691; Case C-256/01, *Allonby v. Accrington and Rossendale College*, [2004] ECR 1328; Case C-151/02, *Landeshauptstadt Kiel v. Jaeger*, [2004] ECR 1528; Case C-313/02, *Wippel v. Peek* and *Cloppenburg GmbH v. Co. KG*, [2005] ECR 1604; and Case C-307/05, *Del Cerro Alonso v. Osakidetza (Servicio Vasco de Salud)*, [2008] ECR 145; as well as observations in the context of Cases C-397–403/01, *Pfeiffer v. Deutsches Rotes Kreuz*, [2005] ECR 1307 and Case C-395/08, *Istituto Nazionale della Previdenza Sociale v. Bruno and Pettini* (unreported).

However, in coming to the view that those questions need to be referred to the Court of Justice, the United Kingdom Supreme Court made a number of observations which suggest that the terminology of the 'employment relationship', and, possibly, the modern approach to considering the scope of individual employment protections (at least, where these derive from the level of the EU – as is the case in a large number of instances) has been placed 'centre-stage' for social policy-makers and the judges who have been charged with the task of 'fleshing out' the content of what has been identified as less than adequate legislative drafting and detailed guidance on this important issue.[87]

While the launch-pad of *O'Brien* would appear to offer an opportunity for the kind of reconsideration and modernisation of the traditional United Kingdom approaches to evaluating personal relationships in the world of work which have regularly been suggested as being sorely needed, one ought, perhaps, not to invest too much hope for such a positive outcome. Indeed, as this author has suggested elsewhere:[88]

> Labour law in the United Kingdom currently stands ill equipped to respond effectively to the swiftly-changing phenomena emerging in a labour market which has changed out of all recognition in the course of a quarter of a century. Unrecognised as a 'discipline' in its own right, and without the institution of a true specialist 'Labour Court', it struggles to deliver the necessary sensitivity to the industrial relations subject matter with which it is so intimately involved. Notwithstanding a proven ability to assimilate the value systems inherent in the regulatory structure and mechanisms of the European Union, the foundations of labour law at the beginning of the 21st century remain

87. In particular, the Supreme Court expressed agreement with observations made earlier by Sir Robert Carswell LCJ, sitting in the Court of Appeal of Northern Ireland, in the case of *Perceval-Price v. Department of Economic Development*, [2000] I.R.L.R. 380, where it was stated that: 'All judges, at whatever level, share certain common characteristics. They all must enjoy independence of decision without direction from any source, which the respondents quite rightly defended as an essential part of their work. They all need some organisation of their sittings, whether it be prescribed by the President of the Industrial Tribunals or the Court Service, or more loosely arranged in collegiate fashion between the judges of a particular court. They are all expected to work during defined times and periods, whether they be rigidly laid down or managed by the judges themselves with a greater degree of flexibility. They are not free agents to work as and when they choose, as are self-employed persons. Their office accordingly partakes of some of the characteristics of employment . . .'.

    It is also noteworthy that, in drawing upon comments from the House of Lords case of *Percy v. Board of National Mission of the Church of Scotland*, [2005] UKHL 73, which was concerned with a claim for sex discrimination by a female associate minister of the Church of Scotland, the Supreme Court pointed out (at para. 24) that: 'In *Percy* the majority held that tenure of an office does not necessarily exclude employment, especially where there is a wide statutory definition of that term. Employment may extend beyond the traditional concept of a contract of service between "master and servant". The degree of control exercised over the employee is therefore less important, and in any case Ms Percy was, in that case, conducting her ministry under the control of a senior minister.'

88. European Commission, *The Evolution of Labour Law (1992–2003), Volume 2, National Reports* (Luxembourg 2005), at 520.

> constrained by traditional Common Law concepts – 'the employee', 'equality of bargaining power', the undesirability of restrictive covenants on grounds of 'public policy', inappropriately applied doctrines relating to 'duress' and to 'illegal contracts', and a whole host of other issues.

Of the 'constraining features' identified there, perhaps the problems surrounding the identification of 'the employee', and the associated issues touching the scope of application of modern statutory employment protections stand as those most urgently in need of re-evaluation in the light of modern labour market conditions.

6. SOME CONCLUDING COMMENTS

It emerges from this survey of the current United Kingdom approaches to relationships in the modern 'world of work' that the pressing challenge is less a problem of finding something which might be described as an 'employment relationship', but rather a problem of differentiating between various groups of persons performing work who are then labelled as either 'employees' or 'workers', and who experience different applicability of employment protection as a consequence.

Since the rapid shift, during the latter half of the twentieth century, to normative regulation of individual employment rights, this 'employee/worker' dichotomy has taken on particular significance, excluding those who do not achieve the status of 'employee' from key protections such as the right not to be 'unfairly dismissed', the right to a redundancy or an insolvency payment, or rights in relation to trade union membership and activities. Yet, there appears to be an absence of any clear overarching policy as to which category of person performing work should receive which 'label' and, thus, be blessed with the wider or the narrower range of employment protections. While there does seem to have been a practice of conferring rights which derive from the level of the EU upon the wider category of 'workers', any more general pattern of 'rights allocation' remains to be discerned inferentially, rather than by reference to a clear set of principles adopted for consistent use on a regular basis.

From a practical perspective – whether from the point of view of employers, persons seeking employment protections, or judges and others charged with the task of determining the appropriate label in particular circumstances – this lack of clarity in terms of either policy or identifiable principle is further hampered by the shortcomings of the available legal analytical tools in undertaking that task. So far as possible, the judicial approach has been to utilise the 'classical' tools of Common Law contractual analysis – and to do so with a remarkable degree of rigidity. Thus, the refusal to treat the relationship of work as any category of 'special contract', but, instead, to deal with this area in line with the principles applicable to 'contracts in general', has deprived the judges of the arguably much-needed flexibility to justify the proposition that:

> over the last 30 years or so, the nature of the contract of employment has been transformed. It has been recognised that a person's employment is usually one

> of the most important things in his or her life. It gives not only a livelihood but an occupation, an identity and a sense of self-esteem. The law has changed to recognize this social reality.[89]

Consequently, problems such as the applicability of the rules on duress, or the consequences of illegality in relation to any element in the relationship, can give rise to especially harsh consequences in terms of deprivation of employment protections when exercised in the context of the individual work relationship. So, too, can this be the consequence of strict adherence to traditional principles governing relationships of 'personal service', as has been seen in the Court of Appeal case of *Tanton*,[90] while only recently have senior judges expressed concern at the widespread practice of drafting terms which seek explicitly to circumvent established notions of the scope of employment protection by reference to 'employee status'.[91] Indeed, the remarkable analytical difficulty which has plagued the Common Law judges in relation to their approach to 'the triangular relationship' serves to highlight just how ill-equipped the United Kingdom is to deal with emerging developments in the shape and nature of working relationships in the twenty-first century.

Nor can such problems be said to reside 'merely at the margins' of Labour Law protection in the United Kingdom, for, where particular rights have been restricted only for the benefit of 'employees', a lack of adequate statutory definitional guidance has resulted in disputes over 'employee status' featuring as key issues in a significant proportion of the cases brought every year before the judicial dispute resolution forum of the Employment Tribunals.[92]

Such a pessimistic conclusion might lead the proponent of effective individual employment protections almost to lose the will to live in the United Kingdom regulatory and judicial environment. Yet, faint glimmers of hope can be discerned – albeit with little prospect of radical change for the foreseeable future. Thus, while the adoption by the ILO in 2006 of its Recommendation (R198) concerning the employment relationship, may not appear, at first glance, to impact substantially upon the world of the Common Law judge in the United Kingdom, it might just be that its timing, coupled with the questions arising in the EU context out of the Supreme Court's reference in *O'Brien v. Ministry of Justice*, could serve to concentrate the minds of those responsible for developing effective labour regulatory policies in this area to come up with something better than the unsatisfactory state of affairs which has prevailed since the 'watershed' which marked the shift towards a dominance for normative statutory provisions as the basis for ensuring 'workplace justice' over the past four decades. Meanwhile, however, while

89. See the Opinion of Lord Hoffmann in *Johnson v. Unisys Limited*, [2001] UKHL 13, at para. 35.
90. *Express and Echo Ltd v. Tanton, supra* n. 56.
91. As, for example, in *Protectacoat Firthglow Ltd v. Szilagyi, supra* n. 58.
92. A feature shared with many other jurisdictions, as evidenced by the ever-present concern with this fundamental issue at annual meetings of the European Association of Labour Court Judges (the most recent of which took place in Rome, in June 2010) or the ILO-organised meetings of European Labour Court Judges (which most recently took place in Jerusalem in October 2010).

possession of the requisite 'label' continues to constitute the key to the riches of effective employment protection in the United Kingdom, the convoluted game of 'hunt the employee' will continue to occupy the time of Employment Judges. At the same time, an uncomfortable juxtaposition of generally-applicable Common Law contractual principles, the special approach to personal services relationships, and judicial reticence to depart from traditional paradigms, will render even more elusive the grail of 'industrial justice' for any individual engaged in modern day employment – that social phenomenon which Lord Hoffmann has seen fit to describe as 'usually one of the most important things in his or her life'.

Chapter 11
Conclusions and Recommendations

Frans Pennings and Claire Bosse

1. GENERAL

The preceding chapters described how countries deal with the problem of disguised employment relationships and the problem of dependent work not covered by an employment contract. In addition the initiatives undertaken by the International Labour Organisation and European Union in these areas were studied. By doing so, the first two questions of our research project, outlined in Chapter 1, were addressed.

In this chapter we will discuss the third question raised in Chapter 1: which conclusions and recommendations follow from these findings?

For this purpose we will consider the proposals, mentioned in Chapter 2, which were made in the literature with the purpose to ensure the protection by labour law. In addition we will refer to Recommendation 198, the Employment Relationship Recommendation (discussed in Chapter 3). The proposals and the recommendation will serve as the framework for discussing both the developments in the various countries and our own recommendations.

We have reordered the proposals and recommendation in order to avoid overlapping discussions and realise a consistent set of proposals to be discussed. This leads to the following order:

(a) The proposal to redefine the subordination criterion.

Frans Pennings & Claire Bosse, *The Protection of Working Relationships*, pp. 173–196.
© 2011 Kluwer Law International BV, The Netherlands.

(b) The recommendations to uncover disguised employment relationships:
   (i) primacy of facts and reclassification of the contract are to be used for determination of the contract of employment;
   (ii) a broad range of means has to be used in order to identify contracts of employment;
   (iii) providing legal presumptions that there is a contract of employment;
   (iv) workers with certain characteristics, in the general or in a particular sector, must be deemed to be either employed or self-employed.

(c) Developing uniform criteria.

(d) The proposal to extend the coverage of labour law.

(e) The proposal to develop a hard core of social rights.

These elements will be discussed in section 2. At the end of that section we will draw conclusions on which approaches seem the most successful given the developments in the studied countries.

In Section 3 we will discuss the role of the international organisations. In this section we will also pay attention to the proposal, mentioned in Chapter 2, to develop an EU definition of employee.

In Section 4 the conclusions on the national and international developments will be drawn and our recommendations will be presented.

2. THE NATIONAL FINDINGS

2.1. Redefinition of the Subordination Criterion

2.1.1. The Contents of the Subordination Relationship

In Chapter 2 we mentioned Perulli's suggestion to redefine the notion of subordinate work by adding other criteria for subordination, in order to have that notion correspond with the changed socioeconomic context.

In the country chapters the authors paid considerable attention to the issue of subordination. They confirmed that the interpretation of the term *subordination* has undergone a major evolution through time. Initially, subordination meant that an employer actually or formally gives or can give detailed instructions to the employee. In the course of time, however, it was acknowledged that employers do not always have the expertise to give such instructions. Sometimes, it is also against the professional code, for example, in the case of medical doctors or researchers (the liberal professions, as they are called in the Belgian chapter) to receive specific instructions.

Gradually it became accepted that also persons with a large freedom in performing their work have a contract of employment. In respect of jobs which have always been performed under a contract of employment, it was acknowledged that supervision by the employer has received a much broader meaning.[1]

1. In Ch. 6 s. 2.2.2, this development is described for France and in Ch. 9 s. 4.1 for Germany.

Another reason why the term *subordination* nowadays does not always mean that employers give detailed instructions to their employees is that more and more work is done outside the workplace. Work has, in other words, become nomadic. This has made supervision often difficult.

These developments mean that a broad interpretation has been given to the term *subordination* in the labour laws of the studied countries. It is the task of the courts to interpret the subordination condition – (sharp) definitions of the employment contract or of subordination are missing and the statutes do not give further criteria. This means that no laws had or have to be changed in order to realise a broader interpretation of the subordination condition.

Thus, where the discussion on subordination concerns the question of the *nature* or *contents* of the instructions that are or can be given, for the large majority of jobs of persons working in dependency there are no principal limits to accept subordination.[2]

2.1.1.1. The Role of the Courts

There can be uncertainty, however, on how the courts will interpret a particular situation when the freedom to do a particular job and the possibility to be replaced are used as arguments by the work providers to deny that the contract is a contract of employment. Thus happens if persons perform work that is to a large extent comparable to that of employees, but when they have considerable freedom to do the job and there are other persons doing the same work who are undeniably self-employed. In such a situation the work provider could come into serious trouble if he is suddenly confronted with claims that persons are employees. An example can be found in the German chapter: teachers at general State schools are employees, whereas teachers at adult educational centres are considered to be self-employed persons. The author added that it is hard to explain this difference. In order not to have to accept a contract of employment it is argued that the owner of the school gives no additional instructions in 'completing' the contract. Such an arbitrary outcome reminds us of the arbitrary 'you know it is one when you see it' test, which was mentioned in the British Chapter.

Uncertainty in this case seems to be mainly due to reticence of the courts to reclassify a particular contract. We see this reticence in particular in the British Chapter. Is it the task of the legislature or of the courts to solve the problem? Traditionally labour law courts have seen a role for themselves, and they can probably find better answers in particular situations than the legislature can by making a general rule. However, the legislature should, if the courts are reticent, make clear – in line with Recommendation 198 – that the courts should indeed take an active role.

2. Cases where subordination is assumed as inconsistent with the job are the obvious ones, like judges, politicians, director/owner of firms. These positions are not problematic from the view of protection, as they are covered by special protective Acts.

In this respect in particular differences in legal positions for which there are no objective justifications may be fruitful to address in court. An example is a more recent decision mentioned in the German Chapter of teachers in vocational education; initially they were treated differently from State school teachers, but in the recent decision they were considered to be employees (see the German Chapter, section 4.2).

The German Chapter also refers to another source for development: if an alleged self-employed freelance journalist is doing an activity that is also performed by employees, he can ask to be considered as an employee, because it would infringe the general principle of equality to make such a distinction in status without any obvious justification. This equality approach can be an important instrument for approaching the issue of disguised employment relationships.

2.1.2. In Case of Absence of the Power to Give Instructions

Different from the situation in which it is difficult to define the contents of the power to give instructions, is the situation in which the work provider *does not have the power at all* to give instructions. It appeared that the subordination relation was not re-interpreted and could not redefined in order to include such situations as well. As a result, in particular in triangular situations, between the work provider and the worker there is no contract of employment; this is, for example, the case for temporary agency workers.[3]

Thus, if the principal cannot instruct the worker or if the worker has the formal freedom not do obey instructions, there is no subordination relationship with the principal and therefore no contract of employment.

Hence, in considering the proposal for redefining the subordination relation we have to distinguish between uncertainty about the contents of the subordination relation and the absence of a formal subordination relationship.

Making a new definition of the contents of the subordination relation is a very interesting topic for handbooks on the contract of employment, but does not appear to be the major solution to the problem of disguised employment relationships and unprotected workers. In the case of the disguised employment relationships the present criteria are adequate.

The problem rests with the position of workers in situations in which a formal subordination relationship is missing. The question is, however, whether redefinition of the subordination relationship can solve this problem. After all, if the principal cannot give instructions to the worker or if the worker has the freedom to do the work in a way that suits him best, it is very difficult to define this situation as one of subordination. Moreover, it is rather problematic to distinguish such a situation from other types of third party relationships or from work whose performance entails a large freedom (the 'genuine' self-employed). No private person who has hired a plumber for a particular job wants to be confronted with a claim

3. As we will see below, sometimes other ways are used to realise that temporary agency workers have a contract of employment.

that there is a contract of employment with this person. Nor do employers who make incidental use of external workers or consultancy workers want to get into such a position.

However, in the latter situation there may be an increasing scale of mutual dependency, if the number of work providers to this person is one or two, the duration and extent of the work is considerable and he has the obligation to do the work personally. It does not seem, however, that situations in which an employment relationship should be accepted or not, can be distinguished by a redefinition of the subordination relationship. Usually, other factors play a role here than the power to give instructions, for example, the duty to perform the work personally, the dependency on each other, the economic position of the parties and their intentions. We will pay attention to these aspects below. Here we can conclude that it is unlikely that a redefinition of the contract of employment can solve the problem of deficiencies in the scope of the employment relationship.

2.1.3. A Tightening of the Subordination Criterion

The country studies also make clear that in some cases there was a retreat from previous case law, where subordination was given less attention, in that the subordination relation was made a key element for determining a contract of employment.

An example is the French *Société Générale* case of 16 November 1996, in which the Court of Cassation decided that providing work in an organised service is merely an indication of subordination, but essential is that the employer unilaterally determines the conditions under which work is carried out.[4] The German chapter also showed a formal approach to the contract of employment: an employee has to perform his services in a work organisation whose structure has been determined by another person. Therefore, in case of on-call workers, not the degree of dependency of the worker, but the formal question whether he may at any time refuse to conclude a new contract is decisive.

The reason why courts have come to put more emphasis on the subordination criterion was not explicitly discussed in the country chapters. Most probably the courts realised that a too broad inclusion of working relationships into employment relationships may lead to situations where 'obvious' self-employed may be covered. Such a broad interpretation – that is, assuming an employment relationship where the principal does not have the power to give instructions – may lead to legal uncertainty.

2.1.4. Tailor-made Solutions

Instead of redefining the subordination relationship, the countries studied appear to make, in particular, use of 'tailor-made' solutions, by which they bring *certain* professions and/or *clearly specified situations* under a contract of employment.

4. Chapter 6, s. 2.2.2.

An example is the temporary agency worker, who is, in several countries, defined as an employee by an Act. Another instrument used is that of the statutory legal presumptions, which involve that a person is considered to have a contract of employment if certain criteria are fulfilled. If for this purpose refutable presumptions are used, the subordination condition as such is not waived, but the burden of proof that there is no subordination rests on the shoulders of the other party.

It is no longer the worker and/or the judge who have to prove or ascertain that there is a subordination relation. The reversal of proof can even mean that the other party rests his case and accepts that there is a contract of employment; he does not take the trouble to claim before the court that there is a subordination relationship.

If the legal presumption is irrefutable, the subordination condition is waived. This means a deviation from, though not a redefinition of, the subordination condition. We will come back to the legal presumptions in section 2.3.3.

We may conclude that the proposal to extend the notion of subordination will lead to more legal uncertainty and possibly lead to wrong effects. Nor is a redefinition of subordination necessary. Instead, in the countries under study other instruments are being used to extend the coverage of labour law, which will be discussed in more detail below.

2.2. Primacy of Facts and Reclassification of the Contract

2.2.1. Examples and Instruments for Reclassification

One of the recommendations of ILO Recommendation 198 is that the determination of the existence of an employment relationship should be guided primarily by the facts relating to the performance of work and the remuneration of the worker. Determination of the contract of employment must be done, notwithstanding how the relationship is characterised in any contrary arrangement, contractual or otherwise, that may have been agreed between the parties (Article 9 of the Recommendation).

Alain Supiot also recommends that the power of the courts to reclassify a civil law contract as an employment contract must be upheld.[5]

The primacy of the facts and reclassification of a civil law contract are closely connected.

This recommendation means that not the name of the contract is decisive, but the facts of the case. In the countries studied, courts indeed reclassify contracts, although with varying intensity, that is, varying between countries and through time.

If a person engaged under a contract which is not an employment contract proves that he is actually working for another person in a subordination relationship, that he has to do the work personally and the work is performed in return for

5. Chapter 2, s. 3.2.

wages, the judge can conclude that there is a contract of employment, even if it is called a civil law contract, unless the contractual party proves otherwise.

This practice of reclassification, 'lifting the veil', is important for the maintenance and sustainability of labour law. Workers may be forced to accept a non-employment contract because they are dependent on work and income. For this purpose it has traditionally been acknowledged that the intentions of the parties and the name of the contract are not decisive for qualifying the contract, since these data may not reflect the real situation.

We see examples of this approach in the country studies. For instance, the Polish Labour Code provides that all remunerated work carried out in Poland under the supervision of an employer should, regardless of the type of legal contract, be regarded as employment based on a contract of employment.[6] The Act also provides that if the execution of the labour relation provides enough elements that are incompatible with the qualification given by the parties, there will be a re-qualification of the labour relation and a corresponding social security system will be applied, without prejudice to the existing rules and regulations. Another example is the French law which provides that the courts are responsible for 'determining the precise classification of the disputed facts and actions, irrespective of the terminology used by the parties'. Irrespective of the will of the parties and the principle of freedom of contract, the decisive factors are the actual conditions under which the work is performed.[7] The Belgian Law provides that if the factual execution excludes the legal qualification chosen by the parties, the qualification which appears from the factual execution should prevail.[8]

The UK situation is to a considerable extent different from those described in the other chapters. On the one hand the common law approach, which leaves it to the judges to decide whether there is a contract of employment, also allows judges here to adjust their 'tests' for deciding whether there is such a contract to changing working relationships. On the other hand it can be seen that judges seem to be much more reticent than those on the European continent to interpret the law in such a way that those who are in a position similar to employed persons are treated in the same way. Judges consider a solution as the task of the legislature, but this party is not really active in realising objectives as such of Recommendation 198.

2.2.2. Limits to Reclassification as Appearing from the Country Studies

Some country studies show that recently some limits have been set to reclassification of contracts as contracts of employment. In Belgium, for instance, the Court ruled that if the parties have characterised their agreement as a contract for

6. In the past judges had some problems with this rule, as can be seen in a 1996 decision of the Polish Supreme Court. Currently, in Polish case law, it is an established presumption that if personal work is performed under supervision for wage there is a contract of employment.
7. Chapter 6, s. 2.2.1.
8. Chapter 5, s. 5.1.

services, the judge may not change that characterisation ex officio. The party who in such a case asserts that there is an employment contract must furnish proof that the contract of services contains elements incompatible with the existence of an independent collaboration relationship.[9] Thus, where earlier the judge had to examine whether or not there was authority or subordination (and thus an employment contract), now a more restricted approach is followed. As is mentioned in the Belgian Chapter, in the Belgian literature the question was raised whether this approach by the Court of Cassation conflicts with ILO Recommendation 198.

Also in the Dutch case law the Court set limits to reclassification of a contract. In the *Groen-Schoevers* judgment, the plaintiff initially claimed he was self-employed. Later he invoked labour law, when this suited him better. The Supreme Court ruled that the intention of the parties when they concluded the contract is decisive, including the way in which they elaborated the agreement. The intention can, however, be contradicted by the existence of a subordination relationship of such a form and extent that, despite the earlier findings of the case, it has to be concluded that there is a contract of employment. In this respect, the Court ruled, the social position of the worker is relevant. The Court found it insufficient that Mr Groen had to be present at fixed times and that he had to follow the guidelines of the training institute he worked for. After all, in case of a contract for services (a contract governed by civil law) the principal can give instructions as well.

Although the actual circumstances of Mr Groen were decisive, the relevance of the judgment is much wider: in later judgments the Supreme Court again referred to the criteria developed in this judgment.

We have to keep in mind, in assessing the *Groen-Schoevers* judgment, that Mr Groen presented himself as a self-employed person, had more than one principal and benefited from his position by having a higher net income (he was not subject to employee insurance contributions). Only when he needed labour law protection (against dismissal), he claimed to be an employee. Thus Mr Groen was far from a person who was forced by an employer into a disguised employment relationship. We can conclude that the Dutch court appeared to be reluctant to accept the opportunistic use of labour law. Instead, its criteria still allow classification in case the intention of the parties is not supported by the form of their relationship and/or parties are not in an equal position.

Another retreat from reclassification, this time initiated by the legislature, was the French Act which introduced a legal regime for managing agents, which was done in order to put an end to reclassifications of their contracts as employment contracts. The new provision introduced more protection for managing agents, but did not include labour law elements which were found inappropriate (i.e., in this case dismissal protection).

9. Chapter 5, s. 4.2.

2.2.3. Assessment of the Limits to Reclassification

At first sight, the retreat from reclassification and the statutory measures meant to reduce reclassification appear not to be in line with the ILO Recommendation. However, this conclusion seems to be too hastily drawn. After all, the facts of the case are still important for the classification of the contract. Thus reclassification of a civil law contract into a contract of employment is still possible.

The case law rather shows the problems which may arise if on the basis of the facts of the case it *always* has to be decided that there is a contract of employment. This is because the criteria for adopting such a contract are not that sharp. If all situations in which there is a certain form of subordination are considered as an employment relationship (i.e., a person works in an organisation and has to follow certain schedules), this does not always lead to a right outcome, since in that case also genuine self-employed situations may have to be treated as employment relationships.. This is not intended by the Recommendation, which focuses on the situation of persons who are really dependent on their employer.

In the Dutch and Belgian cases the intention of the parties is an important element and can even be called a starting point in the consideration of the case. The importance of the intentions can be overruled by the facts of the case, for which the Dutch court mentions several criteria. Relevant here is *inter alia* the position of the parties.

This approach takes into account the difference in positions of the parties and also the complications to which the borderline cases of self-employed and employed activities could give rise.

Thus, if the recommendation that the qualification of a contract is to be guided primarily by the facts relating to the performance of work and the remuneration of the worker, notwithstanding how the relationship is characterised, is interpreted as that the intentions of the parties must not play a role at all, this interpretation needs a refinement. The intentions of the parties may be relevant in so far as it can be ascertained that they are nor in an unequal position and the other facts of the case do not support the assumption that there is a contract of employment.

2.3. A Broad Range of Means Has to Be Used

The Recommendation further recommends that Members should consider the possibility of allowing a broad range of means for determining the existence of an employment relationship (Article 11). It is not exactly clear under which circumstances this recommendation is deemed satisfied.

It is interesting to read in Section 6 of the Belgian Chapter that the Council of State was quite critical in its comments on the draft of the Belgian Employment Relationship Act. This Act bases itself on the agreement between the parties for the characterisation of their legal relationship, which, in view of the Council, runs contrary to Article 9 of ILO Recommendation 198 that gives priority to the factual situation and strong emphasis is placed on the legal relationship of authority alone.

It argued that the Recommendation also allows other criteria, including economic dependency and the indicia criteria.

The Recommendation appears useful since it emphasises the need of different methods to determine whether there is a contract of employment.

Related to this topic is the need to inform the worker on the contents of his contract. Council Directive 91/533/EEC of 14 October 1991 is relevant to this purpose within the EU context, as it contains the obligation of the employer to inform *paid employees having a contract or employment relationship* (our italics) of certain specified elements.[10] For our purpose the title, grade, nature or category of the work for which the employee is employed, or a brief specification or description of the work may be relevant, as these data provides for information useful in disputes on the nature of the contract. If there is no written contract, other means must be admitted by the courts to prove the existence of an employment relationship, such as testimonies or expert-reports.

Although the personal scope of the directive is limited to employees, this directive can still be relevant to disguised employment relationships, as by asking the information required by the directive, the worker can get more certainty on his legal position.[11]

The recommendation can also be read in another way: are there bodies or institutes other than courts which can be addressed in order to decide that a particular agreement is a contract of employment? In most countries it is the court which is asked to decide whether there is a contract of employment or not.

This is a weak element in the protection of workers, since after all, exactly the most vulnerable workers are the ones who work in non-employment relationships. They will often be afraid of losing any further prospect of work when they go to court and often they do not have the funds for paying the costs of the legal proceedings.

Only a few country studies mention alternatives to the courts for determining the nature of the working relationship. In particular, the German report mentions alternatives, but the author of this chapter concludes that these alternatives are not really forceful.

In Belgium the administrative chambers of the Administrative Division Commission for the regulation of the employment relationship have the task of taking preventive decisions concerning the characterisation of an employment relationship (the so-called 'social ruling'); the parties to an agreement – principal and performer – can individually or jointly turn to these chambers and ask for a decision on the qualification of the contract. This decision remains in force for a period of three years. This commission is, however, still in the stage of a proposal; it has not been established yet.[12]

10. OJ L 288, 18 Oct. 1991, 32– 35.
11. From the personal scope are exempted contracts: (a) with a total duration not exceeding one month, and/or – with a working week not exceeding eight hours; or (b) of a casual and/or specific nature provided, in these cases, that its non-application is justified by objective considerations.
12. Chapter 5, s. 5.2.1.

Thus, there are, in practice, at present hardly any alternatives for the courts for deciding on the issue of the employment relationship.

Such alternatives are really worthwhile investigating, although, of course, for them to function well it is also necessary to develop criteria according to which these bodies have to decide. A commission like the Belgian one offers the most accessible prospects, but the main question will be whether decisions of such a condition will be acceptable for both parties.

2.4. LEGAL PRESUMPTIONS THAT THERE IS A CONTRACT OF EMPLOYMENT

2.4.1. Refutable and Irrefutable Presumptions

Article 11 of the Recommendation recommends, as a second method for facilitating the determination of the existence of an employment relationship, the introduction of a legal presumption that an employment relationship exists where one or more relevant indicators is present.

Refutable presumptions are useful, in particular to fight border-line cases, including the bogus self-employed. They may also help persons who are in a dependent situation (e.g., on-call workers) to relieve them from the proof that they work in subordination to the work provider: it is the principal who has to prove that there is not an employment relationship.

The country reports also mention *irrefutable* presumptions. These are – we assume[13] – not different from statutory provisions that a person in a particular situation or profession is deemed to have a contract of employment. For this reason we will discuss these two issues together.

Examples of legal presumptions were given in several of the country chapters.

A presumption based on a particular *situation* can be found in the Netherlands, where the Civil Code contains a general legal presumption that there is a contract of employment if a person is performing work for the benefit of another person against remuneration for at least three consecutive months, on a weekly basis, or for no less than twenty hours per month. This presumption is refutable. Another (refutable) legal presumption provides that, where a contract of employment has continued for at least three months, the contracted work in any month is presumed to amount to the average working period per month over the three preceding months. Thus, these presumptions do not refer to a particular profession nor do they have any conditions related to subordination or doing the work personally. Instead, they refer to circumstances which are not difficult to determine; it is then up to the other party to prove that the criteria for the employment relationship are not satisfied.

13. There may be a difference if a court decides that, despite the fact that the presumption is not refutable, it still does not apply because of the circumstances of the case or because of inconsistency with other standards. Whether this can happen depends on the legal system in question and we have not been informed of such decisions yet.

The objectives of the Dutch presumptions are to avoid uncertain provisions and fake constructions; to solve disputes and to improve the position of persons working under marginal contracts.

In the evaluation studies of the effects of these presumptions (discussed in the Dutch Chapter) it was found that in only a few court cases presumptions are invoked. This may be reassuring for employers (and employees). Thus the presumptions have neither led to difficult and cumbersome (and expensive) procedures, nor did self-employed persons without staff invoke the presumptions. Instead, it appeared that employers have become more precise in defining the conditions of the contract and that the number of on-call contracts was reduced. The latter type of contract was replaced by temporary agency contracts and contracts for a definite period.

Although one might not be too enthusiastic on the finding that one type of flexible contract was replaced by another, this replacement is not without meaning, as there can be important differences between the respective types of contract. In the Dutch system, temporary agency workers often have more protection than on-call workers. Temporary agency workers have a contract of employment with the agency, which means that their social security coverage is clear.

The effect of the legal presumptions is thus a compromise between realising more certainty for the employees while still allowing flexibility for employers. In any case, the effect of the presumptions fits well with the objectives of the Dutch Act concerned and of the Recommendation.

In Belgium, refutable presumptions on the contract of employment were introduced for *particular professions*, that is, commercial travellers, pharmacists, students and sales representatives. For example, a pharmacist working in a pharmacy, which is open to the public, is deemed to be bound by an employment contract with the owner or the lessee of the pharmacy, unless the opposite is proven.

In France persons *in specified professions* are considered as employees: professional journalists, performing artists, fashion models and sales representatives (under certain conditions). The legal presumption places the burden of proof that no employment contract exists on the other party of the relationship (i.e., the employer or client).

In Belgium also *irrefutable* presumptions were introduced. These state that a person cannot do additional services for his employer on a self-employed basis when they are bound by an employment contract for similar services. This rule is a measure to prevent evading labour law (rules on the maximum number of working hours) and social security contributions by both parties rather than to protect workers who are deprived of the protection of a contract of employment. In addition there are irrefutable presumptions on the status of temporary agency workers: they are employees.[14] This is an example of a rule which amounts to the same as a statutory provision as 'Temporary workers work under a contract of employment'. As we have already noticed the Dutch law defines the contract of a temporary

14. Chapter 5, s. 3.2.

agency worker as a contract of employment. This amounts to an irrefutable presumption.

We can conclude that refutable presumptions can have a general character or be related to particular professions. The latter presumptions may be easier to implement, as it is easier to oversee the effects of these presumptions. Such presumptions, however, do not improve the situation of persons outside such professions, even though they need the most protection, for example, home workers and on-call workers, since they may be involved in all kinds of work. General presumptions such as found in the Dutch legislation cover such workers.

2.4.2. Legal Presumptions of Self-employment

A related issue concerns legal presumptions that a person is self-employed. In the French Law of 1994 it was provided that individuals registered in some specified registers are presumed not to be parties to an employment contract for the business activity for which they are so registered. This legal presumption was revoked later, but reintroduced in the same terms by the Act on Economic Initiative of 1 August 2003. It is interesting that initially the presumption caused confusion since it was feared that it would lead to an increase of fake self-employment or outsourcing. However, this did not actually happen, since the legal provision was accompanied by safety nets, among others that a person unsure of his/her precise legal situation could ask the social security organisation for clarification.

In the German system the presumptions are mainly relevant to social security obligations; see below.

The presumptions are both in the interest of workers and employers and enable the authorities to supervise the situation involved. From the facts presented in the application of a person to be considered self-employed it can sometimes be deduced that it is an employment relationship and this can thus help to discover disguised unemployment relationships.

2.4.3. Legal Presumptions in Social Security

German *social security law* contains a refutable presumption that freelancers have a contract of employment. If a person does not employ other persons as employees, works essentially for one single customer, is performing work which is typically done by employees and does not offer his services or his products at the market, the principal has to prove that the person is not an employed person for social security. The first draft of this law was controversial, as small enterprises feared to be too much affected by it. In 2000 the Law was amended by reducing the number of criteria and by introducing the possibility for the employer to ask the benefit administration whether a person was self-employed or an employee. Thus this system of declarations ensured that there is now more legal certainty. As a result, the situation rapidly calmed down and the problem of 'fictitious self-employment' disappeared. As in the case of legal presumptions discussed in the previous section, it is assumed that in some cases the work is now organised in such a way that nobody can pretend that the person concerned is in fact an employee.

The presumptions have led, as in the Dutch case, to contracts which are more clearly drafted. As in the Dutch case, there was a shift to temporary agency contracts. They took over the function of the supposed freelancers.

Also in French law a legal presumption of self-employment was introduced that is mainly relevant for social security reasons. A person who is unsure of his/her precise legal situation can ask the social security organisation for clarification. In the French chapter we can also read that, despite the worries at the time of the introduction of these presumptions, these worked out in the way they were intended.

2.5. Presumption to Be Either Employed or Self-employed

Article 11 of the ILO Recommendation recommends as the third method that Members consider the possibility of determining that workers with certain characteristics, in the general or in a particular sector, must be deemed to be either employed or self-employed. According to Legal Experts in the field of labour law, 'provisions according to which certain persons are legally deemed to be employees are few and far between in the countries covered by the report. They do play a certain role, however, merely with regard to small groups of working persons, for example travelling salesmen'.[15] In the countries studied in this book we can find several examples of such provisions.

One example is, as we already mentioned in the previous section, that in several countries temporary agency workers are considered as employees. For instance, in Belgium the agreement between the temporary agency and the worker is, according to an irrefutable presumption, a contract of employment. In Poland, temporary workers are explicitly deemed to be employees. The same is true for the Netherlands. The Flexibility and Security Act provides that a temporary work agency agreement is qualified as a contract of employment. In other areas there are refutable presumptions, which give less certainty.

2.5.1. The Declaration that a Person is Self-employed

In the previous section we mentioned the legal presumptions assisting workers to assert that they have a contract of employment. However, there is also a group of self-employed persons who wish that their status as self-employed is ascertained. Otherwise it can happen that a person working and treated as self-employed is at a later moment treated as employee. As a result this person is, among other things, subject to social security contributions and fines. Thus it is in his interest that it is clear from the beginning whether he is either an employee or self-employed.

15. *Thematic Report on the Characteristics of the Employment Relationship* (Leiden: Leiden, University, 2009), vi,, (<www.labourlawnetwork.eu/frontend/file.php?id=165&dl=1>).

In several of the country studies we saw measures meant to improve the position of self-employed persons in borderline cases. In the Netherlands, for instance, the Declaration on the Working Relationship (VAR) was introduced. In various Dutch Acts this declaration has been given important legal consequences for the principal who can show such a declaration.

The French Law also introduced a provision for a legal presumption that a person is, in certain circumstances, self-employed.[16]

In Germany, persons can ask the administration for a declaration whether they are employed or self-employed. As a result the problem of fictitious self-employment disappeared.

These declarations can be helpful to ensure legal certainty on whether one is employed or self-employed.

2.6. Developing Uniform Criteria

From the description of the legislation and case law in the countries it appears that it is difficult to make uniform criteria for the employment relationship. The reasons for this have been explained throughout the chapters: a main reason is that the borderline between self-employed and employed persons has become more diffuse through time due to changes in the work to be done and changes in the economy.

Therefore, in order to assess the legal status of a worker, it seems necessary to take all the relevant facts and circumstances into account to assess a particular case: is there really a dependent relationship, are there other principals, how was the use of instruments, materials and the payments arranged?

There were some proposals for checklists, such as the Belgian Unizo formula. In the United Kingdom tests are used by labour judges to determine the existence of an employment relationship.[17] There is no general agreement on the best test to be used, let alone one single test applicable to all cases.

None of the proposals or judiciary tests have received a statutory status. Applying checklists as such may lead to unsatisfactory results in borderline cases. It can also mean that situations are construed to escape the effects of the checklist. Moreover, so far it has not been possible to reach agreement on the exact elements of the checklists or definitions for the elements of the contract of element.

2.7. The Proposal to Expand the Scope of Labour Law

This proposal was made by Supiot.[18] It appears, however, that in none of the countries the existence of economic dependence is sufficient to accept a contract of employment. Instead, the subordination criterion is predominant. In deciding

16. Chapter 5, s. 2.3.2.
17. Chapter 10, s. 4.
18. Chapter 2, s. 3.2.

whether there is an employment relationship or not, the main criterion for the courts is whether the worker is subjected to the supervisory power (the power to give instructions and to control the work) by the presumed employer.

The country studies do not give examples to show that labour law is expanded to cover *all* kinds of contracts. There are some examples, however, that particular contracts are included by labour law, for instance, the temporary agency workers in some countries. However, this is done by means of qualifying these workers as employees by law, and not by extending labour law to contracts other than labour law. The only areas where labour law is indeed expanded to all types of working relationships are health and safety and sometimes the area of working times, exactly those areas where this is demanded by EU directives. In other areas there is little progress in extending the protection by labour law.

Some countries have categories of workers who are assimilated with employees. This is an interesting phenomenon, but although the category was already created a long time ago, it was not considerably extended (see the German Chapter, section 6.5). In order to be included in such a category it has to be possible to define the type of situation which is to be covered. The problem with the workers who are currently not covered by labour law is that they do not fit into specific professions but work in particular situations which are not so easy to define. Therefore it is difficult for the Law to treat them as *arbeitnehmerähnlig*.

2.8. Extension of Protection of Labour Law

This proposal was also made by Supiot,[19] which is in fact a more modest extension of labour law than the previous one. As was discussed in the preceding section, examples can be found of an extension of labour law for workers who are not employees.

In the EU Green Paper, *Modernising labour law to meet the challenges of the twenty-first century*, it was proposed to make rules on a new category of economically-dependent workers, who are neither employees nor self-employed. This was also suggested by Perulli.[20]

Although formally 'self-employed', these persons are economically dependent on a single principal or client/employer for their source of income.

In this view categories of workers must legally be treated in the same way as employees, without reclassifying the work relationship as an employment contract, and disconnecting the work relationship from any legal subordination.

This proposal has not received very much support. To some extent the British category of workers is a third category (see British Chapter), but this group is not really self-employed, but rather resembles that of employed persons. Moreover, in the British context there is even a third category of dependent workers, alongside employees and workers. As was pointed out in the British system, there are no clear

19. Chapter 2, s. 3.2.
20. See Ch. 2, s. 3.3.

cut distinguishing criteria for the separate categories. Therefore this phenomenon cannot be said to be meant to extend the protection of labour law to persons other than employees,

Examples of expansion of labour law to other contracts are the following. Under French law, certain provisions of the Labour Code are applied to professions which are not entitled to an employment contract, but whose business activity is subject to legal conditions. The professions concerned are self-employed managers, distributors, and service providers. These professions are partly covered by labour law and partly by civil or commercial law. Thus independent managers of service stations, other exclusive distributors and franchisees may benefit from this law, as they depend exclusively on a single principal who has an indirect but strong influence on their working conditions and controls the prices of the goods or services they supply to their customers.

Also Germany has a category of persons assimilated with employees (*arbeitnehmerähnliche Personen*); these are regarded as needing protection similar to that of employees. Although labour law is, in principle, not applicable to them, part of the legal protection afforded to employees is extended to these employee-like persons (e.g., the right to annual holiday, prevention of discrimination and collective bargaining).[21]

In the Netherlands chapter the extension of dismissal protection and possibility of making collective agreements to some categories of persons having a contract of services was discussed. In practice, however, very little use is made of this possibility.

Some countries extend parts of social security protection to persons who are not employees, for instance, social security for work-related accidents. Several social security schemes (Netherlands, France) cover categories of workers who do not have a contract of employment. The purpose is both to protect these persons and to prevent them from escaping the contribution for these insurance schemes.

Given the limited scope of our study we will not go into this further, but it is good to keep in mind that social security can compensate some, but not all, deficiencies of the lack of a contract of employment.

2.8.1. Self-employed

A related approach is to develop better protection for particular categories of the self-employed. An example was discussed in the French Chapter, the French amendment to introduce a legal regime for managing agents. This measure introduced more protection for managing agents except from those labour law elements which were found inappropriate (i.e., in this case dismissal protection).[22]

Other countries show similar developments. A country can apply particular parts of labour law to non-employees or it can choose to make a special law for a category of the self-employed. The formal difference between the two approaches

21. See also *Thematic Report, supra* n. 15, 34.
22. See Ch. 6, s. 3.1.2.

does not prevent us from considering this as a (material) extension of labour law. An example is the obligation to pay compensation when a service contract is dissolved.

2.9. The Hard Core of Social Rights

The idea of introducing a hard core of social rights was launched by several authors. One of them was Perulli, who proposed to create a 'hard core' of social rights which are applicable to all work contracts irrespective of their formal qualification in terms of autonomy (self-employment) or subordination.[23] The creation of a minimum floor of rights was also supported by Guy Davidov during the Labour Network Conference. He suggested that 'when the relationship is characterised by dependency but no subordination, it is useful to call the worker a 'dependent contractor' and apply at least some labour laws. In other words, dependency alone should be sufficient to justify a floor of basic labour-related rights, with additional rights (which are tied to subordination) granted only to 'employees'.[24]

In the country chapters we can see that the first initiatives have been taken to introduce a hard core of social rights. Still, these are not given to all workers (including the self-employed) yet; therefore these examples fit better in the proposal to expand part of labour law to all workers.

An example of a social right which has been generally extended is liability of the employer in case of industrial accidents and his obligation to create safe and healthy working conditions. There is certainly not a general social core of social rights yet.

For discussing the core of social rights it may be relevant to look at the Posting Directive, which mentions the following rights which the host country has to apply in case of persons posted to its territory. The hard core of social rights applicable to posted workers consists of: (a) maximum work periods and minimum rest periods; (b) minimum paid annual holidays; (c) the minimum rates of pay, including overtime rates; this point does not apply to supplementary occupational retirement pension schemes; (d) the conditions of hiring-out of workers, in particular the supply of workers by temporary employment undertakings; (e) health, safety and hygiene at work; (f) protective measures with regard to the terms and conditions of employment of pregnant women or women who have recently given birth, of children and of young people; and (g) equality of treatment between men and women and other provisions on non-discrimination.

23. Chapter 2, s. 3.3.
24. Guy Davidov, 'Making Sense of Intermediate Groups in Labour Law: The Distinction between Subordination and Dependency', *Seminar Report of 2nd Annual Legal Seminar of European Labour Law Network*, 24 et seq., (<www.labourlawnetwork.eu/news_and_events/conferences/prm/69/size__1/index.html>).

These rights are selected as being in particular relevant to posted workers, who are by definition only temporarily employed in the host State. For this reason essential elements of labour law, such as dismissal law, are missing.

The example of the Posted Workers Directive in fact involves expansion of part of labour law.

The idea of core rights could also be realised by introducing a *new content* of existing rights, or by introducing a version of an existing right adapted to the special position of the target group. There were no reports of the introduction of a minimum floor of rights for all workers in the countries under study. We found, however, examples of rights adjusted to particular categories. In the French chapter proposals were discussed in which it was argued that some rights may be common to all workers.[25] The authors of these proposals describe that particular developments are already taking place in this area and they make suggestions for their generalisation. An example is the practice to strike which has (in France) become common among self-employed workers. The authors of the proposals propose that these workers should have a recognised right to collective action, which would, in particular, make it possible to maintain the contract in case of a strike and prevent the client from replacing a self-employed worker who was on strike. So here we see an important fundamental right, derived from labour law, but adjusted to the target group. Similarly, the right to collective bargaining is mentioned and has, according to the French report, already been used to negotiate the status of general insurance agents.[26] Also the right to professional training is mentioned. The authors furthermore envisage applying the legal provisions already adopted for sales agents and agency managers concerning notice for termination and severance pay, possibly calculated as a percentage on the order of 10% of the turnover achieved during the contract. In the report it was even discussed whether grounds should be required for unilateral termination by the parent company, which would make the system similar to the law on dismissal. This idea was rejected as it would lead to a too close similarity to the situation of employees; instead it was suggested to adopt a standard for the penalties to be paid for wrongful breach of contract. This is an interesting discussion even though the ideas have not been adopted yet.

An example can also be found in Belgium, where a number of structures have been created which are analogous to those of employees. For example, since 1 July 1997 a bankrupt self-employed person is covered by bankruptcy insurance. He thus maintains his rights to specific benefits and enjoys, during a maximum of six months, a benefit which is equal to the minimum pension of the self-employed.[27]

25. Ch. 6, s. 3
26. In France, apparently such collective bargaining by the self-employed is not seen as problematic in view of competition law; see for the Dutch discussion Ch. 7, s. 6.
27. Chapter 5, s. 6.

2.10. Conclusions

From the developments and the arguments mentioned in the preceding sections we may conclude that a general redefinition or waiving of the subordination criterion for adopting an employment relationship is not feasible, since it will be impossible to distinguish the genuine self-employed from employees if subordination is no longer a decisive criterion.

The countries under study continue to work with the dichotomy of employee and non-employee for persons performing work personally. They take piecemeal measures to increase the protection of the employment contract, such as the introduction of legal presumptions or by defining a particular profession or situation as being under a contract of employment.

The measures which were taken, like in the situation of the temporary agency workers in several countries, had favourable effects since for the group in question the legal uncertainty was taken away. Also small measures may thus improve the fate of many persons.

The drawback of that approach is, of course, that progress is slow and the legislature keeps lagging behind developments. This approach seems not really satisfactory if we wish a rapid expansion of labour law and a general protection of workers. In case of piecemeal expansion of labour law there will always be groups that remain unprotected. However, it seems that the piecemeal expansion fits best with the nature of the problem, that is, the continuing tension between labour law protection and the need for a flexible workforce.

In several countries there are discussions on whether particular distinctions between legal positions are still justified and whether there are objective justifications for the differences. This may mean that a gradual improvement of the position of a particular category may have effects also for other categories of workers, since the distinctions between these categories can no longer be justified. Thus in light of this possibility gradual improvements for particular professions also have an important potential.

Of the instruments mentioned, in particular the legal presumptions seem promising. Remarkable is that in the countries where they were introduced, in particular Germany and France, initially there were confusion and fear about the introduction of the presumptions, since it was feared that the presumptions would include too many situations. This fear existed for the presumptions for employed persons, self-employed persons and for social security. In both countries the presumptions were repealed and reintroduced while some additional safeguards were introduced. After thos there appeared to be no problems.

Also in the Netherlands the presumptions became an accepted instrument. Since their introduction employers tend to draft clearer contracts. In addition they began to make use of other types of contracts, which were still flexible but provide for more certainty for the worker concerned. It is therefore interesting to explore this method further.

Finally, it is good to keep in mind that also employers can benefit from the effect of the presumptions; when they use clearer contracts, the result is more certainty, fewer disputes arise and still the used agreements allow flexibility. Of course, the form and the effect of the presumptions depend on the national context, but these findings are worthwhile to explore.

In addition, the position of the self-employed has also received attention: in several countries there is now a clearer definition to determine when a person is self-employed. Also legal presumptions or declarations that a person is self-employed were introduced.

The discussion on a minimum floor of rights is going on slowly. More progress seems to be reached by gradually extending more rights to particular professions. This is a not an unimportant development.

Although there are some developments in the countries studied, and these developments provide useful materials for further developing instruments to increase the protection by labour law, we cannot conclude that they have all actively investigated all means recommended by the ILO Recommendation. There are also countries where very little progress has been made. For this reason it is useful to look at the role international organisations can play in order to support developments in this field.

3. THE ROLE OF THE INTERNATIONAL ORGANISATIONS

3.1. General

The Chapters on the international organisations showed that there is very little support for making a uniform definition of the contract of employment or to make a binding instrument which decides when a contract of employment exists or not. The employers' organisations have not even supported the adoption of the ILO Recommendation out of fear that the room to manoeuvre for employers would be restricted. This attitude affected later developments, such as discussion on the EU Green Paper on the modernisation of labour law. Employees' organisations in turn have now become reticent to adopt, or even discuss, proposals which might affect the position of the tradition employees, for instance by introducing a third type of contract, by introducing more flexibility in return for more work certainty (*flex-icurity*) or by making a hard core of social rights, out of fear that this may lead to a general deterioration for employees.

This situation will most probably not change in the coming years. Changes in this area may only occur when they are necessary to enforce EU instruments. At present, these instruments have to deal with the different definitions of the personal scope in the Member States, while their objective is to be implemented in the same way.[28]

We can thus conclude that the primary responsibility for realising the uncovering of disguised employment relationships and extending labour law to

28. See also the case law described in the Ch. 10.

non-protected workers lies with the national authorities, rather than with international organisations. Therefore we will pay some attention to how the international organisations studied here can make their Members more active in this area.

3.2. THE EU

A modern EU instrument to realise social policy aims where there are no powers at EU level and where Member States have the sole power to take the decisions is the Open Method of Coordination (OMC). This instrument was developed in the 1990s in the area of employment policy. Later it was also applied in other areas: social inclusion; pensions; immigration; education and culture; and asylum.

In short, the OMC is an instrument meant to meet certain objectives defined by the Council of Ministers. It requires Member States to submit reports on the national state of affairs in the policy area concerned. Subsequently they are given guidelines to improve the situation and then they have to report again. This policy cycle leaves the competences of the Member States intact, but at the same time the States are put under pressure to undertake the desired activities, as their results are subject to 'peer review' in the Council of Ministers.

Initially, it was feared that the OMC would not have much effect. However, in the area of the OMC on employment policy, the Council issued detailed and specific recommendations, which had effect in the actual national policies. Thus, Member States have to consider the recommendations when developing their policies and this makes them quite influential.

It is therefore appropriate to propose that also in relation to the measures they take on unveiling disguised employment relationships, bogus self-employed and persons performing work while not protected by labour law, Member States can be required to make OMC reports. On the basis of these reports, the Council can require from the Member States that they improve the situation. Moreover, the reports can also show best practices, which are useful for other Member States.

Secondly, within the framework of this OMC procedure, Member States can be asked to report which rules and/or principles of labour law can be extended to particular categories of non-employees. They could also be asked to give justifications where such extension is not possible within their system, and what alternatives exist.

3.3. THE ILO

At present the ILO instrument on the employment relationship has the form of a recommendation. This is a rather weak instrument and it is hard to oversee to which extent it is really followed. The reporting procedures on recommendations are also (very) weak.

In order to make this instrument more powerful, we proposed some elements for an ILO Convention on disguised employment relationships (in Chapter 3).

A convention is not only a stronger instrument, but also more focused on particular issues. After all, there is consensus on the unveiling of disguised employment relationships. This Convention will require periodical reports and thus contribute to activities at the national level. An important advantage of this convention is that it is not limited to EU Member States.

4. CONCLUSIONS

From the country studies we can conclude that various measures were undertaken to bring disguised contracts of employment under labour law and to reduce the phenomenon of bogus self-employment. In any case, the need is felt to undertake such actions, but the way they are undertaken vary from country to country, and depends on the structure of the labour law, the civil law system and the economic situation. There are also countries where little has been undertaken by the legislature, even though judges expressed concern at the widespread practice of drafting terms which seek explicitly to circumvent established notions of the scope of employment protection by reference to 'employee status'.

At present there seems to be very little room for initiatives on the part of the European Union and/or International Labour Organisation. They can, however, support and encourage the Members to undertake action and they should do so, since the extent to which national States undertake action varies considerably. The positive effects of best practices should be shared more enthusiastically and the Member States should be pressed to explain the reasons better if they do not undertake action or when the reasons for differences of treatment of groups in comparable situations are unclear.

Since the global approach to this issue is even more complicated than at the EU level, the ILO Convention proposed by us concerns disguised employment relationship only. This convention requires Members to improve the application and enforcement of national laws and regulations in the field of labour law to ensure that persons with an employment relationship have access to the protection they are due at the national level. Member States must develop effective measures, in consultation with employers' and workers' organisations, to unveil disguised employment relationships. For this purpose the suggestions made *supra* are useful to refer to. Member States must also improve the capacity of the labour administration, labour inspection and judiciary to recognise and effectively combat disguised employment. They must inform employers and workers on the negative effects of disguised employment and promote national alternatives which are in the interest of all the parties concerned. Finally, they must maintain a clear distinction between employment relationships and independent contracting.

The EU could go further and ask, within the framework of the Employment OMC, Member States to report their activities to unveil disguised employment relationships and to protect dependent personal workers. For these purposes the Member States should pay special attention to the suggestions made in the preceding paragraph.

From the country reports it follows that in particular the following instruments should be explored:

- the introduction of statutory provisions that qualify particular working relationships as employment relationships;
- the introduction of presumptions that there is a contract of employment if certain conditions are fulfilled;
- refutable presumptions that persons working in a particular profession have a contract of employment;
- creating legal presumptions that a person is self-employed if he satisfies certain conditions;
- extend particular rules and/or principles of labour law to particular categories of non-employees and define these in the Act relevant to them;
- discussions on core social fundamental rights which should apply to all workers.

Given the different position of the ILO and the different nature of the instrument, our suggested contents for the Convention are different from what we suggest for the OMC within the EU context. The principles are the same, however, in that the focus remains on the Member States, and reporting on their efforts is an attempt to realise the objectives underlying the Conventions. For the Member States the findings in this book may at the same time remain useful to take into consideration.

Appendix

R198 Employment Relationship Recommendation, 2006

The General Conference of the International Labour Organization,

Having been convened at Geneva by the Governing Body of the International Labour Office, and having met in its Ninety-fifth Session on 31 May 2006, and

Considering that there is protection offered by national laws and regulations and collective agreements which are linked to the existence of an employment relationship between an employer and an employee, and

Considering that laws and regulations, and their interpretation, should be compatible with the objectives of decent work, and

Considering that employment or labour law seeks, among other things, to address what can be an unequal bargaining position between parties to an employment relationship, and

Considering that the protection of workers is at the heart of the mandate of the International Labour Organization, and in accordance with principles set out in the ILO Declaration on Fundamental Principles and Rights at Work, 1998, and the Decent Work Agenda, and

Considering the difficulties of establishing whether or not an employment relationship exists in situations where the respective rights and obligations of the parties concerned are not clear, where there has been an attempt to disguise the employment relationship, or where inadequacies or limitations exist in the legal framework, or in its interpretation or application, and

Noting that situations exist where contractual arrangements can have the effect of depriving workers of the protection they are due, and

Recognizing that there is a role for international guidance to Members in achieving this protection through national law and practice, and that such guidance should remain relevant over time, and

Further recognizing that such protection should be accessible to all, particularly vulnerable workers, and should be based on law that is efficient, effective and comprehensive, with expeditious outcomes, and that encourages voluntary compliance, and

Recognizing that national policy should be the result of consultation with the social partners and should provide guidance to the parties concerned in the workplace, and

Recognizing that national policy should promote economic growth, job creation and decent work, and

Considering that the globalized economy has increased the mobility of workers who are in need of protection, at least against circumvention of national protection by choice of law, and

Noting that, in the framework of transnational provision of services, it is important to establish who is considered a worker in an employment relationship, what rights the worker has, and who the employer is, and

Considering that the difficulties in establishing the existence of an employment relationship may create serious problems for those workers concerned, their communities, and society at large, and

Considering that the uncertainty as to the existence of an employment relationship needs to be addressed to guarantee fair competition and effective protection of workers in an employment relationship in a manner appropriate to national law or practice, and

Noting all relevant international labour standards, especially those addressing the particular situation of women, as well as those addressing the scope of the employment relationship, and

Having decided upon the adoption of certain proposals with regard to the employment relationship, which is the fifth item on the agenda of the session, and

Having determined that these proposals shall take the form of a Recommendation; adopts this fifteenth day of June of the year two thousand and six the following Recommendation, which may be cited as the Employment Relationship Recommendation, 2006.

I. NATIONAL POLICY OF PROTECTION FOR WORKERS IN AN EMPLOYMENT RELATIONSHIP

1. Members should formulate and apply a national policy for reviewing at appropriate intervals and, if necessary, clarifying and adapting the scope of relevant laws

and regulations, in order to guarantee effective protection for workers who perform work in the context of an employment relationship.

2. The nature and extent of protection given to workers in an employment relationship should be defined by national law or practice, or both, taking into account relevant international labour standards. Such law or practice, including those elements pertaining to scope, coverage and responsibility for implementation, should be clear and adequate to ensure effective protection for workers in an employment relationship.

3. National policy should be formulated and implemented in accordance with national law and practice in consultation with the most representative organisations of employers and workers.

4. National policy should at least include measures to:

(a) provide guidance for the parties concerned, in particular employers and workers, on effectively establishing the existence of an employment relationship and on the distinction between employed and self-employed workers;

(b) combat disguised employment relationships in the context of, for example, other relationships that may include the use of other forms of contractual arrangements that hide the true legal status, noting that a disguised employment relationship occurs when the employer treats an individual as other than an employee in a manner that hides his or her true legal status as an employee, and that situations can arise where contractual arrangements have the effect of depriving workers of the protection they are due;

(c) ensure standards applicable to all forms of contractual arrangements, including those involving multiple parties, so that employed workers have the protection they are due;

(d) ensure that standards applicable to all forms of contractual arrangements establish who is responsible for the protection contained therein;

(e) provide effective access of those concerned, in particular employers and workers, to appropriate, speedy, inexpensive, fair and efficient procedures and mechanisms for settling disputes regarding the existence and terms of an employment relationship;

(f) ensure compliance with, and effective application of, laws and regulations concerning the employment relationship; and

(g) provide for appropriate and adequate training in relevant international labour standards, comparative and case law for the judiciary, arbitrators, mediators, labour inspectors, and other persons responsible for dealing with the resolution of disputes and enforcement of national employment laws and standards.

5. Members should take particular account in national policy to ensure effective protection to workers especially affected by the uncertainty as to the existence of

an employment relationship, including women workers, as well as the most vulnerable workers, young workers, older workers, workers in the informal economy, migrant workers and workers with disabilities.

6. Members should:

(a) take special account in national policy to address the gender dimension in that women workers predominate in certain occupations and sectors where there is a high proportion of disguised employment relationships, or where there is a lack of clarity of an employment relationship; and

(b) have clear policies on gender equality and better enforcement of the relevant laws and agreements at national level so that the gender dimension can be effectively addressed.

7. In the context of the transnational movement of workers:

(a) in framing national policy, a Member should, after consulting the most representative organisations of employers and workers, consider adopting appropriate measures within its jurisdiction, and where appropriate in collaboration with other Members, so as to provide effective protection to and prevent abuses of migrant workers in its territory who may be affected by uncertainty as to the existence of an employment relationship;

(b) where workers are recruited in one country for work in another, the Members concerned may consider concluding bilateral agreements to prevent abuses and fraudulent practices which have as their purpose the evasion of the existing arrangements for the protection of workers in the context of an employment relationship.

8. National policy for protection of workers in an employment relationship should not interfere with true civil and commercial relationships, while at the same time ensuring that individuals in an employment relationship have the protection they are due.

II. DETERMINATION OF THE EXISTENCE OF AN EMPLOYMENT RELATIONSHIP

9. For the purposes of the national policy of protection for workers in an employment relationship, the determination of the existence of such a relationship should be guided primarily by the facts relating to the performance of work and the remuneration of the worker, notwithstanding how the relationship is characterized in any contrary arrangement, contractual or otherwise, that may have been agreed between the parties.

10. Members should promote clear methods for guiding workers and employers as to the determination of the existence of an employment relationship.

11. For the purpose of facilitating the determination of the existence of an employment relationship, Members should, within the framework of the national policy referred to in this Recommendation, consider the possibility of the following:

(a) allowing a broad range of means for determining the existence of an employment relationship;

(b) providing for a legal presumption that an employment relationship exists where one or more relevant indicators is present; and

(c) determining, following prior consultations with the most representative organisations of employers and workers, that workers with certain characteristics, in general or in a particular sector, must be deemed to be either employed or self-employed.

12. For the purposes of the national policy referred to in this Recommendation, Members may consider clearly defining the conditions applied for determining the existence of an employment relationship, for example, subordination or dependence.

13. Members should consider the possibility of defining in their laws and regulations, or by other means, specific indicators of the existence of an employment relationship. Those indicators might include:

(a) the fact that the work: is carried out according to the instructions and under the control of another party; involves the integration of the worker in the organisation of the enterprise; is performed solely or mainly for the benefit of another person; must be carried out personally by the worker; is carried out within specific working hours or at a workplace specified or agreed by the party requesting the work; is of a particular duration and has a certain continuity; requires the worker's availability; or involves the provision of tools, materials and machinery by the party requesting the work;

(b) periodic payment of remuneration to the worker; the fact that such remuneration constitutes the worker's sole or principal source of income; provision of payment in kind, such as food, lodging or transport; recognition of entitlements such as weekly rest and annual holidays; payment by the party requesting the work for travel undertaken by the worker in order to carry out the work; or absence of financial risk for the worker.

14. The settlement of disputes concerning the existence and terms of an employment relationship should be a matter for industrial or other tribunals or arbitration authorities to which workers and employers have effective access in accordance with national law and practice.

15. The competent authority should adopt measures with a view to ensuring respect for and implementation of laws and regulations concerning the employment relationship with regard to the various aspects considered in this Recommendation, for

example, through labour inspection services and their collaboration with the social security administration and the tax authorities.

16. In regard to the employment relationship, national labour administrations and their associated services should regularly monitor their enforcement programmes and processes. Special attention should be paid to occupations and sectors with a high proportion of women workers.

17. Members should develop, as part of the national policy referred to in this Recommendation, effective measures aimed at removing incentives to disguise an employment relationship.

18. As part of the national policy, Members should promote the role of collective bargaining and social dialogue as a means, among others, of finding solutions to questions related to the scope of the employment relationship at the national level.

III. MONITORING AND IMPLEMENTATION

19. Members should establish an appropriate mechanism, or make use of an existing one, for monitoring developments in the labour market and the organisation of work, and for formulating advice on the adoption and implementation of measures concerning the employment relationship within the framework of the national policy.

20. The most representative organisations of employers and workers should be represented, on an equal footing, in the mechanism for monitoring developments in the labour market and the organisation of work. In addition, these organisations should be consulted under the mechanism as often as necessary and, wherever possible and useful, on the basis of expert reports or technical studies.

21. Members should, to the extent possible, collect information and statistical data and undertake research on changes in the patterns and structure of work at the national and sectoral levels, taking into account the distribution of men and women and other relevant factors.

22. Members should establish specific national mechanisms in order to ensure that employment relationships can be effectively identified within the framework of the transnational provision of services. Consideration should be given to developing systematic contact and exchange of information on the subject with other States.

IV. FINAL PARAGRAPH

23. This Recommendation does not revise the Private Employment Agencies Recommendation, 1997 (No. 188), nor can it revise the Private Employment Agencies Convention, 1997 (No. 181).

Bibliography

M. Aarts. *De zelfstandige in het sociaal recht* (Deventer: Kluwer, 2007).

P.H. Antonmattei & J.C. Sciberras. *Le travailleur économiquement dépendant: quelle protection?* (Paris: La Documentation française, 2008).

I.P. Asscher-Vonk. 'Flex en zeker: de uitzendkracht'. *SMA* 1997, 376.

P. Auer & S. Cazes. 'The Resilience of the Long-Term Employment Relationship: Evidence from the Industrialized Countries'. *International Labour Review* 139, no. 4 (2000), 379–407.

I. Baeke et al. 'Werknemer of zelfstandige: met vragenlijsten en puntensysteem naar een voorafgaandelijk bindend advies?'. *Tijdschrift voor Sociaal Recht/ Revue de Droit Social* (2001) 107–299.

J. Barreau & M. Del Sol. 'Les formes hybrides de travail; de nouveaux rapports entre précarité et situations professionnelles'. In : J. Barreau & M. Del Sol (ed), *Nouvelles dimensions de la précarité* (Paris: PUR, 2001).

J. Barthelémy, 'Réflexions à propos des accords du 16 avril 1996 fixant le statut des agents généraux d'assurance'. *Droit social* (1997).

J. Barthélémy. 'Une convention collective de travailleurs indépendants? Réflexions à propos des accords du 16 avril 1996 fixant le statut des agents généraux d'assurance'. *Droit social* (1997), 40.

J. Barthélémy. 'Essai sur la para-subordination'. *Semaine Sociale Lamy* (2003), 6.

J. Barthélémy. 'Qualification de l'activité du participant à une émission de téléréalité'. *Semaine sociale Lamy*, 1382 (2009), 8.

R. Bellace & M.G. Rood. *Labour Law at the Crossroads: Changing Employment Relationships* (The Hague: Kluwer Law International, 1997).

Berenschot. *Flexibiliteit en zekerheid, effecten en doeltreffendheid van de Wet Flexibiliteit en zekerheid* (Utrecht: Berenschot, 2002).

L. van den Berg. *Tussen feit en fictie* (Den Haag: Boom, 2010).

L. Betten. *The Employment Contract in Transforming Labour Relations* (The Hague: Kluwer Law International, 1995).

W. Beveridge. *Social Insurance and Allied Services* (Cmnd 6404, HMSO, London, 1942).

R. Blanpain. 'Ondergeschikt verband: de sleutel op de deur van het arbeidsrecht'. *Tijdschrift voor Sociaal Recht/Revue de Droit Social (Special Issue)* (1998), 1–14.

J. Boissonnat. 'Le travail dans vingt ans'. In O. Jacob (ed.), *Rapport pour le Commissariat général du Plan* (Paris: La Documentation française, 1995).

G.C. Boot. 'Rechtsvermoedens'. *Sociaal Recht* (1997), 198.

G.C. Boot. 'Weerlegbare rechtsvermoedens'. *Arbeidsrecht* (1998), 53.

R. Böheim & U. Muehlberger. *Dependent Forms of Self-employment in the UK: Identifying Workers on the Border between Employment and Self-employment.* Working Paper No. 91 (Vienna: University of Economics and B.A., 2006).

C. Bosse. *Bewijslastverdeling in het Nederlandse en Belgische arbeidsrecht* (Deventer: Kluwer, 2003).

E. Breways. 'Cassatie velt principearrest over arbeidsstatuut advocaten'. *De Juristenkrant* (2006), 138.

S. Brissy. 'L'application du droit du travail aux travailleurs indépendants, un régime juridique cohérent?'. *JCP Social* 5 (2006), 1093.

J. Buelens. 'De normatieve afdeling van de Commissie tot regeling van de arbeidsrelatie: een niet-evidente zoektocht naar specifieke criteria'. In M. Rigaux and A. Van Regenmortel (eds), *Rechts(on)zekerheid omtrent (schijn)zelfstandigheid* (Antwerp: Intersentia, 2008), 159–176.

B. Cantillon. 'The Failures of Bismarck and Beveridge: The Case of Old-Age Pensions for the Self-employed in Belgium'. In E. Overbye (ed.), *Pensions: Challenges and Reforms* (Ashgate: Aldershot, 2004), 131–147.

B. Cantillon et al. 'Propositions de réformes dans le régime de pension des travailleurs indépendant: deuxième rapport du Groupe de travail Cantillon'. *Revue belge de sécurité sociale* 2 (2002), 229–263.

R. Castel. *Métamorphose de la question sociale.* 2d. (Paris: Fayard, 1995).

J.-P. Chauchard. 'Le rescrit social, procédure d'interrogation de l'URSSAF'. *Droit social* (1995), 642.

J.-P. Chauchard. 'Entre travail salarié et travail indépendant: l'émergence du travail autonome'. In *Du travail salarié au travail indépendant: permanences et mutations* (Bari: Cacucci Editore, 2003).

J.-P. Chauchard. 'Eléments pour une définition d'un contrat de travail indépendant'. n° 24 *JCP* (June 2007), 1761.

J.-P. Chauchard. 'Les avatars du travail indépendant'. *Droit social* 11 (2009), 1065.

J.-P. Chauchard & A.C. Hardy Dubernet (eds). *La subordination dans le travail* (Paris: Cahier Travail et Emploi, 2003).

C.E. Clesse. 'L'Ordre des avocats peut-il imposer une relation de travail indépendant malgré les dispositions impératives et d'ordre public?'. *Jurisprudence de Liège, Mons et Bruxelles* (2006), 32–43.

J. Clesse. 'La qualification juridique de la relation du travail'. In J. Clesse & F. Kefer (eds), *Questions de droit social* (Liège: Anthémis, 2007), 232.

C. Clesse. 'Chronique de jurisprudence. Aux frontières de la fausse indépendance', *Orientations* 2 (2009), 1–11; and *Orientations* 3 (2009), 1–9.

N. Countouris. *The Changing Law of the Employment Relationship – Comparative Analysis in the European Context* (Burlington: Ashgate, 2007).

I. Daugareilh & Ph. Martin. 'Les intermittents du spectacle: une figure du salariat entre droit commun et droit spécial'. *Revue française des affaires sociales* 3–4 (2000), 77–92.

M. Davagle, *Vrijwillige arbeid* (Mechelen: Wolters Kluwer, 2008), 214.

P. Davies & M. Freeland. 'Employees, Workers, and the Autonomy of Labour Law'. In H. Collins, P. Davies and R. Rideout (eds), *Legal Regulation of the Employment Relation* (The Hague: Kluwer Law International, 2000), 267–286.

P. Davies & M. Freedland. *Towards a Flexible Labour Market: Labour Legislation and Regulation since the 1990s* (Oxford: Oxford University Press, 2007).

J.L. Dehaene. 'Financiële participatie van werknemers'. *Economisch en Sociaal Tijdschrift* (1998), 331.

S. Deakin. 'The Contract of Employment: A Study in Legal Evolution'. *Historical Studies in Industrial Relations* 11 (2001), 1.

S. Deakin, *Evolution for Our Time: A Theory of Legal Memetics*. ESRC Centre for Business Research, University of Cambridge, Working Paper No. 242 (Cambridge: September 2002).

S. Deakin. *Interpreting Employment Contracts: Judges, Employers, Workers*. ESRC Centre for Business Research, University of Cambridge, Working Paper No. 267 (Cambridge: June 2003).

S. Deakin and G. Morris. *Labour Law*, 5th edn (Oxford: Hart Publishers, 2009).

D. Delvax. 'Le recours au contrat de travail ou au statut de la fonction publique. Prolégomènes'. In J. Jacqmain (ed.), *Une terre de droit du travail: les services publics* (Brussels: Bruylant, 2005), 1–30.

Department of Trade and Industry. *Discussion Document on Employment Status in Relation to Statutory Employment Rights* (URN 02/1058) (HMSO, London, July 2002).

V. Dooms & T. Messiaen. *Schijnzelfstandigheid*. Bibliotheek Sociaal Recht Larcier (Ghent: Larcier, 2009).

J.J. Dupeyroux, M. Borgetto & R. Lafore. *Droit de la sécurité sociale* (Paris: Dalloz, 2008).

W. Däubler. *Arbeitsrecht 1*, 16th edn (Hamburg: Rowolt, 2006).

W. Van Eeckhoutte. 'Advocaat-medewerker is geen medewerker: een schot naast de roos'. *De Juristenkrant* 87 (2004), 1.

W. Van Eeckhoutte. 'La formule dite d'UNIZO'. In X., *Le lien de subordination. Actes du colloque organisé le 19 mars 2004 par l'Ordre des Avocats du Barreau de Tournai et le Jeune Barreau de Tournai*. Etudes pratiques de Droit Social n° 18 (Brussels: Kluwer, 2004), 165–179.

W. Van Eeckhoutte. 'Gezag' in de cassatierechtspraak. Een kwestie van bewijs, interpretatie en kwalificatie'. *Nieuw Juridisch Weekblad* 95 (2005), 2–17.

W. Van Eeckhoutte & G. De Maeseneire. 'Arbeidsrelatieswet. Het bepalen van de rechtsaard van arbeidsrelaties'. *Nieuw Juridisch Weekblad* (2007), 98–119.

C. Engels. *Het ondergeschikt verband naar Belgisch arbeidsrecht* (Bruges: die Keure, 1989).

C. Engels. 'Subordinate Employees or Self-employed Workers?'. In R. Blanpan (ed.), *Comparative Labour Law and Industrial Relations in Industrialized Market Economies* (The Hague: Kluwer Law International, 2004), 275–291.

European Commission. *Information Note Prepared by the Services of the European Commission on the Provisions of the Proposed ILO Recommendation on the Employment Relationship* (Brussels: European Commission, 2006).

European Commission. *The Evolution of Labour Law (1992–2003), Volume 2, National Reports* (Luxembourg: European Commission, 2005).

European Commission. Directorate General Employment, Social Affairs and Equal Opportunities. *Termination of employment relationships. Legal situation in de Member States of the European Union* (Brussels: European Commission, 2006).

European Network of Legal Experts in the Field of Labour Law. *Characteristics of the Employment Relationship*, s.l., 2009, <www.labourlawnetwork.eu> (under Publications)

Expert Group. *Transformation of Labour and Future of Labour Law in Europe* (Brussels: European Commission, 1998).

M. Fabre-Magnan. 'Pour une obligation de motiver la rupture des contrats de dépendance économique'. *Revue Droit commercial* 2 (2004), 573.

W.J.P.M. Fase. 'De gefaseerd afnemende flexibiliteit van uitzendarbeid'. In F.J.L. Pennings (ed.), *Flexibilisering van het sociaal recht* (Deventer: Deventer, 1996).

W.J.P.M. Fase. 'De uitzendkracht wordt een normale werknemer, al duurt het even'. *Arbeid Integraal* (1997), 12.

A. Fossaert. 'Télé-réalité et contrat de travail'. *Semaine sociale Lamy* 1403 (2009), 3–4.

M. Freedland. *The Contract of Employment* (Oxford: Oxford University Press, 1976).

M. Freedland. *The Personal Employment Contract* (Oxford: Oxford University Press, 2003).

M. Freedland. 'From the Contract of Employment to the Personal Work Nexus'. *Industrial Law Journal* 1 (2006), 1.

D. Frère. 'La loi du 3 juillet 2005 relative aux droits des volontaires'. In J. Clesse & F. Kefer (eds), *Questions de droit social* (Liège: Anthémis, 2007), 7–48.

J. Fudge, E. Tucker & L. Vosko. *The Legal Concept of Employment: Marginalizing Workers* (Ottawa: Law Commission of Canada, 2002).

C. De Ganck. 'Intellectuele onafhankelijkheid van de advocaat verhindert de uitoefening van een "vrij beroep" in dienstverband'. *Rechtspraak Antwerpen, Brussel* (Gent: Uitgeverij Larcier, 2004).

F. Gaudu. 'Du statut de l'emploi au statut de l'actif'. *Droit social* (1995), 535.

F. Gaudu & R. Vatinet. *Le contrat de travail* (Paris: LGDJ, 2001).

B. Gazier. 'Transitional Labour Markets: From Positive Analysis to Policy Proposals'. In G. Schmid & B. Gazier (eds), *The Dynamics of Full Employment. Social Integration through Transitional Labour Markets* (Cheltenham and Brookfield: E. Elgar, 2002).

B. Gazier. 'Flexisécurité et marchés transitionnels du travail: esquisse d'une réflexion normative'. *Travail et emploi* 113 (2008), 117.

D. Ghai. 'Decent Work: Concept and Indicators'. *International Labour Review* 142, no. 2 (2003), 113–145.

H. Gilbert. 'Contrat et production: l'agriculteur intégré ou un exemple de la dépendance dans l'indépendance'. In J.P. Chauchard & A.C. Dubernet (eds), *La subordination dans le travail* (Paris: Cahier Travail et Emploi, 2003), 227.

J.M. Goerloch & A. Guamán. 'Le règlement de 2009, une nouvelle étape dans la règlementation espagnole de l'hybride'. *Revue de droit du travail* (2009), 337.

M. Goldfays. 'Assurance sociale et travailleurs indépendants faillis'. *Journal des Tribunaux de Travail* (1997), 317–322.

K. Goossens. *Het vrijwilligersstatuut* (Mechelen: Kluwer, 2006).

K. Goossens. 'Spelregels voor organisaties en hun vrijwilligers'. *Or.* 5 (2007), 103–114.

Z. Górlal. Prawo do pracy. Studium prawa polskiego w świetle porównawczym (*The Right to Work. A Study of Comparative Polish Law*) (Lodz: Lodz University, 1994).

F.B.J. Grapperhaus & M. Jansen. *De uitzendovereenkomst* (Deventer: Kluwer, 1999).

M. Hascoët. 'Le contrat de projet: le nouveau visage de la para subordination en Italie' *Droit Social* (2007), 879.

D. Hay & P. Craven (eds). *Masters, Servants, and Magistrates in Britain and the Empire, 1562–1955* (Chapel Hill, NC: University of North Carolina Press, 2004).

F. Héas. 'Etre ou ne pas être subordonné'. *Droit social* (1995), 405.

P.F. van der Heijden. *Naar een nieuwe rechtsorde van de arbeid* (Den Haag: Sdu, 1999).

J. Heynen. 'Schijnzelfstandigheid aan banden. De ervaringen van de inspectiediensten'. *Arbeidsblad* (1995), 17–23.

K.M. van Holten. 'Detachering als alternatief voor uitzendarbeid: een valkuil'. *TVVS* (1994), 121.

H. Van Hoogenbemt. 'Zelfstandigheid en schijnzelfstandigheid na de Programmawet (I) van 27 December 2006'. *Oriëntatie* 3 (2007), 49–65.

P. Humblet. *De gezagsuitoefening door de werkgever. Een juridische analyse* (Antwerp: Kluwer rechtswetenschappen, 1994).

P. Humblet. 'Gezag en ondergeschiktheid in de 21e eeuw. Van werknemer naar medewerker?'. In M. Stroobant & O. Vanachter (eds), *Honderd jaar Arbeidsovereenkomstenwet* (Antwerp: Intersentia, 2001), 85–96.

P. Humblet. 'Employment through Temporary Staff Agencies in Belgium'. *Europäisches Arbeits- und Sozialrecht.* 10 (2002), 183–196.

P. Humblet & T. Martens. 'De normatieve afdeling van de Commissie ter regeling van de arbeidsrelatie: het organisatorische kader'. In M. Rigaux & A. Van Regenmortel (eds), *Rechts(on)zekerheid omtrent (schijn)zelfstandigheid* (Antwerp: Intersentia, 2008), 145–158.

International Labour Organisation (ILO). *Contract Labour.* Report V (2A) (Geneva: ILO, 1998).

ILO. *Decent Work.* Report of the Director-General (Geneva: ILO, 1999).

ILO. *Basic Technical Document.* Meeting of experts on workers in situations needing protection (the employment relationship: scope) (Geneva: ILO, 2000).

ILO. *Provisional Record 26* (Geneva: ILO, 2003).

ILO. *The Scope of the Employment Relationship*, Report V (Geneva: ILO, 2003).

ILO. *Provisional Record 21* (Geneva: ILO, 2006).

ILO. *The Employment Relationship*, Report V (1), (Geneva: ILO, 2006).

ILO. *The Employment Relationship*, Report V (2A), (Geneva: ILO 2006).

ILO. *The Employment Relationship. An annotated guide to ILO Recommendation No. 198* (Geneva: ILO, 2008), <www.ilo.org/public/english/dialogue/ifpdial/downloads/guide-rec198.pdf>.

International Organisation of Employers. 'The employment relationship', preparatory note for the 95th Session of the International Labour Conference (Geneva: ILO, 2006).

International Society of Labour Law and Social Security. 'Problemática actual del contrato individual de trabajo: la frontera entre el trabajo subordinado y el trabajo ind/ependiente'. V Congreso Regional Americano de derecho del trabajo y de la seguridad social (Lima: ISLLSS, 2001).

A. Jacobs. *Labour Law in the Netherlands* (The Hague: Kluwer Law International, 2004).

M. Jamoulle. 'La notion de subordination et son évolution'. In *Seize Leçons sur le droit du travail* (Liège: Coll. Scientifique de la Faculté de droit, 1994), 109–136.

M. Jamoulle. 'Le contrat de travail à l'épreuve du temps'. *Chroniques de Droit Social* (1998), 473.

R. Janvier. 'Over vrijheden, contractanten en ambtenaren: geen vrijblijvende "ménage à trois" '. In M. De Vos & I. Plets (eds), *Contractuele tewerkstelling in de overheid* (Bruges: die Keure, 2005), 1–35.

A. Jeammaud. 'L'assimilation de franchisés aux salariés'. *Droit social* (2002), 158.

O. Kahn-Freund. 'Servants and Independent Contractors'. *Modern Law Review* 14 (1951), 504.

O. Kahn-Freund. 'Blackstone's Neglected Child: The Contract of Employment'. *Law Quarterly Review* 93 (1977), 508.

Sir Otto Kahn-Freund. *Labour and the Law.* Hamlyn Lectures (London: Stevens and Sons, 1972).

J.Y. Kerbourch. 'Le portage salarial: prestation de services ou prêt de main-d'œuvre illicite?'. *Droit social* (2007), 72–80.

J. Kerremans. 'De wet betreffende de aard van de arbeidsrelaties: kroniek van een aangekondigde dood?'. *Journal des Tribunaux de Travail* (2007), 149–155.

P. De Keyser. 'Un avocat peut-il être un employé? Révolution ou fin d'une hypocrisie'. *Journal des procès* 408 (2001), 26–27 and 30–31.

P. De Keyser & N. Beaufils. 'Agence commerciale et représentation commerciale. La loi du 13 avril 1995'. *Journal des Tribunaux du Travail* (1996), 1–13.

C. Kilpatrick. 'Has New Labour Reconfigured Employment Legislation?'. *Industrial Law Journal* 32 (2003), 135.

M. Kittner. *Arbeits- und Sozialordnung*, 35th edn (Frankfurt am Main: Bund-Verlag 2010).

R. Knegt et al. *Tweede evaluatie Wet flexibiliteit en zekerheid* (Amsterdam: HIS and TNO, 2007).

Robert Knegt (ed.). *The Employment Contract as an Exclusionary Device* (Antwerp: Intersentia, 2008).

T. Koopmans. *De begrippen werkman, arbeider en werknemer* (Alphen aan de Rijn: Samsom, 1962).

J.J.M. de Laat. 'De rechtsvermoedens van het bestaan en de omvang van de arbeidsovereenkomst'. *Sociaal Recht* (2006), 266.

F. Lagasse. 'Les faux indépendants et le droit du travail: les frontières du lien de subordination'. *Orientations* 5 (2003), 3–15.

F. Lagasse. 'Les faux indépendants et le droit du travail (II), quelques cas d'espèces'. *Orientations* 5 (2003), 16–24.

F. Lagasse. 'Les faux indépendants et le droit du travail (IV). Les projets de réforme de la ministre Onkelinx'. *Orientations* (2003), 16–18.

K. Van den Langenbergh. *Les Faux Indépendants. La différence entre le travail indépendant et le travail dans les liens de subordination* (Brussels: Ministère fédéral de l'Emploi et du Travail, 1999), 252.

K. Van Den Langenbergh. 'Basisprincipes van de Arbeidsrelatieswet: herkomst en kritische analyse'. In M. Rigaux & A. Van Regenmortel (eds), *Rechts(on)zekerheid omtrent (schijn)zelfstandigheid* (Antwerp: Intersentia, 2008), 36–37.

K. Van den Langenbergh & A. Van Regenmortel. 'De UNIZO-formule kritisch bekeken. Brengt deze formule de gewenste rechtszekerheid en wordt, gelet op het beschermend karakter van het sociaal recht, voor deze (schijn van?) rechtszekerheid geen al te hoge prijs betaald?'. *Tijdschrift voor Sociaal Recht/Revue de Droit Social* 3 (2002), 27.

K. Van den Langenbergh & A. Van Regenmortel. 'Schijnzelfstandigheid na de arbeidsrelatiewet: een eerste evaluatie'. In X., *CBR Jaarboek 2008–2009* (Antwerp: Intersentia, 2009), 503.

O. Langlet. 'L'existence du lien de subordination: recherche d'équilibre entre la Cour de Cassation, le juge du fond et l'exécutif'. *Chroniques de Droit Social* (2006), 245–263.

M. Laroque. 'Présentation introductive de la loi du 11 Février 1994 relative à l'initiative et à l'entreprise individuelle'. *Droit social* (1995), 631.

G. Lauwers. *Schijnzelfstandigheid bij advocaten* (Antwerp: Maklu, 2008).

P. Leighton. 'The European Employment Guidelines, "Entrepreneurism" and the Continuing Problem of Defining the Genuinely Self-employed'. In H. Collins, P. Davies and R. Rideout (eds), *Legal Regulation of the Employment Relationship* (The Hague: Kluwer Law International, 2000), 287–303.

G. Lenaerts '(Schijn)werknemer of (schijn)zelfstandige?... Soms een moeilijke evenwichtsoefening!'. *Pacioli* 225 (2007), 1–6.

A. van Leur. *De reikwijdte van de arbeidsrelatie* (Amsterdam: HIS, 2004).

R. Leysen. 'Het Arbitragehof: 15 jaar rechtspraak in sociale zaken'. *Tijdschrift voor Sociaal Recht/Revue de Droit Social* (2000), 546.

H. L'Homme. 'Casuïstiek omtrent enkele aspecten van sociale fraude in het rechtsgebied van het Arbeidshof te Antwerpen'. *Rechtskundig Weekblad* (1997–98), 657–665.

C. Lhoste. 'La loi relative à la nature des relations de travai: vers une plus grande sécurité juridique dans l'exercice d'une activité professionnelle'. *Orientations* (2007), 9–15.

C.J. Loonstra. 'De gezagsverhouding ex artikel 7:610 BW'. *Sociaal Recht* (2005), 96.

C.J. Lorré. 'Aard van de arbeidsrelaties als *deus ex machina*'. *Rechtskundig Weekblad* (2006–2007), 1662–1676.

G. Lyon-Caen. *Le droit du travail non salarié* (Paris: Sirey, 1990).

G. Lyon-Caen. 'Où mènent les mauvais chemins'. *Droit social* (1995), 647.

P.M. Menger et al. 'Travailler par mission: qui et comment? Le cas du portage'. *Droit social* (2007), 46–57.

E.M. Meijers. *Ontwerp van een Nieuw Burgerlijk Wetboek* ('s-Gravenhage: Staatsuitgeverij, 1972).

Ministerie van Sociale Zaken en Werkgelegenheid. *Flexibiliteit en zekerheid, Effecten en doeltreffendheid van de Wet Flexibiliteit en Zekerheid. Eindrapport* (Den Haag: Ministry of Social Affairs, 2002), I-20.

M.L. Morin, 'Partage des risques et responsabilité de l'emploi. Contribution au débat sur la réforme du droit du travail'. *Droit social* (2000), 736.

K. Mortier. 'Arbeidsrelatieswet. Twee jaar na de inwerkingtreding'. *Nieuw Juridisch Weekblad* (2009), 382–386.

Brian Napier. *The Contract of Service: The Concept and its Application* (Cambridge: PhD, 1975).

Alan C. Neal, 'Atypical Workforms and European Labour Law'. *Recht der Arbeit* 45 (1992), 115.

Alan C. Neal. 'Public Sector Industrial Relations – Some Developing Trends'. *The International Journal of Comparative Labour Law and Industrial Relations* 17 (2001), 233.

Alan C. Neal. 'We Love You Social Dialogue – But Who Exactly Are You?'. In Fondazione Giulio Pastore (ed.), *La contrattazione collettive europea: Profili giuridici ed economici* (Milan: FrancoAngeli, 2001), 113.

K. Nevens. 'De betekenis van de kwalificatiearresten verduidelijkt'. *Rechtskundig Weekblad* (2007–2008), 782–783.

K. Nevens. 'De transformatie van het rechtsbegrip "ouvrier": van het Burgerlijk Wetboek naar de eerste arbeidswetgeving (1804–1900)'. *Brood en Rozen* 1 (2009), 46.

A. Patulski. Wolność pracy – próba ujęcia wielopłaszczyznowego (*Freedom of Work – An Attempt at a Multi-level Analysis*) (Warszawa: Warsaw University, 1992).

R. Pedersini. *Economically Dependent Workers', Employment Law and Industrial Relations*. European Industrial Relations Observatory, online 2005.

J. Pélissier, A. Supiot & A. Jeammaud. *Droit du travail*, 24th edn (Paris: Dalloz 2008).

A. Perulli. *Economically Dependent/Quasi-subordinate (Parasubordinate) Employment: Legal, Social and Economic Aspects* (Brussels: European Commission, 2002).

A. Perulli. *Forms of Non-standard Work and the Role of the EU*, presented at the *Conference on labour law in Europe, steps towards 2010* (Leiden, 2004).

E. Peskine, 'Entre subordination et indépendance: en quête d'une troisième voie'. *Revue de Droit du Travail* (2008), 371–377.

Frans Pleijster & Pim van der Valk. *Van onbemind tot onmisbaar. De economische betekenis van ZZP'ers nu en in de toekomst* (Zoetermeer: EIM, 2007).

Th. Priestley. 'A propos du "contrat d'activité" proposé par le rapport Boissonnat'. *Droit social* (1995), 955.

Ch. Radé. 'La possibilité d'une île'. *Droit social* (2009), 930.

Meenakshi Rajeev. *Contract Labour Act in India: A Pragmatic View, IGIDR Proceedings/Project Reports Series PP-062-33* (August 2009), available at <www.igidr.ac.in/pdf/publication/PP-062-33.pdf>.

W. Rauws. 'De kwalificatie van de (arbeids)overeenkomst'. *Journal des Tribunaux de Travail* (2006), 93–101.

J.E. Ray. 'De Germinal à Internet. Une nécessaire évolution du critère du contrat de travail'. *Droit social* (1995), 634.

J.E. Ray. 'Sea, sex . . . and contrat de travail'. *Semaine sociale Lamy* (2009), 1403.

A. Van Regenmortel. 'Onderscheid tussen werknemer en zelfstandige'. In J. Van Steenberge and A. Van Regenmortel (eds), *Actuele problemen van het sociale zekerheidsrecht* (Bruges: die Keure 1995), 31–100.

A. Van Regenmortel. 'De Arbeidsrelatieswet: continuering van de cassatierechtspraak'. In M. Rigaux & A. Van Regenmortel (eds), *Rechts(on)zekerheid omtrent (schijn)zelfstandigheid* (Antwerp: Intersentia, 2008), 91–143.

M. Rigaux. 'De gespannen verhouding tussen artikel 1134 BW en de sociaalrechtelijke finaliteit. Inleidende beschouwingen'. In M. Rigaux & A. Van Regenmortel (eds), *Rechts(on)zekerheid omtrent (schijn)zelfstandigheid* (Antwerp: Intersentia, 2008), 20.

M. Rigaux & A. Van Regenmortel (eds). *Rechts(on)zekerheid omtrent (schijn)-zelfstandigheid* (Antwerp: Intersentia, 2008).

M.G. Rood & M.J van der Ven. *Flexibele arbeidsrelaties* (Alphen aan den Rijn: Samson, 1988).

D. Roulive. 'Les sanctions à charge de l'employeur dans le cadre de la réglementation du chômage'. *Orientations* 10 (2008), 10–18.

G. Schmidt. 'Le plein emploi est-il encore possible? Les marchés du travail "transitoire" en tant que nouvelle stratégie des politiques d'emploi'. *Travail et Emploi*. 65 (1995), 5–17.

J. Schatteman & P. Vanden Broeck. 'Schijnzelfstandigheid aan banden. Het onderscheid tussen werknemer en zelfstandige in de rechtspraak'. *Arbeidsblad* (1995), 24–47.

Johannes Schregle. 'Labour Relations in the Public Sector'. *International Labour Review* 113 (1974), 381.

A. Sciarra. *The Evolution of Labour Law (1992–2003)* (Brussels: European Commission, 2004).

J.M. Servais. *International Labour Law* (The Hague: Kluwer, 2005).

S. Simitis. 'The Case of the Employment Relationship: Elements of a Comparison'. In W. Steinmetz (ed.), *Private Law and Social Inequality in the Industrial Age: Comparing Legal Cultures in Britain, France, Germany, and the United States* (Oxford: Oxford University Press 2000), 181.

Bruce Smith. 'Imperial Borrowing: The Law of Master and Servant', *Comparative Labor Law and Policy Journal* (2005), 447.

J. Stevens. 'De uitoefening van het beroep van advocaat in dienstverband'. *Rechtskundig Weekblad* (2005–2006), 1–21.

A. Supiot. *Au-delà de l'emploi* (Paris: Flammarion, 1999).

A. Supiot. 'The Transformation of Work and the Future of Labour Law in Europe: A Multidisciplinary Perspective'. *International Labour Review* 138, no. 1 (1999), 31–46.

A. Supiot. 'Les nouveaux visages de la subordination'. *Droit social* (2000).

A. Supiot. *Beyond Employment. Changes in the Work and the Future of Labour Law in Europe* (Oxford: Oxford University Press, 2001).

A. Supiot. 'Revisiter les droits d'action collective'. *Droit social* (2001), 687.

A.M. Świątkowski. Polskie prawo pracy (*Polish Labour Law*) (Warszawa: LexisNexis, 2003).

A.M. Świątkowski. *Międzynarodowa polityka społeczna wobec świadczących pracę w niezorganizowanej gospodarce* (*International Social Policies for Workers Working in Unorganized Markets*), vol. 4 (Warszawa: Polityka Społeczna (*Social Policies*), 2003).

A.M. Świątkowski. *Kodeks pracy. Komentarz* (*Labour Code Commentary*) (Warszawa: C.H. Beck, 2006).

A.M. Swiatkowski. 'Poland'. In R. Blanpain (ed.), *European Framework Agreement and Telework: Law and Practice, a European and Comparative Study*, Bulletin of Comparative Labour Relations, vol. 62 (The Hague: Kluwer Law International, 2007).

A.M. Świątkowski. Ograniczenie swobody zawierania umów o pracę na czas określony jako alternatywa koncepcji flex-security (*Limiting the Freedom to Enter into a Work Agreement for a Non-permanent Period of Time, as an Alternative to the Flex-Security Concept*) (Warswaza: Monitor Prawa Pracy, 2008), No. 11.

A.M. Świątkowski. *Międzynarodowe prawo pracy* (*International Labour Law*), vol. I *Międzynarodowe publiczne prawo pracy* (*International Public Labour Law*), vols 1–3 (Warszawa: C.H. Beck, 2008).

A.M. Świątkowski, 'Poland'. In R. Blanpain and C. Gramt (eds), *Fixed-Term Employment Contracts. A Comparative Study* (Bruges: Vanden Broele Publishers, 2009), 377.

A.M. Świątkowski. 'Ochrona praw człowieka w świetle przepisów prawa pracy i zabezpieczenia społecznego' ('Human Rights Protection in Light of Labour Law and Social Security). In A.M. Świątkowski (ed.), *Każdy ma prawo do* ... (*Everyone Has a Right To* ...) (Warszawa: C.H. Beck, 2009).

T. Teklè (ed.). *Labour Law and Worker Protection in Developing Countries* (Geneva: ILO, 2010).

J.P. van den Toren, G.H.M. Evers & E.J. Commissaris. *Flexibiliteit en zekerheid: effecten en doeltreffendheid van de Wet flexibiliteit en zekerheid* (Den Haag: Minsitry of Social Affairs, 2002).

F. Valdés dal Ré & O. Leclerc. 'Les nouvelles frontières du travail indépendant. A propos du statut du travail autonome espagnol'. *Revue de droit du travail* (2008), 296–303.

V. Vannes (ed.). *Le lien de subordination dans le contrat de travail* (Brussels: Bruylant, 2005).

A. Veldman. 'Tijdelijk besluit arbeidsovereenkomst post: de goede weg om loonconcurrentie in een geliberaliseerde markt tegen te gaan?'. *Tra* (2011), no. 3.

C.E. Vercammen. 'Beoordelingsvrijheid in dienstverband: na de geneesheer, ook de advocaat onder arbeidsovereenkomst'. *Rechtskundig Weekblad* (1992–93), 1353–1366.

P. Verdonck (ed.). *La nouvelle loi sur les relations de travail. Premier état et perspectives* (Louvain-la-Neuve: Anthémis, 2007), 171.

J.P. Vendrig et al. *Evaluatie Wet uitbreiding rechtsgevolgen verklaring arbeidsrelatie* (Zoetermeer: EIM, 2007), 6.

E. Verhulp. 'Een arbeidsovereenkomst? Dat maak ik zelf wel uit!'. *Sociaal Recht* (2005), 87.

M. Vericel. 'Le rétablissement de la présomption de non salariat, Art. 23, loi du 1er August 2003 pour l'initiative économique', *Droit social* (2004), 297.

J.Y. Verkindt. 'Debout! Les damnés de la terre'. *JCP* (2009), 25.

Ch. Vigneau. 'Les travailleurs précaires face à l'exigence de continuité de l'emploi'. *Semaine Sociale Lamy* (2003), 5.

M. De Vos. 'Het Arbitragehof en het arbeidsrecht'. In M. Rigaux & P. Humblet (eds), *Actuele problemen van het arbeidsrecht VI* (Antwerp: Intersentia, 2001), 89.

M. De Vos. 'De advocaat: zelfstandige of werknemer? Het dogma van de zelfstandige advocaat en het enigma van de ondergeschikte advocaat-stagiair'. *Nieuw Juridisch Weekblad* (2004), 542–545.

P. Vroonhof et al. *Zelfstandigen zonder personeel* (Zoetermeer: EIM en Bureau Bartels, 2008).

B. Waas. 'The Legal Definition of the Employment Relationship'. *European Labour Law Journal* no. 1 (2010), 45.

R. Wank. *Arbeitnehmer und Selbständige* (München: C.H. Beck, 1988).

P. Wedde, *Telearbeit*, 3rd edn (München: C.H. Beck 2002).

C. Willems, 'Le contrat d'agence commerciale: la formation et l'exécution du contrat'. *Orientations* 2 (1996), 25–40.

Diana de Wolff & Frans Pennings. 'Dienstbetrekking of zelfstandig ondernemerschap, de reikwijdte van de sociaalrechtelijke bescherming van de zelfstandige zonder personeel'. In S.S.M. Peters & M.S. Houwerzijl (eds), *Exit: Onderneming, werknemer en het einde van de dienstbetrekking* (Deventer: Kluwer, 2009), 363–388.

X. Le lien de subordination. Actes du colloque organisé le 19 mars 2004 par l'Ordre des Avocats du Barreau de Tournai et le Jeune Barreau de Tournai, Etudes pratiques de Droit Social n° 18 (Brussels: Kluwer, 2004).

X. *Vade Mecum van de financiële en statistische gegevens over de sociale bescherming van België* (Brussels: Federale Overheidsdienst Sociale Zekerheid, 2009).

J.P.H. Zwemmer. 'Rechtsvermoeden, omvang arbeidsduur, een updating'. *ArbeidsRecht* (2005), 50.

Index

STUDIES IN EMPLOYMENT AND SOCIAL POLICY

1. W. Beck, L. van der Maesen & A. Walker (eds), *The Social Quality of Europe*, 1997 (ISBN 90-411-0456-9).
2. R. Blanpain, M. Colucci, C. Engels, F. Hendrickx, L. Salas & E. De Smyter, *Institutional Changes and European Social Policies after the Treaty of Amsterdam*, 1998 (ISBN 90-411-1018-6).
3. V. Lo: *Law and Industrial Relations: China and Japan after World War II*, 1998 (ISBN 90-411-1075-5).
4. A. Den Exter & H. Hermans (eds), *The Right to Health Care in Several European Countries*, 1998 (ISBN 90-411-1087-9).
5. M. Biagi (ed.), *Job Creation and Labour Law from Protection towards Pro-Action*, 2000 (ISBN 90-411-1432-7).
6. W. Beck, L. van der Maesen, F. Thomése & A. Walker (eds), *Social Quality: A Vision for Europe*, 2000 (ISBN 90-411-1523-4).
7. F. Pennings, *Introduction to European Social Law*, 3rd ed., 2001 (ISBN 90-411-1628-1).
8. J. Murray, *Transnational Labour Regulation: The ILO and EC Compared*, 2001 (ISBN 90-411-1583-8).
9. R. Blanpain & C. Engels (eds), *The ILO and Social Challenges of the 21st Century*, 2001 (ISBN 90-411-1572-2).
10. M. Biagi (ed.), *Towards a European Model of Industrial Relations? Building on the First Report of the European Commission*, 2001 (ISBN 90-411-1653-2).
11. J. Clasen (ed.), *What Future for Social Security? Debates and Reforms in National and Cross-National Perspective*, 2001 (ISBN 90-411-1671-0).
12. A. Numhauser-Henning (ed.), *Legal Perspectives on Equal Treatment and Non-Discrimination*, 2001 (ISBN 90-411-1665-6).
13. R. Blanpain (ed.), *Labour Law, Human Rights and Social Justice* 2001 (ISBN 90-411-1697-4).
14. M.-C. Kuo, H.F. Zacher & H.-S. Chan (eds), *Reform and Perspectives on Social Insurance: Lessons from the East and West*, 2002 (ISBN 90-411-1819-5).
15. P. Foubert, *The Legal Protection of the Pregnant Worker in the European Community*, 2002 (ISBN 90-411-1842-X).
16. M. Biagi (ed.), *Quality of Work and Employee Involvement in Europe*, 2002 (ISBN 90-411-1885-3).
17. F. Pennings, *Dutch Social Security Law in an International Context*, 2002 (ISBN 90-411-1887-X).
18. T. Carney & G. Ramia, *From Rights to Management: Contract, New Public Management and Employment Services*, 2002 (ISBN 90-411-1889-6).
19. R. Blanpain & M. Colucci, *European Labour and Social Security Law, Glossary*, 2002 (ISBN 90-411-1905-1).
20. I.U. Zeytinoglu (ed.), *Flexible Work Arrangements: Conceptualizations and International Experiences*, 2002 (ISBN 90-411-1947-7).

21. J. Berghman, A. Nagelkerke, M. Boos, R. Doeschot & G. Vonk (eds.), *Social Security in Transition*, 2002 (ISBN 90-411-1969-8).
22. R. Blanpain, *The Legal Status of Sportsmen and Sportswomen under International, European and Belgian National and Regional Law*, 2003 (ISBN 90-411-1980-9).
23. R. Blanpain & M. Weiss (eds.), *Changing Industrial Relations & Modernisation of Labour Law, Liber Amicorum in Honour of Professor Marco Biagi*, 2003 (ISBN 90-411-2008-4).
24. J. Malmberg (ed.), *Effective Enforcement of EC Labour Law*, 2003 (ISBN 90-411-2160-9).
25. M. De Vos (ed.), *A Decade Beyond Maastricht: The European Social Dialogue Revisited*, 2003 (ISBN 90-411-2163-3).
26. M. Sewerynski (ed.), *Collective Agreements and Individual Contracts of Employment*, 2003 (ISBN 90-411-2190-0).
27. R. Blanpain & M. Van Gestel, *Use and Monitoring of E-Mail, Intranet and Internet Facilities at Work: Law and Practice*, 2004 (ISBN 90-411-22-66-4).
28. A. C. Neal (ed.), *The Changing Face of European Labour Law and Social Policy*, 2004 (ISBN 90-411-2312-1).
29. E. Sol & M. Westerveld (eds), *Contractualism in Employment Services: A New Form of Welfare State Governance*, 2005 (ISBN 90-411-2405-5).
30. F. Pennings (ed.), *Between Soft and Hard Law – The Impact of International Social Security Standards on National Social Security Law*, 2006 (ISBN 978-90-411-2491-3).
31. L. Dickens & A. C. Neal (eds), *The Changing Institutional Face of British Employment Relations*, 2006 (ISBN 978-90-411-2541-5).
32. G. Sebardt, *Redundancy and the Swedish Model in an International Context*, 2006 (ISBN 978-90-411-2503-3).
33. A.M. Swiatkowski, *Charter of Social Rights of the Council of Europe*, 2007 (ISBN 978-90-411-2608-5).
34. M. Sargeant (ed.), *The Law on Age Discrimination in the EU*, 2008 (ISBN 978-90-411-2522-4).
35. G. Di Domenico & S. Spattini (eds), *New European Approaches to Long-Term Unemployment: What Role for Public Employment Services and What Market for Private Stakeholders?*, 2008 (ISBN 978-90-411-2614-6.)
36. C. Welz, *The European Social Dialogue under Articles 138 and 139 of the EC Treaty: Actors, Processes, Outcomes*, 2008 (ISBN 978-90-411-2744-0).
37. M. Rönnmar (ed.), *EU Industrial Relations v. National Industrial Relations: Comparative and Interdisciplinary Perspectives*, 2008 (ISBN 978-90-411-2770-9).
38. F. Pennings, Y. Konijn & A. Veldman (eds), *Social Responsibility in Labour Relations: European and Comparative Perspectives*, 2008 (ISBN 978-90-411-2783-9).
39. F. Pennings & C. Bosse (eds), *The Protection of Working Relationships: A Comparative Study*, 2011 (ISBN 978-90-411-3289-5).